Inman's War

A Soldier's Story of Life in a Colored Battalion In WWII

Inman's War

A Soldier's Story of Life in a Colored Battalion In WWII

Jeffrey S. Copeland

First Edition 2006

Published in the United States by
Paragon House
1925 Oakcrest Avenue, Suite 7
St. Paul, MN 55114

Library of Congress Cataloging-in-Publication Data

Copeland, Jeffrey.
  Inman's war : a soldier's story of life in a colored battalion in WWII /
   Jeffrey S. Copeland. -- 1st ed.
     p. cm.
  ISBN 1-55778-860-X (pbk. : alk. paper) 1. Perkins, Inman. 2.
     World War, 1939-1945--Participation, African American. 3.
     United States. Army Air Forces--African Americans--Biography.
     4. African American soldiers--Biography. 5. Soldiers--United
     States--Biography. I. Title.
  D810.N4P473 2006
  940.54'4973092--dc22
  [B]
                            2006013077

The paper used in this publication meets the minimum requirements of
American National Standard for Information Sciences—Permanence
of Paper for Printed Library Materials, ANSIZ39.48-1984.

Manufactured in the United States of America
10 9 8 7 6 5 4 3 2 1

This book is dedicated to the men who served in the 449th Signal Construction Battalion, Army Air Corps.

CONTENTS

AUTHOR'S NOTE

The seeds of this book were planted on a blistering hot Sunday morning in the fall of 2002. While at an outdoor flea market in Belleville, Illinois, I came across a dusty suitcase full of old letters from a Sgt. Inman Perkins to a Miss Olivia Merriwether of St. Louis, Missouri. Intrigued, I read a few of the letters, and the voice in them touched something deep in me. After acquiring the letters I determined to find out who these people were and what had happened to them. With that, I began a journey I couldn't have imagined in my wildest dreams.

All major events of *Inman's War* are true. The background details for the story were gathered from the original letters, through official military records, most of which had been sealed and locked away since the end of World War II, historical records of the city of St. Louis, museum archives in five states, conversations with relatives and others who knew those involved, and interviews with current military personnel and those who served during World War II.

The time period involved was compressed to allow the story to unfold as presented.

Also, for the obvious reasons, some of the names have been changed, and other characters are composites of several. I've given additional information on the sources in a section at the back of the book.

—JSC

INTRODUCTION

Very seldom does a book come along that is so many stories—and is so important—to so many people. *Inman's War* is such a book.

Inman's War, by Jeffrey Copeland, is a true story, an honest story, one without any hidden agendas.

It is on one level an ugly story about America and racism and prejudice and discrimination and sexism.

But it is also a human story, a story about real people, a story of friendship and loyalty, a story of the human spirit as it tries to overcome adversity.

It is also a love story, a story of two teachers in Sumner High School in St. Louis, Missouri, Inman Perkins and Olivia Merriwether, who were forced by rules of the day to keep their love secret—to keep it only within their own hearts.

On another level it is also a tragedy, a story of soldiers in a "colored battalion" who were serving for and were willing if necessary to die for their country—and who never felt equal to others until they drove the few miles from where they were once stationed in Texas across the border into a foreign country, where they could feel the freedom and equality they were fighting for. They were nothing but strangers in their own country, and they knew it, knew it in their hearts and souls. They also knew they were unwelcome strangers.

It is also a magnificent slice of history, a story of America and its Negroes. It is a story that reminds us we must say to Dr. Martin Luther King Jr. and all those who were, and still are, the core of the civil rights movement, "Thank you. Because of you, 90 percent of the suffering and injustice described in this book no longer exists today."

I would like to say myself "Thank you" to the author, the publisher, and all the people who were involved in seeing to it that this very important part of our past, this very important piece of one of the darkest sides of American history, has been brought from the darkness into the light. Thank you for filling a silence, for telling the world what has been kept behind doors for so long. For *too* long.

Americans of all ages and all races and all religions need to read this book. It should be in all schools and libraries across this country. I hope *Inman's War* will help create an atmosphere where the discussions of freedom and dignity and human rights and equality of all people will be put above all else where they belong.

—Dick Gregory

1

DESTINATIONS

OCTOBER 2, 1943

I couldn't help but smile. As St. Louis's Union Station disappeared from view, I eased back in my seat, folded my arms, closed my eyes, and lost myself in the sounds of the troop train, a converted streamliner in the Missouri-Pacific Line. This was my first time aboard a train. Before tonight, the longest trip I ever made in my life was during my move from Des Moines to St. Louis, and that had been by Greyhound bus.

It was only a week before that I reported to Jefferson Barracks for induction into the army. And now here I was on my way from St. Louis to assignment at Davis-Monthan Field in Tucson, Arizona. As the last twinkling lights of the city began to disappear, the steady *click-clack, click-clack* of the rails seemed to be matching the rhythm of my own heart. At once I felt the excitement of the unknown and more than a little sadness for the life I was leaving behind. I didn't know what the future would hold, but I was already aching for what was fading into the distance.

St. Louis was my home. It was also where I found my first job after graduating from college. I was a science teacher at Charles Sumner High School, the first high school for Negroes built west of the Mississippi River. Through the years Sumner earned the reputation as one of the finest schools in the city, if not the entire Midwest. Its faculty came from all regions of the country, eager to establish a climate at 4248 West Cottage Avenue where students were taught not just the contents of books, but also to be proud of themselves, their families, and their heritage.

And I was proud to be a part of this: Room 231. Science Lab. Teacher: Mr. Perkins.

St. Louis was also where I fell in love with Olivia Merriwether. The first time I saw her, the morning of my first day working as a substitute teacher at Sumner, I thought she was a student in my first-period class. Olivia taught biology and chemistry, but she also showed up an hour early each day to work with students who needed extra help with their studies, science-related or not. That first morning she was wearing a white lab coat as I walked into the science lab a few minutes before the first period of the day was to begin. Her back was to me as she stood on tiptoes, erasing the blackboard behind my desk. She was so petite I just assumed she had to be an early-bird student trying to earn brownie points.

Without giving her so much as a second glance, I said, "I'm chasing my tail today. I really appreciate you doing that. When you finish, would you also please help me put these books on the desks before you take your seat."

When she turned around she smiled at me and responded coyly, "Well, I'll help you with the books, but I think people would start to talk if I took a seat and stuck around, don't you?"

Seeing the confused look on my face, she laughed, extended her hand, and said, "I'm Miss Merriwether. Room 232. I heard you were coming. Just thought I'd help get you off to a good start by tidying up a bit. I don't think this room has been cleaned since last spring."

Then, eyeballing me up and down, she winked at me and added, "By the way, I'll be in the next room over if you need someone to clap your erasers later."

And with that, as the first bell rang, she hurried from the room, her lab coat dragging the floor behind her. I started after her to apologize, but the students began rushing in before I could even get halfway to the door.

During the lunch period that day I decided the least I could do was return the favor, so I snuck into her classroom to clean the blackboard before her next class started. I was feeling pretty smug about my own act of kindness and how sneaky I'd been to pull it off until I looked up a few minutes before that next class was to begin and saw her leaning against the doorway of my classroom. As she stood there, she had one of those squinty "You'll get yours!" looks on her face.

"Cleaned my blackboard, did you?"

She pointed to the chalk dust covering the front of my trousers.

"I want you to know those were my notes for my next class. Took me about fifteen minutes to get them all up there. Do me a favor, will you? The next time you decide to clean something, take a good look at yourself first."

I was caught. Guilty as charged.

I started to apologize again, but the bell sounded and my students poured into the room. Olivia waved and smiled insincerely, then disappeared into the crowd of students rushing up and down the hall.

The rest of the afternoon I tried my best to concentrate on making a good first impression with my students. Goodness knows I had flopped at that with Olivia. But I just couldn't get her out of my mind. I must have looked at my watch a hundred times that afternoon, but the hands seemed to be moving slower every time I looked. I thought the day was never going to end.

As soon as the students were dismissed, I rushed to her classroom, only to discover she taught in a different room the last period of the day. Dejectedly, I walked slowly down the front steps of the school and headed for home. About halfway down the block I saw her talking to someone at the streetcar stop up at the corner. Fitting perfectly with my luck that day, the streetcar pulled up and they got on before I could get there.

For the next two days it seemed like I saw her constantly all over the school building, but every time I started to walk over to her either the bell would ring again or she'd get up and leave before I could get her attention. I was beginning to wonder if I'd ever be able to talk to her again. The odds of that were beginning to seem smaller and smaller with the passing days, but there was one thing I did know for sure. I was already falling for her—and I was hoping nothing would break that fall.

* * *

My thoughts of Olivia were interrupted when a young lieutenant came over, tugged lightly on my sleeve, and instructed me to follow him. As

..de our way toward the back of the train, we passed through car
..ter car packed with soldiers. Finally he said to me, "Soldier, I have an
important job for you. You're going to guard the mail."

"Yes, Sir!" I replied, excited to be given so much responsibility so
soon.

We walked the rest of the way in silence, rocking back and forth
with the motion of the train. At the end of the last car, he opened the
rear door and we stepped outside onto a small platform. The evening
air was cool as it swirled around us.

"Watch your step," he said as he jumped the short distance to the
caboose's matching platform.

I followed him across, noticing the railroad ties zipping by below
me. The lieutenant opened the door of the caboose and motioned me
inside.

"There's your station," he said, pointing to a small, wooden desk
by the window. "Sit there and keep an eye on these bags of mail."

As I looked at the dozen or so large duffel sacks piled in the middle of the floor, my eyes caught movement in the shadows in the back
of the caboose. Two other colored soldiers were sitting on the floor
and suddenly stood up and snapped to attention at the sight of the
lieutenant.

"At ease," he said without looking directly at them. "I'm giving
you three a very important job—watch this mail. I'll have some chow
sent to you later. Whatever you do, don't leave this car."

And with that, he turned and walked out, not returning our
salutes.

The taller of the two men came forward and extended his hand.
"I'm Taylor. Call me Doc. Everybody does. This is Williams. Looks
like we'll be traveling together."

His handshake was strong. "I'm Perkins," I replied. "Nice to meet
you. Where you two from?"

Just then the train lurched and I half fell back and half sat down
in the little chair by the desk. At the same time, my new traveling
companions awkwardly sat back down on the floor as Doc replied,
"We're both from St. Louis. Kinloch. North part of the city. Where
you from?"

"I'm from St. Louis, too," I said. "Easton Avenue. Just a few blocks from Sumner High School. In the Ville."

Williams looked up and said in a soft voice, almost a whisper, "I went down to Sumner once. I took my sister there to see one of her friends who was in some kind of school play. Did you go to Sumner?"

"No, I'm a teacher there. Well, at least I was until now. I teach science mostly, but it seems like they have me teach just about everything they can think of—and then some."

Williams replied, "No fooling? A teacher? You know, that science is a rough subject. I just barely passed it by the skin of my teeth."

Doc laughed out loud and said, "You barely passed everything."

Turning to me, he added, "You see, Williams isn't exactly the sharpest knife in the drawer, if you know what I mean."

I looked at Williams and noticed his uniform was hanging so loosely on him that it seemed to flap as he moved his arms. He wore round, gold-rimmed glasses that were so scratched I could barely see his eyes even when he looked right at me. It didn't take long to tell he was more than a little shy—and more than a little scared.

After a little prodding to get him talking again, he admitted this trip would be his first away from home, that he had never been very far out of St. Louis. He said he once went with his family to see some cousins across the river in East St. Louis, but that had been the extent of his travel.

He also explained how he had been working as a cook in a diner on the south edge of Kinloch right next to the main streetcar stop. The more he talked about his former job, the more excited he got, his voice rising sharply. He finally stood up, gesturing wildly, and moved back and forth in front of us at an imaginary grill, demonstrating how he could prepare several different orders at the same time.

He was practically out of breath when Doc shouted at him, yanking on his arm at the same time, "Sit down, Houdini. That'll be enough of that. Besides, the waitresses there tell me you're a better tip-stealer than cook anyway. I heard about what happened there last month."

"Now look here—I didn't steal nothin'!" he protested. "I thought that money was for me. You know, 'compliments to the chef' and all that. That customer was loaded—a regular Daddy Warbucks. So how was I supposed to know the money he left on that plate wasn't for me? The waitress left it there when she shoved the tray in to me. And besides, I finally gave it back to her, didn't I?"

"That's not the way I heard it," Doc teased. "I heard you practically wrestled that poor waitress to the ground to get that five-spot. Darn near broke her arm!"

Williams screwed up his face and made a fist, shaking it at Doc. The sight of that fist swirling around in that baggy sleeve was too much. Doc and I looked at each other and cracked up.

"Why, I've never stolen a tip in my life," he continued, his voice rising even more. "Well, none that amounted to anything anyway."

He smiled and winked at me. I didn't know what kind of cook he really was, but I knew a good sense of humor when I saw it.

I had the feeling I was going to like him.

As soon as Williams sat back down, I turned to Doc and asked, "So how about you? What are you leaving back there?"

Doc, unlike Williams, wasn't bashful in the least. As a matter of fact, he had a booming voice, one that commanded attention. He was also a powerfully built man, almost to the point of being muscle-bound.

"I was a mechanic," he said. "At my uncle's garage. I don't know if it was fate or what, but it all just sort of happened. When I was a junior in high school my uncle's mechanic just up and quit on him one day, leaving him with five cars parked out front that needed to be worked on. I didn't know much about cars, but I knew how to operate the gas pump, so I said I'd pitch in and do that while my uncle tried to catch up. Well, one day he had to go tow in a car that had just died down by the park, so he left me there by myself. An old lady brought in a car that was backfiring so bad I thought I was being shot at when she pulled up. I didn't have anything else to do, so I took her carburetor apart and cleaned it. Then I took the spark plugs out and cleaned them, too. After that, it ran just fine. I was just lucky. Beginner's luck, that's all. My uncle came back just as she was ready to leave and she made such a big deal out of it he offered me a job right after she left. I told him I really didn't know what I was doing, and I'll never forget what he said. He said, 'Son, if you find a mechanic who thinks he knows everything, stay the hell away from him. He's an idiot.' Anyway, I hated to quit school, but he is family and needed the help. I started working for him full-time the next day and never looked back."

"The heck you haven't," Williams cut in. "You've been sorry you quit school from the minute you took that job."

He turned to me and continued, "You should have seen this guy in sports. By the time he was a sophomore he already had just about every school record in everything from baseball to basketball. People used to come from miles around just to see him play, and he never once disappointed them. Shoot, I once saw him hit a home run that went so far nobody ever found the ball."

"I think it rolled into a sewer," Doc said, grinning.

"I'm not kidding," Williams continued. "This guy was great. No telling what he could have done if he'd stuck around a little longer. He might even be playing now for the Homestead Grays!"

"Yeah, right," Doc said sarcastically. "Besides, it's all water under the bridge. I get just as much fun now setting the timing on a car or blowing out a clogged gas line. That may be a little different than club-bing a baseball, but they're still a pretty good challenge, too."

"Is he half as good as a mechanic as he was in sports?" I asked Williams.

"Better. I'll tell you how he got his nickname, and I think that'll explain it all. Right from the start he was a pretty good shade-tree mechanic, but he had this really peculiar habit that we all used to laugh about behind his back."

Here he paused and scooted away from Doc before continuing, "But we didn't dare let him see us laughing or he'd have killed us dead. He had to wash his hands over and over, like he was getting him-self all sterilized, every time he got ready to take something apart. Just like a doctor. And he'd always say the same thing over and over when he popped a hood, 'Well, I'm going to have to cut her open, but I think she'll live.' Pretty soon everyone in Kinloch was calling him 'Doc.' Their cars are like his patients. And you know what, I sure don't remember many he couldn't save."

The admiration in Williams' voice was touching. It was clear the two had been friends for a long time, but a more unlikely pair I couldn't have imagined. The high school athletic hero and the fry cook. Yet there was a common bond there somewhere, possibly a mutual respect, that linked the two.

Doc, embarrassed by his friend's words, mumbled, "Well, I've been lucky a time or two. That's all."

"It takes more than luck," I said. "Sounds to me like you've got a gift. A very special one."

"And one more thing," Williams interrupted. "There's something else I can tell you about Doc. Now I wouldn't tell this to just anybody."

He leaned forward and motioned me to come closer to him.

Almost in a whisper he said, "He's got six toes on his left foot."

"Jesus!" Doc yelled. "I can't believe you said that. Why don't you just tell him I'm a fiend or Jack the Ripper while you're at it."

He shook his head, looked at me, and added, "I do *not* have six toes on my left foot. I was chopping firewood one time and the ax skidded off a piece of wood. I caught my left foot just below the little toe. Hurt like hell, and you should have seen the blood. I about fainted. When it healed, I ended up with a great scar and this little flap of skin there where it healed funny. That's all. I thought maybe it would keep me out of the army, but the doctor who looked at me just said, 'Hmmmmm.' That's all he said. Just 'Hmmmmm.' And, well, here I am."

"Six toes!" Doc repeated again, raising his hand like he was going to slug Williams.

Williams quickly crab-walked to the back of the caboose and then let out his high-pitched laugh.

I laughed, too—at Williams.

The three of us sat there a while in silence, swaying back and forth with the motion of the caboose, staring at the bags of mail on the floor in front of us. Through the window on the door we could also see into the car behind us. It looked like a party was in full swing in there. We couldn't hear them, but we could see the soldiers in that car were clapping for a redheaded private who was swaying back and forth, singing to and dancing with an invisible partner. By the laughter and frequent shocked expressions on all of their faces, I gathered it must have been a pretty risqué song.

I was just about to ask what song Doc and Williams thought it might be when Williams, who was thumbing through a newspaper, suddenly starting singing quietly to himself his own version of a popular ditty of the day:

> You're in the army now,
> You'll never get rich, and how,
> You'll never get rich,
> Diggin' a ditch,
> We're in the army now.

He folded over a page of the paper, looked up, and realized we were staring at him. Innocently, and more loudly than he had spoken all night, he said, "Well, we WON'T!"

Doc and I howled.

We spent the rest of the evening talking about our families, friends, and favorite places we were leaving behind. Every once in a while we'd spot lights off in the distance and make a game out of guessing what they were attached to—whether it was a farmhouse, a business in some small town, or maybe even a car driving down a lonely road. We were all getting pretty sleepy, and when Doc suggested we use the mail sacks as pillows, we each quickly grabbed one. I reminded them that we were supposed to be guarding the mail and that one of us should be awake at all times. I volunteered to take the first watch and told them to get as much shuteye as they could.

When Doc was finally finished shifting around and was as comfortable as he was going to get, he said, almost as if he were speaking to himself, "You know, it's funny the three of us were chosen to guard the mail."

I looked out the side window of the caboose at the lights of what I imagined was a small farm off in the distance. Then I looked back through the window of the car behind us and watched the soldiers milling around, drinking coffee, and eating sandwiches as they visited with each other.

I looked again at the sacks of mail and said, "If you ask me, 'funny' isn't the right word."

And for the rest of the night as the three of us watched the mail, our thoughts were punctuated by the steady *click-clack, click-clack* of the rails.

2

ARRIVALS

I t took three days and four changes of train before we arrived at our destination, Davis-Monthan Field in Tucson, Arizona. By the time we made it there I felt like I had been riding all the way across the country in an old Conestoga wagon. My back was absolutely killing me. The seats on those trains were hard as a hammer, and that, combined with the jerky motion of the train, made every muscle in my body strain for the entire three days.

The motion of the train was also so different for us that after the first day we were swaying back and forth even when the train wasn't moving. Williams got "train-sick" twice, and Doc, who had also never been on a train before, said the eyestrain from constantly staring out the window so he wouldn't miss anything had given him a headache the size of St. Louis. As we left the train, we were a fine sight. One looked sick as a dog and was holding his stomach, one was squinting like a man just entering the sunlight after working three days in a coal mine, and one—me—was hunched over like a man with lumbago. I looked at my traveling companions, laughed out loud, and said, "What a fine first impression we're going to make."

At least we hadn't been asked to ride in the caboose and guard the mail after we changed trains in Kansas City. From there on, each time we got aboard the next troop train, Doc, Williams, and I had the rearmost car next to the caboose to ourselves. We also noticed that each time we made a stop, the number of soldiers who got back on the train with us kept getting smaller and smaller. When we finally arrived in Tucson, there were only seven of us who got off, and we hadn't even seen the other four soldiers traveling with us the entire last leg of the journey. They had obviously been riding in an entirely different part of the train.

A light rain was falling in Tucson as we left the station. The sky was darkening quickly, and I could hear the faint sound of thunder rumbling over the mountains off in the distance. We weren't sure exactly where to go or what to do next because nobody met us when we got off the train. Doc finally suggested we sit on a bench outside the main entrance and wait for orders, especially since the other soldiers had already sat down in chairs along the wall on the other side of the entrance.

It wasn't long before several army transport trucks pulled up. These trucks were called "six-by-sixes" and "six-bys" by the veteran soldiers. Part of the name came from the fact they did have six wheels, two up front and double sets of two at the rear. Story had it they were geared so low and had so much traction they could pull a tree stump right out of the ground. But that wasn't the main reason they were called "six-by-sixes." The cramped riding area in the back, which was covered by a thick canvas tarp, definitely wasn't for the claustrophobic because it seemed only six by six feet square at best. Several of these trucks were filled with supplies and pulled away before a sergeant came over to us, pointed to the last truck in the line, and barked, "You three—in here." As we climbed in, I saw the other soldiers who had gotten off the train with us getting into the truck in front of ours.

The ride to camp was as bumpy as the train ride had been, but we were all so excited we hardly noticed. We couldn't have been riding more than ten minutes when Davis-Monthan Field came into view. Williams, who liked to read at every opportunity, looked up from his newspaper and said, "Holy mackerel! Would you look at that."

The camp could only be described as a swarm of activity. Soldiers were marching in formation on the parade ground. Planes were zooming in just over our heads as their pilots practiced takeoffs and landings on the airstrip to our left. Six-by-sixes, jeeps, and other types of trucks were all honking as their drivers tried to part the steady stream of soldiers moving back and forth from building to building. We had been stopped for a few moments when shots suddenly rang out, causing us to duck back in our seats. A soldier walking by saw us flinch and said, "That's incoming! Better watch out!"—and he laughed and slapped a buddy on the shoulder as they just avoided being hit by a jeep. The crack of rifle shots continued and Doc rolled his eyes and pointed across the way to the rifle range where soldiers were practicing. "Incoming," he said drolly.

Our truck continued to inch through the camp, and I, too, was stunned by the activity around us. The only time I ever saw this much activity in one place was during the halftime spectacular at the Iowa-Michigan football game in Iowa City when I was a student there. As I looked around I thought to myself, "Beehive…"

The three of us were entranced. We passed an infirmary with a huge red cross painted above the door. As clumsy as I am, I figured I'd get to know that place really well. Then the main base headquarters went by. It was smaller than I expected it to be, a small frame building wedged between two metal Quonset huts. It had a small porch on the front, and soldiers with rifles were stationed on either side of the door. We passed three mess halls, designated A, B, and C. They were wooden buildings, rectangular in shape, with flat roofs, which I thought was odd. We passed half a dozen large Quonset huts that appeared to be serving both as workstations and hangars for some of the planes assigned to the field. I could see sparks from welding torches lighting the shadows inside as we passed. Off in the distance, across the road and just to the side of the main runway, I could see the outline of a baseball field and pointed it out to Doc and Williams. Both had been unusually silent the whole time we had been making our way through camp. "That looks right up your alley, Doc," I said while making the motion of swinging a bat. Doc started to say something, but then just sat back against the canvas and shook his head like he couldn't believe what he was seeing before him. Williams, too, just leaned back and stared out at the camp as we inched along.

"What do you think?" I asked.

"It's bigger than all of Kinloch," Williams said, blinking his eyes rapidly. "This is a damn city. And what do you suppose that is?" he pointed and asked as we passed a building marked Service Club.

"I'm not sure," I replied. "It sort of sounds like the army version of a nightclub, doesn't it? I sure hope it is."

As we turned a corner, we also noticed the obstacle course off to our left. Soldiers were crawling, running, and diving in all directions as gunfire blasted away. "If it ever gets quiet here, I'll be shocked," I said.

We finally came to the barracks, which were very similar in size and shape to the mess halls we had passed. Actually, there were several rows of barracks, each set designated by a letter and a number. Our truck stopped between Barracks A-3 and Barracks B-1. The four soldiers who had been on the last train with us hopped out of their truck and were directed toward Barracks A-3.

Doc started to climb out of our truck when a sergeant standing to the side called out, "Wait one. This isn't where you'll bunk." Doc sat down again as the truck lurched forward. We passed Barracks B-2 and B-3 and kept going. About two football field lengths from Barracks B-3 we came to Barracks C-3, the barracks that appeared to be most distant from the front gate.

A sergeant was waiting there, evidently expecting us. He was using his tongue to roll a toothpick back and forth in his mouth.

"OK," he said. "You three. This way—and I mean right now." He scrunched his face and motioned impatiently for us to follow him as he growled, "Come on, come on!"

We followed him up a gravel path strewn with weeds. When he got to the entrance of the barracks, he opened the door and said, "Find yourselves some bunks and then stow your gear. And for God sake get cleaned up. You look like boxcar bums. You've got one thing and one thing only to do today. Report to the infirmary back by the gate so the doc can check you out. Chow is at seventeen hundred. You report to Mess C. Got that?"

He paused and then repeated more slowly this time, "Mess C. Got that?"

"Yes Sir!" I said as I snapped to attention and saluted. Doc and Williams caught this out of the corner of their eyes and followed suit.

The sergeant immediately paced back and forth right in front of us, getting right in our faces as he shouted. "You idiots! You don't salute sergeants! Where do you think you are, in the damn Boy Scouts?"

Before any of us could open our mouths he said, "At ease. Now get your asses in there and get organized. After you get checked out by the doc, you can either come back here and crap out or look around the camp—but don't bother anybody for criminy sakes. And don't be late for chow or you'll go hungry. Get in there and get going," he said as he ushered us into the building.

"One more thing," he added. "Your barracks sergeant will be by sometime later today to get you organized. Try not to get yourselves in trouble until then. OK?"

I nodded back at him and unconsciously started to salute as he turned and walked away, but I put my arm back down when I saw he had already started yelling at a young private who had flipped a cigarette butt right in the middle of the road. "You stupid idiot!" he screamed at the stunned soldier. "Where do you think you are, in your living room at home? Pick that up and put it in your pocket."

The soldier, who looked like he was going to throw up by this time, picked up the lit cigarette and put it into his shirt pocket.

"Oh, no respect for your uniform either!" the sergeant yelled right in his face. "Why you dumb jackass...."—and his voice trailed off as he ushered the soldier up the road like a dog herding a sheep.

"Nice guy, isn't he?" Doc said as we headed toward the barracks.

"Yeah. Maybe our sergeant will be just as nice," Williams said dryly.

Our surprise at our first glimpse of Davis-Monthan Field was suddenly matched by the expressions on our faces as we entered the barracks.

"Holy smokes," Williams said. "What the..."

"It's like a ghost town," Doc added solemnly.

He walked over to the window and rubbed a peephole in the thick layer of dust covering it. "Will you look at this," he said, "This place is filthy. My uncle's garage isn't half this bad."

"And it looks like it is all ours, " I added.

Canvas cots were lined up about three feet apart on both sides of the barracks all the way back to an open area at the far end of the room. There were plenty of windows along the outer walls, but the dust on them was so thick they didn't let in much light. We walked the length of the cots to the open area. There we found a small hand-painted sign on the wall that said, "Recreation Area—Keep It Clean!" In this recreation area we found an ancient pool table. Closer inspection revealed the felt covering on it was ripped in three places. The pool cues were also missing their tips. There was something that resembled a Ping-Pong table lying across two sawhorses, but it was as warped as a record left sitting in the sun too long. We found paddles under the table, but there were no Ping-Pong balls in sight. To the right of this there were also a couple of tables with wooden folding chairs around them. We sat at one of the tables and took stock of the situation.

Williams was the first to break the silence. "I don't think anyone else is staying here."

Doc frowned and said to me, "See, I told you he wasn't the sharpest knife in the drawer."

"No, I'm serious," Williams continued. Nobody has slept in these cots in ages. And look at that sink." He gestured toward a lone sink on the wall next to the pool table. "It's dirty as an old toilet."

"Sure looks like it has been used as one," I added.

"What do you suppose that is?" Doc asked as he got up and walked through a door behind the recreation area and into the only part of the barracks we had yet to explore. I was just about to say, "It's probably the latrine" when he immediately came back out, eyes closed, holding his nose.

"I thought so," I said. "Pretty clean, huh?"

"Yup, clean like the city dump," he replied.

"Well, what do we do?" Williams asked. "Do we clean it up or what?"

"I'm no psychic," Doc said, "but I don't think any maids are going to come in and clean it up for us."

I reminded them that we were to report to the infirmary right away. "It'll keep," I said. "We'll worry about housekeeping later."

Williams, who really was shaping up to be quite an optimist, said, "You know, I don't think it will be too bad after we clean it up a little."

Doc and I just groaned.

We chose the three cots nearest the recreation area and put what few items we had with us into the footlockers next to them.

I took one last sweeping glance around the barracks and said, "Well, it isn't much, but I guess it's home. I've been in worse places."

Doc quickly added, "Yeah, but recently?"

* * *

We walked the reverse of our entrance into the camp until we came to the infirmary. On the way there we all talked about getting a pretty good going over during the physicals we had received after reporting for induction. Williams said it was the first time a doctor had taken a look at him since he had the measles when he was five years old. The more we talked, it also finally dawned on us we had all had our physicals at Jefferson Barracks in St. Louis—but on different days during the same week.

The doctor at the infirmary, a short balding man with a thin mustache, lined us up and checked our hearts, lungs, reflexes, and eyes—all without saying a word to any of us other than "Uh-huh" as he finished each test. When he checked Williams' eyesight, he noticed how scratched up his glasses were. He held the glasses up to the light and said, "Well, I think we can do something about these. How in the world can you even see to walk, soldier?"

Williams responded, "I only have trouble seeing at night, Sir."

The doctor replied, "If you're going to be in the army, you've got to see all the time. Especially at night. You report back here tomorrow morning and I'll see what I can do for you."

I guessed we all passed because he wrote a few notes on a clipboard and instructed us to get dressed up to our shirts. We all knew what was coming next. More shots. I had already had so many shots before we left St. Louis that I was starting to feel like a man thrown onto a cactus. Doc leaned down to Williams and whispered to him, "I heard about this guy who had arms that were so skinny—about like yours—that the needle went all the way though and the doctor ended up giving himself a shot instead."

Williams, who was already looking queasy, just smiled sickly and closed his eyes tightly as he received the first shot, during which he let out a yelp that shocked even the doctor.

* * *

By the time we finished our physicals it was only about fifteen minutes before mess call. We walked over to "Mess C" and matched pennies outside until a corporal standing by the door motioned us in. Williams was still rubbing his arm when we entered the building.

No one else was there.

The corporal showed us where to sit and then walked back and stood by the door. We each looked at each other, but none of us knew what to say. A minute or so after we sat down, a soldier wearing a well-soiled cook's apron came in carrying a tray of food for each of us. He put the trays in front of us, turned around, and without comment left the building.

"Should we just dig in?" Williams asked.

"Might as well," I said. "I get the feeling we're going to be dining alone this evening."

The food was actually pretty good. Either that or we had just worked up healthy appetites during the long trip to camp. On our trays we had some kind of meat loaf, mashed potatoes and gravy, creamed corn, and a roll. I wanted salt for my corn, but other than the corporal at the door, who stood there watching us eat, there wasn't anyone else around to ask for it.

While I ate my nonsalted corn, I thought about the irony of the colorful posters on the walls between the windows of the mess hall:

"Eat All You Want, But Eat All You Take."

"Loose Lips Sink Ships."

"They May Be Listening."

The last poster had a picture of Hitler, Tojo, and Mussolini all cupping their ears as they leaned toward a group of Allied soldiers who were talking to each other.

"They May Be Listening," I read aloud to the amusement of Doc and Williams. "Somehow, gentlemen, I don't think we have to worry about that tonight."

When Williams and I finished eating, our plates were so clean they could have been reused right away.

The corporal at the door came back over to our table and asked,

"You want any more?"

Williams and I were leaning back in our chairs and patting our stomachs when Doc said, "If it's OK, I could stand some more of that meat loaf. And could you throw in some more of that corn and maybe some potatoes, too?"

A few minutes later another tray of food was brought in by the soldier wearing the soiled apron. Williams and I sat there and watched Doc do what the sign on the wall behind him said to do—"Eat All You Want, But Eat All You Take." He was taking that literally.

As Doc dug into his second helping of food, I said to Williams, "You know, I don't even know your first name. What is it?"

My question nearly caused Doc to choke on his food. When he regained his composure, he laughed and said, "Yeah, Williams. Why don't you tell him your real name?"

"I don't like my name much. I'd rather you just call me Williams."

"OK with me, " I replied. "Just curious, that's all."

Doc swallowed a huge bite of mashed potatoes and said, "His name is Percival. Percy for short."

I could tell how uncomfortable Williams was becoming, so I quickly added, "Most people back home call me Perc. I think it would be too much confusion if we had a Percy and a Perc in the same outfit. I'll just call you Williams if that's OK with you."

Williams nodded his head in approval.

Doc finally finished his food and we got up to put our trays away—but we couldn't figure out what to do with them.

"That's OK," the corporal said. "Just leave 'em on the table. If you're finished, you can go back to your barracks now. I was instructed to tell you that your sergeant will be there to see you soon. He'll take care of you from here on."

We left Mess C and started walking back to the barracks. Before we had gotten too far Doc said, "Wait a minute. Look at that."

He was pointing to Mess B. Through its windows we could see it was well-lit and appeared to be full of soldiers.

"You see any colored soldiers in there?" Williams asked.

"You're right," I said to Doc. "He isn't the sharpest knife in the drawer."

A little farther down the road Williams started singing again,

"You're in the army now,

You'll never get rich, and how…"

And at that point Doc grabbed him, turned him upside down, and over Williams' protests pretended he was going to stuff him into a trash can on the side of the road. When Doc finally put him down, Williams put up his fists and said, "One of these days, Doc."

He looked so silly, his uniform flapping in the evening breeze, all we could do was laugh.

I looked over my shoulder one last time at Mess B.

We walked the rest of the way to the barracks in silence.

3

GHOSTS

D oc was right. Barracks C-3 "was" a ghost town.
And we were the ghosts.

At least we might as well have been. For the next three days we were pretty much holed up there, doing the best we could to make the barracks livable. The flurry of activity around camp continued nonstop during the days, but we weren't asked very often to be part of it. Instead, we had been given a specific job—barracks duty.

Our barracks sergeant had been waiting for us that first night when we returned from chow, and we were glad to see him. His name was Sergeant Ingram. His was the first black face we had seen since arriving. He had been transferred to Davis-Monthan from Fort Leonard Wood in Missouri, so, in an odd sort of way, we felt he was also something like family. One of the first things I asked him was why he wasn't staying in the barracks with us, and he said for some reason he had been quartered by himself in a small Quonset hut behind headquarters. It didn't make any sense to any of us, but, as Sergeant Ingram said, "The army never explains."

That first night he also had us sit with him at a table in the recreation area so he could go over the rules of the camp, and especially about places that were off-limits. Sergeant Ingram, who told us just to call him Sarge when others weren't around, appeared to be in his mid-forties. He had short-cropped hair that had already receded halfway toward the back of his head. His eyebrows were bushy and turning lightly gray, and if I knew for sure it wouldn't have gotten me thirty days in the stockade I would have made fun of the fact that it looked like they were almost growing together above his nose. He was soft-spoken to the point that it was often difficult to make out what he was saying. In every respect he was the opposite of the sergeant who led us to the barracks that first afternoon. And the difference made me smile as I listened to him go over our orders.

We had all originally been told we'd be taking our basic training at Davis-Monthan, but Sergeant Ingram said that wouldn't be happening, that we'd be shipping out pretty soon. I asked where we might be going next, and again, only Uncle Sam knew for sure. Sergeant Ingram had replied, "Son, when you have been in the army as long as I have, you'll learn not to ask questions. You'll be told where to go, what to do, and when to do it all. THAT is life in the army. And you better get used to it."

Still, it was odd watching other soldiers around camp getting their training while we were pushing brooms and rakes.

Our orders had been simple. The three of us, under the supervision of Sergeant Ingram, were to clean the barracks and police the outer grounds. Basically we were to get the barracks ready for the next group of soldiers coming in. No one knew exactly when they would arrive, but we were told to get on with the cleaning as quickly as we could. So we did.

We followed the same routine in the mornings for the next three days. Sergeant Ingram came and rousted us at 0600. We dressed quickly and headed to the mess hall for breakfast, where we continued to eat alone. Back at the barracks, we put on our work clothes, which looked like painter's coveralls, over our uniforms. We then got to work. I suggested, just to give us some variety, that every thirty minutes or so we rotate our jobs. I started out cleaning the sinks and stools in the latrine, Doc worked on scrubbing the floor, and Williams tried to make headway on the dusty windows. Then, after half an hour or so, we'd switch off. Sarge came in once in a while to check on us and see if we needed anything, but he stayed outside, smoking and reading a stack of old *Stars and Stripes* newspapers.

The crud and stains built up on the sinks proved too much for the old toothbrush and small tin of cleaning paste I had been given. No matter how hard I scrubbed, they just weren't coming clean. I smelled the cleaning paste, and it had just the faintest odor of soap. What I needed, I decided, was something much stronger, much more caustic. At midmorning, at the start of my second round of working on the latrine, I asked Sarge if I could go look around for some other type of cleaner. I don't think he really heard me because he kept right on reading his paper and just nodded and said, "Uh huh."

I walked over to a Quonset hut where I had seen welder's sparks flying when we first came into camp. When I entered the hut, one of the mechanics came over, continuing to wipe grease off his hands with a rag, and asked me, "Is there something you want?"

"Very much," I said. "I'm working over in Barracks C-3. I'm trying to clean it up, but all they gave me was this paste that works about as good as spit. Can I look around for a few things to add to it—to juice it up a little?"

The mechanic looked warily at me. "I don't have anything but degreaser in here."

He stopped short of offering me some of it. I could tell he still didn't quite understand what I was doing there.

"Look," I said, holding out my hands. "Ever seen hands that black before? If I don't get something else to use on those sinks, I'll never get them—or these hands—ever clean again."

The mechanic looked at my hands, then at me, and started laughing. "Go ahead. Be my guest," he said. "I'll get you some degreaser, and if you can find anything else you can use, help yourself."

I thanked him and hurried inside before he changed his mind. After looking around, I filled small cans with everything from airplane fuel to motor oil. I put the cans in a small box and tried my best to keep them from spilling. When the mechanic saw me about to leave he yelled, "Keep those hands clean!"

I laughed, waved back to him, and, gingerly holding the box against my chest, headed back to the barracks, dodging soldiers and trucks as I went.

Sergeant Ingram was still completely absorbed in his *Stars and Stripes* and didn't even seem to notice when I stepped around him on my way back up the walk.

When I entered the barracks, Doc and Williams asked what I had in the box, and I replied, "Our salvation—I hope." Each one just shook his head as I disappeared into the latrine. There, I quickly set up my lab. I knew I had gathered plenty of petroleum-based materials, but I wasn't sure if I had enough in the way of reactionary agents to mix with them. I closed my eyes a minute and wondered what Professor Johnson would have done. Professor Johnson had been my "chemistry lab" teacher, and my favorite teacher, at the University of Iowa. I owe him so much. He not only gave me constant encouragement, but he also gave me something I needed more than that—a job. He hired me as his lab assistant, a job that paid just enough to keep me from getting the heave-ho at my rooming house. My main job was to keep the lab in tip-top shape, but he also had me tutor some of the slower students in his classes when I had the time. I never dreamed, while working for Professor Johnson, that one day I'd be using the knowledge he shared with me to clean toilets....

As I looked at the tins set up before me, I also remembered a warning he had always given us in the lab: "In chemistry it isn't always just what you mix together, it's 'how' you mix them together. Never, ever think of one without the other."

The only thing I was worried about was mixing the cleaning paste with the other items. I could also smell ammonia in it, and I didn't want to turn the barracks into a gas chamber. "It's 'how' you mix them together," I said to myself as I mixed the ingredients, adding the petroleum-based items last. The cleaning paste combined with airplane grease made a concoction as gritty as sandpaper. However, when I added the airplane fuel and the motor oil, the result was a brown glob that had the consistency of mud. I dipped the toothbrush into my makeshift science experiment and headed over to the worst of the sinks. A few circular scrubs later I watched the crud on the sink sliding down the drain. To be honest, it was probably the airplane fuel, all one hundred–plus octane of it, that had more effect on the dirt and grime than anything else. All I knew for sure was that this concoction worked. The only downside, as far as I could tell, was that it smelled more than a little like carp left in the sun too long. If it saved us time, I really didn't care.

I asked Doc and Williams to keep at their present duties for an extra half hour so that I could get more of the new cleaner ready to go.

When we finally did switch off, I handed Williams the can of cleaner and said, "Whatever you do, don't get it on your hands. And don't light any matches or turn on any radios. If you do, we'll all go up like the Fourth of July."

"What is it?" Williams asked. He took a good whiff of it, turned his head to the side, and said, "Dead fish?"

"No," I replied. "It's our new cleaner for the latrine—and probably for the windows too, although it might eat away the grout holding them in place. Just hold your nose and be careful with it."

Doc, who had already moved over to the windows, shouted back, "Geez-Louise. I can smell that shit over here. I'm opening some windows."

It may have reeked of dead fish, but it also helped Williams clean the rest of the sinks in less than half an hour. When we went outside for a smoke, I said to myself, "Thank you, Professor Johnson. Thank you."

* * *

The next day we finished the inside of the barracks. Since we didn't have to work on the latrine anymore, we concentrated on the floors and the windows. The cleaner worked fine on the windows, but I told Doc and Williams not to bet any money they'd still be there in three months. When Sarge came in to look around, he couldn't believe the change. "Well I'll be damned. You guys are really good," he said. "I've still got some doubts, but just maybe there's hope for you yet."

We didn't tell him about the new cleaning product. Sarge had already advised us not to ask questions while in the army, but we were all figuring out something else equally as important: Don't volunteer information. What others didn't know, we figured wouldn't hurt us.

At about four in the afternoon, 1600 army time, on the third day of barracks duty, Sergeant Ingram came in and told us to knock off for the day.

"Come on outside, boys. Light 'em if you got 'em."

I didn't want to tell him, but there was no way on this earth we were going to light up a smoke inside the barracks where the cleaning fumes were still pretty thick. I looked at Doc and Williams, and they must have been thinking the same thing because they were both grinning like idiots as they reached for their cigarettes.

When we got outside, two baseball gloves, a bat, and a ball were on the ground in front of us.

"I heard you guys talking about the baseball field last night," Sergeant Ingram said softly. "Well, I look at it this way. You three have been working your tails off. I don't think a little ball will ruin you."

Doc had already picked up a glove and was pounding a fist into its pocket.

"It's close enough to chow that I don't think anyone else will show up, but if they do, you'll have to get off the field. Understand?"

"Got it, Sarge," I responded, picking up the ball and bat. "Can we go now?"

"Go ahead. Get the hell out of here. But be back in time to get cleaned up for chow!"

With that, we took off running toward the field, whooping and hollering like kids let out at recess.

Doc suggested we play something called "Indian ball," and Williams quickly seconded the idea. Both said it was "the" game to play back in St. Louis. I'd never heard of the game before, so I asked them how it was played.

Doc, itching to get started, quickly explained the rules. As it turned out, Indian ball was the perfect game for three players. All three players played against each other—each was his own team. Doc wanted to be the St. Louis Browns. Williams decided to be the St. Louis Cardinals, the rival team in St. Louis. I became the Kansas City Monarchs.

Doc quickly explained that when three play the game, one bats, another pitches, and one plays a combination infield/outfield position. The first thing he did was walk off about thirty feet from third base over toward second base. When he stopped, he yelled at Williams, "Hey, find something I can use to mark this spot."

Williams looked around the field and spotted an empty Coke bottle. He picked it up and tossed it underhand over to Doc. Doc stood the bottle up on the spot he had just marked. "OK," he said, pointing to Williams. "You bat first. I'll pitch. Perc, you play just behind the infield between those two markers," pointing again to third base on the left and the bottle on the right.

The rules of the game were simple enough. Each batter got two outs per inning. Each swing and miss was an out, so making contact with the ball was a must. However, the batter didn't just have to hit the ball, he had to hit it between the markers, in this case third base and the Coke bottle, or the result was an out.

Doc rounded out the rules by saying, "This is all pretty easy. A ground ball past the pitcher and past the line between the two markers is a base hit. If the fielder catches it before it gets beyond that line, it's an out, but if it makes it past the line before being caught, it is a single. If it gets by the outfielder, it is a double or triple depending on how far it goes—we can argue about that later. A fly ball caught in fair territory by anybody is an out. A fly ball that lands in front of the outfielder is a single. If it is over the outfielder's head, it's a home run. Anything hit anywhere on either side of the markers is an out, no matter if it is a grounder or a fly. Got that?"

It didn't seem all that complicated, so I said I was ready to give it a try. "Let's go," I said, looking again at my watch. "We don't have much time."

Doc moved from the regular pitching mound over toward the left-field line so that he was roughly between the markers but still the same distance from home plate as the regular mound. From there, he threw the first pitch to Williams, who swung and missed.

"Hey, I wasn't ready!" he yelled.

"That's one out," Doc replied.

"All right. You asked for it now. Bring it in," Williams shot back.

He swung and clobbered the next pitch, sending a line drive to my left that I got my glove on but couldn't catch. The ball rolled halfway to the fence before it stopped rolling.

"That's a triple," he shouted.

"No way," Doc yelled back. "Double at best. Didn't make the fence."

When they finally quit arguing, Doc double-pumped his windup, kicked his leg high in the air, and threw a pitch that whizzed right past a swinging Williams.

"Garden gate," Doc teased. "Looked like my garden gate."

Doc rotated in to bat, and suddenly I was pitching. Williams moved to the fielder position.

"This guy can't hit. Easy out. Easy out," Williams encouraged. I had the feeling, watching Doc taking his warm-up swings, that he was going to be anything but an easy out. I hadn't thrown a baseball in a long time, and my first pitch bounced before it got to Doc. He stuck one hand out, caught it on the bounce, and fired it back to me.

"Two balls is a walk," he reminded me.

My next pitch was close enough to the strike zone for him to whack it down the third base line. Williams hustled over to catch it on a bounce in fair territory, but it was past the invisible line between the two infield markers, so it was a single. I was impressed by Williams' athletic ability. For someone so slight, he ran like a gazelle. I did suppress a laugh, though. While running, his clothes flapped like there was a kite following him.

Doc drilled my next pitch right over the Coke bottle, and the ball didn't stop rolling until it hit the fence. A triple.

"One run in," Doc shouted to us. "Invisible man on third."

"Who do you think you are, Josh Gibson?" Williams quipped.

Josh Gibson was Williams' hero, the star of the Homestead Grays of the Negro National Leagues. Gibson was a power-hitter who struck fear into every pitcher in the league. Williams called him "the black Babe Ruth," and the name was fitting. It was said that he once hit a line drive so hard it knocked a hole in the outfield wall during an exhibition game at Forbes Field in Pittsburgh.

"Just call me Stephens," Doc responded, alluding to Vern Stephens, his favorite player, the power-hitting shortstop of the St. Louis Browns.

My next pitch was a ball, but I teased, "Say, didn't that hit the corner?"

"My ass. I couldn't have hit that with a broom."

He added, chuckling, "Who do you think you are—Satch?"— referring to Satchel Paige, the star pitcher for the Kansas City Monarchs.

The minute I threw the next pitch I instinctively started ducking—and it was a good thing. Doc swung on and smacked the ball just past my head. It was so close I could hear the ball sizzle as it went by. By the time I got myself off the ground I saw Williams picking the ball up back at the fence.

"Easy triple. Ought to give me a home run for that one, " Doc laughed. "What's the matter, Perc? Part your hair with that one?"

"Very funny," I said dusting the dirt from my clothes. "Very funny."

Williams called time out and ran in while motioning me to meet him at the edge of the infield.

"Look," he said. "You're going to get killed if you're not careful. Can you throw a curveball?"

"Nope."

"A sinker?"

"Nope."

"The spitter?"

"No."

"Well, what can you throw?"

"Just base hits, I guess." I thought that was pretty funny, but Williams was taking this all seriously and just stared blankly at me. While he and Doc were good friends, it was also obvious there was a long-standing competition between them. I just figured that anything between them on a playing field would probably end up looking like David playing Goliath, but it was clear Williams had other ideas. Williams was shy, but I was starting to see he was what my father always called "sneaky-shy." When it counted, Williams could come out of his shell in a hurry.

"Look, I've seen him knocking hits all my life. He's great. But there is one thing he can't hit, and that's a curveball. I've got a fair one, so after five runs, I'm relieving you. I'll get him out."

Their rules permitted a change of pitchers after the batter had plated five runs. To this point only two runs had scored, and there was a runner on third.

One pitch later it was four runs in. Doc pounded the ball well over a backpedaling Williams. The ball took one bounce and hit the fence.

"Home run!" Doc shouted. "Circle the bases, boys," he motioned to the imaginary runners.

"My next pitch ended up in almost exactly the same spot. Five runs were now in.

"Relief pitcher!" Williams practically screamed while running in. "You go take the outfield," he said to me as he took the ball and started rubbing it up. It was obvious I reeked as a pitcher, and I had also just about had my hair parted by a line drive, so I was relieved, in both senses of the word. I shrugged and trotted out to the edge of the outfield grass.

"Oooohhhh, I'm scared now," Doc said as he shivered at the plate.

Williams wound up, put all of his weight behind the pitch, and followed through so far he actually slipped and fell down as he threw the ball. I was watching him fall when I heard the *whack* of bat on ball. I never saw the ball. I "heard" it hit, on the fly, the fence behind me. If it had hit me, it would have killed me.

Williams called me back in and said, "Tell you what. Forget playing short outfield. Move all the way back to the fence and come in on a fly ball. We'll give him all the singles he wants, but he's too proud to settle for that. Eventually he'll hit one you can catch."

"Eventually" was the right word. Eleven runs scored before Doc got under a pitch and popped it right to me. I didn't have to take two steps before it settled into my glove. Doc, probably still shocked that I had caught the last ball, swung at the next pitch, a sharp breaking curve, and missed. I then rotated in to bat. Two swings later I was back pitching, much to their laughter and delight.

Indian Ball turned out to be a fast game. With only two outs per at-bat, it seemed like Williams and I spent more time changing positions on the field than we actually spent in the batter's box. After Williams started pitching to him, Doc's turns at bat also sped up. Still, Doc had enough bat control that he could pretty much place line drives wherever he wanted on the field. We were just about out of steam from chasing them down when Doc looked at his watch and called out, "Hey you guys—it's chow time. Let's move it. I'm starved."

Doc had won the game, 17 to 3 against Williams—17 to 0 against me. I had lost the game, but I was feeling the glow of a winner and the warmth of new and sincere friendship. As we left the field, Doc and Williams came over, patted me on the back, smiled broadly, and each slung an arm up over my shoulders. We may have been three teams on the field, but we were one leaving it. And it felt good. Damn good.

We barely had time to take the baseball equipment back to the barracks before we had to rush over to the mess hall. Again, we had the entire place to ourselves. This time we were served chipped beef in a heavy gravy on slices of toasted bread, with a heaping mound of mashed potatoes on the side. The corporal who watched us eat called it "SOS"—which Sergeant Ingram later told us stood for "shit on a shingle."

We all thought it tasted pretty darn good.

* * *

Just before taps we decided to go out into the cool night air to have a last smoke. Doc and I were Lucky Strike men. Williams had no choice—he kept bumming cigarettes from us.

"Good grief, can't you get your own smokes?" Doc whined.

As I held a match over to light Williams' cigarette, he inhaled the first drag and started choking and coughing. "When did you start smoking?" I asked, more worried about his health than interested in when he first picked up the habit.

"When we got here," he replied.

"Yeah, he's a tough guy now," Doc needled. "Smokes cigarettes and eats SOS. Better watch him. He might stab you in your sleep tonight."

"Ha ha," he responded—and choked again as he took another puff.

As busy as the camp had been during the day, it was equally quiet at night. An occasional plane would take off or land, but other than that, there was very little commotion. We weren't under blackout rules, but it was understood by all on the base there would be no lights on at night unless absolutely necessary. As the crow flew, we weren't actually all that far from the Pacific Ocean. There were always rumors of Jap carriers lurking near the coast. I don't think any of us actually believed Jap planes could make it this far inland, but who knew for sure? Extra fuel tanks on a plane just might make it possible, and that thought alone kept men reaching for the light switches as soon as dusk fell.

I took a long draw on my cigarette. I had been thinking about something ever since we arrived at camp. I wasn't sure I should bring it up, but it was becoming a thought like an itch that I just couldn't quite scratch.

"OK, I can't stand it anymore. I've just got to ask you something. Didn't you think they'd put us all together—because of the war and all?"

By the way Doc and Williams turned and looked at me, I knew I didn't have to explain what I was talking about.

I continued, "Call me stupid, but I didn't think it would be like this."

"You're stupid," Doc almost whispered.

"I mean, I thought we were all fighting this together. If Hitler and Tojo marched right into my backyard, they'd be marching into everybody else's too, wouldn't they?"

"My uncle said it would be just like this," Doc said. "It was the same for him in the Big War back in '18. While others pulled triggers, he skinned mules."

Williams, who was practically choking to death, snuffed out his cigarette and said, "Maybe they are saving us for special duty."

Doc and I looked at each other and said, in chorus, "Not the sharpest knife in the drawer."

"No, maybe we're being saved for something really important."

"Like skinning mules?" Doc replied sarcastically.

"I thought I'd be put in a lab or something," I said.

"I want to get my hands on those planes," Doc added.

"I just want to cook," Williams whined softly.

"Well, let's not get too low just yet. After all, I suppose Williams could be right. Remember, here we have the best mechanic and the best cook in all of Kinloch, maybe in all of Missouri. And don't forget, I can make toilet cleaner out of grease, spit, and airplane fuel. I guess we're just going to have to wait and see what happens."

I could tell there was more Doc and Williams wanted to say, but both suddenly became very quiet and just stared back toward the main entrance to the base. Without speaking, we shared one more cigarette, Williams nearly coughing his head off each time his turn for a puff came around, and then headed inside.

I wrote Olivia a quick letter before turning in. I was missing her so much. I could still smell her hair, taste the softness of her lips, feel the small of her back as she hugged me. I was also regretting not asking her to marry me before I left St. Louis. The letter from the draft board, full of instructions to "get your affairs in order" just in case we didn't return, didn't exactly light any romantic fires on my part the last night we were together before I left. I had decided it would be better to wait until I returned from service to propose, but now I was feeling I had made a mistake.

I was right on the edge of sleep when a bugler released the melancholy notes of taps. I sat up in my cot and looked out the east windows in the direction of St. Louis.

My heart was a long way from home.

4

TRANSITIONS

J ust a week and a day after arriving at Davis-Monthan Field, Sergeant Ingram told us to keep sharp and get ready to ship out. He wasn't sure exactly when the word would come, but he said to keep our gear close at hand and be ready to leave at a moment's notice. He said "scuttlebutt," the army version of the gossip one would hear on a telephone party line, said we were going west, with the two most likely choices being somewhere in California or up in Seattle, Washington. Sergeant Ingram was going with us. He said word also had it that we would be joining some type of special unit.

"See," Williams said after hearing Sarge mention the possibility of a special unit. "I told you they were saving us for something special."

Doc and I groaned and shook our heads in response.

We didn't have much time to debate possible destinations. Our orders came in the middle of that same afternoon. Sergeant Ingram, out of breath and waving a sheet of paper in his left hand, came rushing into the barracks.

"This is it, men. We pull out at 0600 tomorrow. Get packed tonight and get some shut-eye. I still don't know exactly where we're going, but I do know we 'are' going—and that's all we need to know for now."

He continued as he looked around the barracks, "You know, I'm actually proud of you three. This place looked like a flophouse. And now look at it. You can be proud. Good job. Damn good job."

We thanked him, not just for the compliment, but also for all he had done for us the past week.

Doc then asked him, "Sarge, you think we'll all be kept together wherever we're going? I'm kinda getting used to these knuckleheads."

"I don't know. No way to tell. We could all be split up, or we could end up in the same outfit for the duration. Uncle will decide that. Whatever happens, I just want you to know I've enjoyed meeting you. You three are still green as corn, but now I'm pretty sure there might be some hope for you yet. Just remember in case we do get split up, don't ask so many damn questions, keep your mouth shut, and don't volunteer for anything, no matter how good it sounds. Got that?"

We all nodded.

"OK then. Police the barracks this afternoon, but other than that, you can write letters, get packed, do anything you want. This is probably the last day of your military service you'll be able to call your own. When we get wherever we're headed, Uncle will own our time from then on out. So, kick back while you can."

Then he added, "Oh, before I forget it, there's one more thing. If you get bored out of your skulls tonight, I hear some engineers got a projector and are going to show a movie against the outside of the motor pool. Some Bogart movie. I think it'd be OK if you went, but sit off to the side somewhere and not in the chairs. If I don't see you there, I'll see you first thing in the morning."

When Sergeant Ingram left, the three of us sat on our cots, not really knowing what to say or do next. The barracks was in good order. The day before we had even pulled the weeds in the walk outside. We were now in "army limbo," a state of being where we were neither fish nor fowl. Like musicians without instruments. Or, closer to home, a cook without a kitchen. A mechanic without a garage. A teacher without a classroom. At that moment, we were nothing. We were nothing until the army said we were something, and we had no clue what that would end up being. All Williams wanted to do was cook. Doc was itching to get his hands on trucks or airplanes. And me? I hoped I would be involved in training programs of some type so I could use my teaching experience. I was *really* hoping the army would use my science background somehow, but I knew that was probably too much to hope for. I could tell similar thoughts were going through Williams' and Doc's minds because they both were sitting on the edge of their cots, staring at the floor, chins resting in their hands.

"I don't know about you two," I said. "But now that I've got some time, I'm going to write a letter back home."

"Me, too Williams said. "My parents are probably worried to death about me."

"I'm not much on writing," Doc said. "But I guess I better give it a shot."

Doc and Williams sprawled out on their cots and started writing letters to their parents. I moved over to the table in the recreation area and started writing first to my parents, and then to Olivia.

In the letter to my parents I told them about cleaning the barracks and learning to play Indian ball. I wanted to tell them about Davis-Monthan Field, but we had already been warned not to include in our letters any specific information about where we were stationed. And we were specifically warned not to describe the layout of the base. Sergeant Ingram told us that all our mail would be read by the censors before it was mailed out. The censors, he said, actually took black markers to the letters and covered any lines that contained information that might hurt us if it fell into enemy hands. On occasion, he said, they took scissors and cut out whole sections of letters before letting them be mailed. He said he once saw a letter that had been cut so many times it ended up looking like a Shirley Temple paper doll. He said all this fell into the "Loose Lips Sink Ships" area.

"Men," he had said. "Don't you complain about what these censors do. The threat of sabotage is real. Remember December 7? How do you think our fleet at Pearl Harbor got its tail kicked? It was all those damn spies who took pictures of the ships and wrote letters back home that made us sittin' ducks. Remember that when you write to your folks back home. Tell 'em you love them. Tell 'em you miss them. And then tell 'em you'll write more later. That's enough."

I didn't figure the rules of Indian ball would betray any national secrets, so I spent most of the letter to my parents talking about the game we played earlier in the week. I really did miss them. I hadn't had time to get back to Des Moines before my travel orders came, so it had actually been almost a year since I was last home. My dad was a high school teacher, and I knew, because this was approaching the middle of the term, he was probably swamped with work at school. My mom was a nurse, and she was always busy trying to juggle her work at the hospital and what needed to be taken care of at home. My brother, James, had just finished high school after a stint in summer school. He had decided to start college at the University of Iowa, as I had many years earlier, but at the last minute he changed his mind. He said he just didn't know what he wanted to do with his life yet. I told him in a letter I sent to him before leaving St. Louis that if he didn't get into college, and fast, Uncle Sam would be making up his mind for him.

As I sat there in the barracks, I could suddenly see the three of them sitting on the front porch and enjoying the cool evening air. My dad, in a heavily starched white shirt, would be giving the newspaper a good going-over. He'd turn a page roughly as he would growl, "Nothing but bad news in this rag." My mom would look up from reading a book, usually a mystery story, shake her head, and respond, "Then why read it?" But Dad never responded. He'd just keep thumbing through the paper until he found more bad news he couldn't pass up. My brother would be in the porch swing, seeing how long it would take ten cars that weren't painted black to go by on our street. It was a game we played as we talked about sports and events of the day. Something to help pass the time. I missed those quiet nights together on the porch. I missed them all.

My letter to Olivia didn't contain any military secrets, but I was still wondering if the censors wouldn't just shred it up after reading it because it was written so lousy. I missed her so badly I couldn't even begin to capture it in the right words. I sat there wondering, "How do you tell someone you love her without making it sound like it's the distance talking?" We were over a thousand miles apart, and I felt every mile between us as I tried to scratch out a few sentences. As I stared at the paper, my mind kept drifting. I knew she was probably just getting home from teaching at Sumner, and here I was, sitting in an army barracks in Tucson, Arizona. And I ached to be with her. Finally, taking a variation of Sergeant Ingram's advice, I told her I loved her, I missed her, and I'd write more later. The words I wanted to send just wouldn't come, so I sent my own "censored" version instead and hoped she'd be able to read between the lines.

We finished our letters, put them in addressed envelopes, but, as instructed, did not seal them. The censors would do that for us after they checked them over. We were also told postage would be free, so we didn't have to worry about getting stamps.

I was still thinking about Olivia and unconsciously tapping the envelope on the table when Doc broke the silence. "I suppose I should write a letter to my uncle, too. He said I could be his partner in the garage when I get back home. I've been thinking a lot about that lately."

"Be honest, Doc. Is that what you'd really like to do—or is that still something you feel you should do because he's family?" I asked.

"I'm not sure. I love working on cars. I really do. I'm just not sure I want to spend the rest of my life in Kinloch. Don't get me wrong. Kinloch is my home. My family is there, and most of my friends still live there. But I don't think there's a car or truck in town that I haven't been under the hood. Before I left, it just about got to the point where I could tell what was wrong with a car as it pulled into the garage because I had worked on it so many times before."

"I think I know what you mean," I said. "When I first started college I worked part-time at a cleaners. Same thing, day in, day out. I got to the point where I could press shirts with my eyes closed, which I think I often did because I usually stayed up too late studying and had to sleep sometime."

"It isn't just that," Doc continued. "I don't know if I can say this right. Ever since I was a kid I've wanted to travel, to see what's outside my own backyard. My family never had the money to go anywhere, and even if we would have, there weren't many places we could go. You know what I mean. I hated it when my dad would say, "Son, we can't go there." I knew it wasn't just money he was talking about. I don't know.... I can't..."

"I know," I said reassuringly. "I know."

He continued, "The reason I've still got a headache is I couldn't stop looking out the window of the trains on the way down here. Everything we went by was new to me. And some of the cars we saw driving along next to the tracks—you ever see anything like those before? I want to work on 'those' cars. I want to see what's under 'those' hoods. Does that make any sense at all?"

"I know what you mean," Williams jumped in. "Cooking is in my blood now. But you know what? I've never cooked anyplace other than the diner. Hell, I've never even been *in* any restaurant other than the few we've got in Kinloch. I swear just about every night I dream about those fancy restaurants you hear about on the radio. You know - those clubs. Now there's where I'd like to cook. I talked about this one time with my dad, and he told me I should just be happy with what I've got. Maybe he's right. I don't know. It's just that I've always dreamed about cooking someplace grand. Someplace where people don't want gravy on everything."

That last comment got a laugh out of us.

"Isn't gravy *supposed* to be on everything?" I asked.

Williams just glared at me in mock disgust.

"How about you, Perc?" Doc asked. "What do you want to do when you get back home?"

I had been thinking about this ever since our train pulled out of Union Station and didn't have to think twice before responding.

"You guys probably won't believe this, but all I want is my old job back. I just want to go back to Sumner. In so many ways, that school *is* my home now. While I was finishing school at Iowa I kept hearing about this great school for Negroes down in St. Louis. It seemed like everyone I talked to had something to say about the place, and it was never anything but positive. Most said it was one of the best schools in the entire country."

I laughed, then continued, "I still can't believe how I got that job. I found out they got about ten times as many applications as they had jobs. Heck, *everybody* wanted to teach there. I knew a letter wasn't going to get me so much as an interview, so one day I packed a few things, got on the bus, and just went down there to see the principal. I told him I had just come nearly four hundred miles just to tell him the school needed me—that I could put together a science lab that would knock his socks down. I even gave him a copy of my chemistry thesis. Know what he said? He said he already had a first-rate lab, but he didn't have a driver's training teacher. The former one had just joined the army. He asked if I could teach that class. I said yes. He then asked if I could also teach math. I said yes. Science? Of course. History? Naturally. Physical education? Absolutely. Finally, he looked me right in the eye and said, 'Son, you're either one whale of a fibber or the greatest teacher since

Socrates. I'll put you on as a substitute teacher for driver's training and science, if you don't think that is too much beneath you, and we'll see which it is.' And that's how I got the job."

"That's when you moved to St. Louis?" Williams asked.

"No, that's when I went back to Des Moines to learn to drive. I had never driven a car in my life. I was pretty sure I could stay a day or two ahead of the students in those other subjects until I got the hang of things, but I figured the principal would want to check my driving skills when I got back and doubted that was something I could fake. Actually, for days after I talked to him I had dreams of wrecking a car and killing us both."

"So who taught you to drive?" Doc asked.

"Of all people, our minister's wife."

Doc and Williams scooted closer as I told the story.

"My parents didn't have a car. Hell, nobody I knew had a car. In Des Moines, the streetcars ran everywhere, so there wasn't a need for anybody to have one of their own. But our minister had one. He was either too busy—or too scared—to teach me himself, so he volunteered his wife, Mrs. Livinia Lucille Little. Her name may have been 'Little,' but I'm telling you right now, that woman was anything but."

I spread my arms to indicate her size and continued, "She was an enormous woman. I mean B-I-G. Must have weighed in at three hundred pounds. When she got in the car it seemed like the car just sort of formed around her. Her chest actually stuck through the steering wheel. That made it really tough for her to turn the car quickly, so I spent most of the time trying not to swear in front of her while she dodged other cars. But that didn't stop her. The funniest thing was how she talked to herself while she drove. She didn't exactly use swear words. She had this sort of vocabulary all her own. But by the way she used the words, I could tell it was just the same as swearing. When she'd just miss hitting a car or miss running off into a ditch she'd howl, 'Puttin' on a hat! Puttin' on a hat!' Or 'Watch that dog! Watch that dog!' One time she did slip and said, 'Hell's on fire! Hell's on fire!' But her all-time favorite swearing was 'Jumpin' the fence! Jumpin' the fence!'—which we almost did every time she turned a corner. She also wore these huge hats loaded with hatpins, and that got to be really dangerous. When she'd take a hard right turn she'd lean over so far toward me that I actually got poked one time. Darn near put my eye out. I'm not kidding."

Doc and Williams were howling. I reassured them the story was true and continued, "After she showed me how she drove, she then told me to get behind the wheel. We were on a dirt road about two miles from town. I didn't know anything about a clutch, so I kept grinding the gears like coffee. Finally, and to this day I don't know how she did it, she reached over with her left leg and showed me how to use the clutch—but she got stuck. And her leg was over mine, so I was stuck, too! Neither one of us could get out of the car!"

Williams was laughing so hard it looked like he couldn't catch his breath. Doc was shaking his head and rolling his eyes.

"I finally got unpinned and quickly learned to drive before she killed me. I learned out of self-preservation. Seriously. I'm not kidding about any of this. After all that, I figured that teaching kids to drive couldn't be that bad. And that's how I learned to drive—and how I ended up teaching driver's training."

"Yep," Doc said, still shaking his head. "I think we're definitely going to have to keep an eye on you. Perc, you're what my uncle calls 'slick as okra.' It's hard to tell when you're really pulling our legs. But that's OK. I bet you'll never tell us a dull story, either."

"It's all true!" I protested. "So help me."

We then sat a few more minutes in silence, each of us lost in our own thoughts of what the future might hold. I probably should have just kept my mouth shut, but I decided I just had to get something off my chest that had been bothering me ever since leaving St. Louis.

"You know what really gets my goat? When I first started at Sumner, I was technically hired as a substitute teacher. That meant I didn't exactly have a permanent job. Basically, I taught on days when a teacher got sick. Luckily for me, one of the science teachers always seemed to have something wrong with her, and the driver's training teacher was off in the army, so I did end up teaching most days. After a few months I was made what they called at Sumner a 'permanent substitute.' That meant I could just about count on being called every morning, and it sure made the bills easier to pay. I didn't know it at the time, but that was also like a probationary period when the principal could decide if he liked me enough to make me part of the regular faculty. We were already losing teachers right and left because of the war, so he finally called me in one day and offered me a full-time position. He asked me if I'd like to be the new general science teacher—and still teach driver's training on the side. I was so happy I actually went behind his desk and hugged him. I think he thought I had lost my mind. Anyway, this is what really gets my goat. I was finally just getting settled into the job of my dreams when the draft board came knocking. I still can't believe it. What luck. What timing. And now look at me. Here I am—sitting with two chuckleheads in Tucson, Arizona."

"Who you calling a chucklehead?" Doc asked. "I think I count three of us sitting here. Right?"

He had a point.

As I sat there I took a close look at my companions. I was really starting to like them. They were good men. And more than that, they were becoming good friends. In the short time that I had known them we had been traveling companions, baseball players, barracks cleaners—and even ghosts together. My father used to tell me it was friendship, not money, that made one rich. In that case, I was feeling wealthy.

Very wealthy.

5

DEPARTURES

The next morning at exactly 0530, Sergeant Ingram threw open the door of Barracks C-3 and shouted, "OK you goldbricks. Off and on! Off and on!"

There was something decidedly different about his demeanor as he urged us to get our gear ready. He had told us we would be pulling out at 0600, so we had exactly half an hour to get rid of the cobwebs, get cleaned up a little, and be outside the barracks.

Sergeant Ingram had been right. When the army said move, we moved. And we were learning not to waste time by asking questions.

We dressed quickly and made it outside just as a six-by-six pulled up and skidded to a halt right in front of us. Sergeant Ingram, who was doing one last general inspection of the barracks, had to run toward the truck and hop in as we were pulling away. Even though it was early morning, we still had to inch our way through the mass of humanity clogging the road.

"Hey, I just thought of something. We didn't get breakfast!" Doc whined.

Sergeant Ingram responded, "You probably won't get lunch, either."

Doc rolled his eyes and plopped back against the canvas.

Williams, who earlier looked like he was sleepwalking, suddenly came to life, "And my glasses! The doc said I'd get new glasses! Maybe they're ready. Can we stop?"

Doc and I looked at each other and, again at the same time, said, "Not the sharpest knife in the drawer."

Sergeant Ingram leaned forward and took a quick look out both sides of the truck. He then sat back down and said to Williams, "I can't do anything about your glasses, but…"

He pulled a paper sack out of his shirt.

He smiled, put a finger to his lips to make the "Shhhhh!" sign, and pulled from the bag warm biscuits and a large slice of ham.

"Look at that!" Doc shouted.

The rest of us quickly, and in unison, whispered, "Quiet!"

Using his pocketknife, Sergeant Ingram then cut the ham into square pieces and, slicing open the biscuits, made each of us a sandwich. "Eat fast, and eat quiet," was all he said as he handed them to us.

At least we wouldn't go hungry.

"You know," I whispered. "As sergeants go, I guess you're really not half bad. Thanks for doing this."

Even through the chewing I could see him smile.

As we pulled up to the station I looked off in the distance and watched a plane land at Davis-Monthan Field.

I wasn't going to miss that place.

* * *

At the station we sat on a bench and waited. Then we waited some more. I was finally starting to understand the old expression that all one did in the army was "hurry up and wait." Several trucks pulled up to the loading area and boxes of varying sizes and shapes were transferred to the train cars in front of us. Every once in a while another truck or jeep would pull up and soldiers hopped out and got right on the train. But we didn't. We were told to hurry up and wait.

When a lieutenant finally came over and told us to get aboard, we were instructed to get in the last car before the caboose. That was getting to be a familiar order.

I claimed a window seat on the side nearest the station so I could watch the comings and goings of the early morning travelers. I was surprised that so many women were there to say good-bye to their men. Long kisses followed by quick hugs seemed to be the order of the day, but one exception in particular caught my eye. The soldier, a corporal, was quite animated, arms waving wildly, as he tried to explain something to his girl. She was wearing a simple green dress with a matching hat. She also had striking features, and even from where I was sitting I could see she had what my dad called an "Italian nose." She stood in front of the soldier, obviously enjoying his performance. Every once in a while she would appear to stop paying attention to him and would look down and pretend to swat wrinkles from her dress. The corporal was becoming more and more frustrated. I couldn't make out his words, but his voice was getting louder and louder. I motioned for Doc to take a look, and he said, "Looks to me like a 'Dear John' letter happening before the poor guy even gets out of town. Damn."

"I don't think so," I replied. "She's enjoying it too much. If she was going to get rid of him, she would have just kissed him and walked away, or not come to the station at all."

"You're an expert on women, too?"

"Hardly. Just the opposite. I was just thinking it wasn't that long ago Olivia dropped me off at Union Station. Those two just reminded me of that."

I started to elaborate but changed my mind for the present. Instead, I pointed out the window and added, "I can tell that guy is crazy about her. Flipped over her. But she's played him like a trout, and now he's just about out of gas."

The corporal was slowing down. Finally he took her by the hand, said something, and she jerked her hand away, obviously taken back by whatever he'd said. Then he took off his cap, slowly got down on one knee, took her hand again, and looked up at her.

"Don't do it!" Doc yelled through the glass of our window. "Run buddy! Get the hell out of here!"

I smacked him playfully on the shoulder. "What you are witnessing," I said, "is true love unfolding right before your very eyes."

"What I am witnessing," Doc responded, "is a man taking his own life. Hell, he might just as well jump under the damn train!"

At that moment we could feel the floor under us start to bounce as if an earthquake was taking place. Almost instinctively, Doc and I started getting up to rush somewhere—anywhere—other than the train. We stopped when we heard the whistles and catcalls of soldiers in the other cars. They were stomping the floors in their cars to serenade the poor corporal on the platform. By this time, Williams and

Sergeant Ingram had come over to our side of the train to see what was going on, and we all joined in with the stomping and hooting. Williams also whistled so loudly the rest of us winced and covered our ears.

Finally the train whistle blew. The woman in the green dress kept playing the soldier, but it was time to let her fish go. We could see her mouth the words "I'll think about it" as the soldier, responding to shouts from the train, turned and ran just as we started moving. A chorus of "boos" welcomed him aboard. The woman in the green dress wasn't embarrassed by all this attention. Not in the least. She blew one final kiss in the direction of the train, turned, and walked away.

As we all returned to our seats, I wandered off into thoughts of the last night I saw Olivia. Union Station was packed that night with servicemen saying their good-byes to family and sweethearts. We were bumped and jostled like pinballs as we tried to get one last private moment alone in that sea of bodies, but before long it became obvious it just wasn't going to happen. Olivia grabbed my hand and urged me to follow her up the long steps behind us.

Once we were upstairs, she pointed to a small alcove just to the right of the main Market Street entrance and instructed, "You stand in here. Put your ear next to the wall and just wait—just listen."

She then moved as quickly as she could to a matching alcove directly across from me on the other side of the entrance hall. I watched her turn around and face the marble wall inside that alcove. In a voice as clear as if she were standing right in front of me I heard her say, "I love you, Inman Perkins. Heaven help me, but I know I always will. Always."

Startled, I turned and looked over at her, but she was still facing away from me. For the life of me I couldn't figure out how her words had come through so crystal clear. The flow of travelers making their way between us as they entered the station had not let up for a second. There was no way her voice should have been able to carry through all that commotion. I then heard her say, playfully scolding me, "Inman Perkins, did you hear me?"

I turned to face the wall in my alcove and said, "I... I love you, too," but I'm afraid my voice was tinged more with curiosity than love.

"That's more like it," she responded. "But you could say it like you mean it." Her words were again crisp and perfectly clear.

I felt like an idiot, standing there talking to the wall, but I leaned forward again and whispered, "I love you with all my heart. How's that?"

I waited for her response. A few moments later I was being tapped on the shoulder. I jumped and turned around to see Olivia smiling at me.

"How in the world does that work? That's amazing!" I said.

"You didn't grow up in St. Louis, so I'm not surprised you don't know about these," she began. "These are the famous Whispering Arches. No one seems exactly sure how they work. It's something to do with the way the building was put together. All you have to do is whisper in one of the arches, and every word of what you say can be heard all the way across the room in the other. Legend has it that if you say 'I love you' to someone you really and truly love in the Whispering Arches, the two of you will meet again right here within the year. I'm counting on that, you know."

Then, mischievously, she added, "And most get married, too. Well, at least that's what I've heard."

"Let's do it again!" I practically shouted, caught up completely in the mystery of the arches.

"We'll have to make it quick or you'll miss your train," she cautioned.

We both moved to our original positions. I faced the wall and said, slowly and clearly this time, "I really do love you—everything about you." I then added, laughing, "Well, *almost* everything about you."

She then replied, "And I love you. So much. So much more than you'll ever know." And then she added, playfully, "And so much more than you deserve!"

We turned and faced each other, catching glimpses only when the steady stream of travelers would part for a second. We made our way to the center of the room where, without saying a word, I took her hand and gently squeezed it. We walked back down the steps to the waiting area just as a soldier and his family moved off a bench. I motioned for her to sit down quickly before someone else jumped in.

We sat there for a few minutes without saying a word to each other. She finally leaned over and nestled herself against my shoulder. I could feel the warmth of her cheek through my uniform, and I pulled her closer just as "All aboard!" rang into our ears.

As we stood up I said, "I'll write as much as I can"—then quickly added, "And twice on Sundays," which got a little smile out of her.

"Come here," I said as I pulled her closer, looking deeply into her eyes. "This kiss has got to last a long, long time."

Olivia started to say something but I pressed my lips to hers and kissed her as hard as I could. Too hard. I then gently kissed her forehead, her nose, her cheeks, and finally her lips again. I didn't know when we'd next be together, and I wanted to remember every feature of her face. As I headed toward the train I turned around one last time and said, "Keep me in your heart" as I pounded a fist to my chest.

Olivia mouthed back, "I love you."

A group of soldiers marched between us and I lost sight of her. Entering the train, I ran my tongue across my lips, tasting her lipstick one last time.

* * *

As we left Tucson, we were all still thinking about where "scuttlebutt" said we were headed. A few minutes after we left the train yard we could tell by the sun we were traveling north.

Noting this fact, Doc said, "I'd say we're headed to that airfield up in Seattle. That's 'way' north of here. Long train ride," he groaned as he rubbed his back.

We then rode in silence until we suddenly started veering slightly west.

"California!" Williams shouted as soon as our direction changed. "Always wanted to see the ocean. Ever since I was a little kid."

At that moment it didn't much matter to me where we were going. Each passing mile was one more chunk of distance between Olivia and me, and that was all I could think about, especially after seeing the soldier and his woman in the green dress that morning at the station.

The train then settled into a steady northwesterly progression. The part of Arizona we were moving through was dry and unpopulated.

We seldom saw any signs of life other than cactus, some of which appeared to be well over ten feet tall, much taller than any I had ever seen in books. Scrub grass and small bushes also dotted the landscape. I thought it odd I never saw any ponds or streams. At one point a dog ran beside the train for a minute or so until it tired itself out. It then sat down, breathing hard, and watched us continue past. The scrub bushes we were passing became almost hypnotic, and I warned Doc to look away once in a while or he'd again have another headache, in his words, the size of St. Louis.

Half an hour or so into our journey Sergeant Ingram broke the silence. He motioned us to lean toward him and whispered, "I guess we're far enough out. I can tell you now where we're going. I'm sorry, but I was under strict orders—*strict* orders—not to say anything until we got away from Davis-Monthan. Security reasons, you understand. Hell, I didn't even know until an hour before we left. No one is supposed to spill the beans about troop movements. No one."

"And we're so important," Doc interrupted sarcastically.

Sarge shot him a cold stare and continued, "Like I was saying. Now I can finally tell you. To be honest, I don't know why we're going north. We're supposed to be going east—to Fort Bliss in El Paso, Texas. That's where Biggs Field is. Men, we've been assigned to a brand-new outfit, the 449th Signal Construction Battalion of the Army Air Corps."

We all took turns questioning Sergeant Ingram about the 449th and what our duties might be, but either he couldn't, or wouldn't, provide much information. Our orders had just been to report. Exactly what we would be doing after we got there would be told to us when the army decided it was time for us to know.

"All I know, " Sergeant Ingram continued, "is that there'll be no more playing around. Looks like we'll probably learn communications and air support, two of the most important duties in this man's army. And a little construction work will probably be thrown in, too. I'm betting so. Hell, to be honest, we'll probably do a little of everything before all's said and done."

"And we're going to be kept together?" Doc asked.

"As far as I know," Sarge replied. "At least we'll be together until

Uncle decides what he wants us to do next."

Doc and Williams then settled into sharing opinions about what specific duties we should be assigned. Sarge finally couldn't take it anymore and said, "Opinions are like assholes. Everybody has one."

That shut them up—until they started laughing.

It took several hours before we learned the reason we were headed north. Our first stop was Phoenix, which was "not" in the right direction for us to be headed to El Paso. As a matter of fact, it was almost in the opposite direction. A sergeant at the station came into our car just long enough to announce we'd have about a two-hour stop there and that we could get off the train to stretch our legs and have a smoke if we wanted. We stepped out onto the platform and watched most of the soldiers traveling with us get off the train. They headed either out of the station or over to other areas to board trains bound for different destinations. Sergeant Ingram told us to stick near the train while he went inside to get a newspaper.

I lit my cigarette and then held my match over to light Doc's. I noticed Williams pulling a cigarette from his shirt pocket, so I held the match over his direction.

"Not on your life!" he shouted. "Three on a match! Get that away from me. You know what that would mean."

"What?" Doc asked drolly. "That you'll get pregnant?"

"No. Third guy on a match always has something horrible happen to him. I've seen it a thousand times. Not me. No way."

"Superstitious, are we?" I added, smiling.

"No," he said. "Not at all. Just not taking any chances."

Williams took a deep drag on his cigarette and started coughing and gagging again.

"Smooth, eh?" Doc teased.

We had been stretching our legs for about thirty minutes when the station suddenly came to life again. Once the activity started, we could hardly believe what we were seeing. The trickle of soldiers was slow at first. The first of them, maybe nine or ten, all privates, had gotten off a train that we watched ease into the station from the west. The soldiers stood on the platform close outside their train and appeared to be waiting for further orders. They also appeared more than a little anxious. They smoked and chatted quietly—and kept together. Very close together.

Within fifteen minutes, two more trains arrived, and this time dozens and dozens of soldiers carrying their gear hopped from those trains and headed into the waiting area near the front of the station. I thought the Phoenix station was starting to resemble Union Station in St. Louis, at least as far as the foot traffic was concerned. Normally, seeing this many soldiers moving around in a train station wouldn't be cause for a second look.

But all the faces in front of us were now colored.

Sergeant Ingram finally came back. He handed us each a section of his newspaper, admonishing us not to rip it up as we read it. But none of us were interested in reading. The colored soldiers who were now moving through every part of the station had our complete attention.

"What's going on, Sarge?" I asked. Doc and Williams asked the same thing almost at the same time.

"Looks like we are getting some company. After the second train came in I asked one of their sergeants where they were headed. Well, guess what? They're coming with us. That's why our train is being held up. We're *all* going to Fort Bliss."

The way he emphasized the word *all* indicated he was just as confused and curious as the rest of us.

After studying the crowd, Williams asked, "Do you see anybody we know?"

Doc and I didn't answer him. It was a ridiculous question, but at the same time we knew what he meant. So far we hadn't seen too many black faces in "this man's army." The odds of seeing someone from St. Louis seemed a long shot at best, but I also caught myself studying the group, just in case....

* * *

Half an hour later all were climbing aboard our train. Our car filled up quickly, and as soon as all were seated the questions rang out around us: "Where you from?" "Where you been?" "What've you heard?" "Where we going?"

Again, scuttlebutt had all the answers—in fact, too many answers.

The soldiers from the different trains, all from different parts of the country, had all "heard" something more than the others, so each group tried to top each other with new information. One group said they "heard" we were going to be trained as a ground combat unit and then sent to the Pacific. Another "heard" we were all destined for construction work, especially the building of airfields. A small group of soldiers from Los Angeles "heard" we were all going to be part of a transportation unit. Still another, the wildest of the stories, had us all, after a short stop for training at Fort Bliss, going to protect the Panama Canal. They had "heard" we were chosen because of our dark skin and the fact we'd blend right in with the locals down there. Therefore, the enemy wouldn't be able to tell the soldiers from the Panamanians, which would give us a tremendous advantage in case of an attack. That was so wild it actually seemed plausible. However, the more I listened to the conversations around me, the more I understood that nobody really knew anything. But the stories made the time go quickly. There was also something comforting about hearing the speculation. It gave us a strange kind of common bond. Soldiers united by gossip.

And Sergeant Ingram had been right. Everybody had one of each.

The soldiers in our car were young. Too young, I thought. The private sitting in front of me looked like he wouldn't have known a razor if it bit him. Even in his crisp new uniform he still looked like he belonged more in the Boy Scouts than in the army. Every once in a while he pulled a picture from his shirt pocket, snuck a quick glance at it, and then put it back. I didn't want to appear like I was spying on him, but I leaned forward, tapped him on the shoulder, and asked, "Your family? Can I see?"

He was embarrassed at being caught. "Yes," he said quietly, handing me the picture. "My mom and dad and my brother."

I glanced at it, handed it back, and asked, "First time away from home?"

"First time anywhere."

I saw his eyes were starting to well up as he looked at the picture.

"Well, stick close to us veterans," I said motioning to myself and to Doc, who was sound asleep and snoring like a wild buffalo. "We'll take care of you, soldier."

"Thanks," he said in a relieved tone. "I don't mind telling you I'm scared. Real scared."

"Ah, you aren't scared. You're just excited like the rest of us. Wouldn't be human if you weren't. Look at Doc here," I said pointing to my dead-to-the-world and snoring traveling companion. "He's excited, too."

The soldier laughed softly.

"He's a tough guy, too. Why, I once saw him break two of his toes with a hammer just to make his shoes fit better!"

He laughed out loud.

"That's better," I said. "You stick close to us. You'll be OK."

"Thanks," he said again. He then pulled the picture from his pocket, not caring if anyone else saw it, and held it on his lap. Soon I saw that he had fallen sound asleep.

I looked around the car again. Yes, I decided, our new traveling companions looked just like a Boy Scout troop. And not a very experienced one even at that.

We then traveled due east to Albuquerque, where we picked up about three dozen more soldiers. The cars were getting crowded. When we first started out from Phoenix, we had the luxury of space, so soldiers put their duffel bags on the seats next to them. Now, however, the bags had to be moved to the aisles so that the new arrivals could have places to sit. In our car, two soldiers stacked their duffels together to the side of the aisle and sat on them. They probably had the only comfortable seats on the train.

Socorro, New Mexico, due south, was our next stop. The train pulled to a side spur and the engines were stopped, which meant we were likely to be there a long time. It was 2:00 A.M. and the New Mexico night air was unusually cool, even for October, as it seeped into our car. By this time the men were talked out, and the only sounds that could be heard were snores and an occasional cough. Sergeant Ingram suggested to all who were still awake that we try to get some shut-eye. Before I drifted off to sleep a white lieutenant making a head count walked through our car. He counted me as "eighty-seven" and continued toward the back of the train. I closed my eyes and never saw him come back through.

* * *

At exactly 0500 the train's engines rumbled to life, shaking the train, waking most of us from an uneasy, and very uncomfortable, slumber. Apparently, even the trains were now on military time.

It wasn't long before the sun started coming up off to our left. A few pulled down window shades to block the morning rays, but Doc asked if he could switch places with me so he could look out the window. Socorro had been a strange stop. As near as any of us could tell, no one either got on or off the train there. The only thing I could think of was we were kept there so that we wouldn't arrive at Fort Bliss before reveille.

I asked Doc what he thought, and he joked, "Listen, if they had brought this many of us into camp in the middle of the night, it would have scared 'em half to death."

He may have been right.

My stomach was growling, but I didn't see any signs that food would be brought to us anytime soon. Someone "heard" we'd be fed once we got to the base. Williams said he was going to go up into the cars ahead of us to see if he could scrounge something for us to eat.

It wasn't long before he came back, empty-handed.

* * *

When we finally pulled into the station at El Paso, about a dozen six-bys were already there waiting for us. We quickly poured out of the train and headed for them. An occasional white soldier was salted into the mix, but most of the faces were black. Doc, Williams, and I followed Sergeant Ingram to a truck near the front of the line and settled in for the ride. I saw the young soldier who had been sitting in front of me on the train and motioned him to join us. I held out a hand and pulled him in.

The ride didn't take long at all because we didn't have to go through the town of El Paso. The base was on the outskirts of town, and a new road had been built around the town just for transport to and from the station. As we approached Fort Bliss, Sergeant Ingram pointed ahead and said, "Gentlemen, you're in the army now."

The minute he said it, Doc and I knew what was coming next. Doc looked at me, slapped his forehead, and said, "Oh, no…"

Williams, without looking up from his comic book, started singing, "You're in the army now…"

"Oh what the hell," I said as I looked over at Doc. And we both joined in, "You'll never get rich, and how…"

As we continued to sing, Sergeant Ingram just shook his head and spit disgustedly out the back of the truck.

Yes, we were in the army now.

6

BASICS

Sergeant Ingram was right. From the minute we entered the gates at Fort Bliss, there was no doubt about it: We "were" in the army now. Davis-Monthan had actually been little more than a relocation center for us, a brief stop on the journey to our real destination and purpose. Of course, this had been planned all along by the higher-ups. We found out about it only when it was time for us to know about it. That was the army way.

We were now assigned to the 449th Signal Construction Battalion, Army Air Corps. Those of us on the train had been brought together to form what the army called a "support" battalion. We were told that support battalions were usually created to help ease the growing pains of an outfit that either through dramatic increase in size or through an expansion of its mission suddenly found itself in serious need of additional help. And we were now going to be providing this additional help, at least temporarily, to the 20th Bomber Command and the 16th Bombardment Operational Training Wing, both headquartered at Biggs Field.

We were also told our primary responsibilities down the road would be in the areas of communications, construction, and air-ground support. However, Sergeant Ingram had also been right about something else. We learned quickly that our group would also be expected to provide everything from transportation to maintenance to security—and pretty much anything else that needed to be done. In other words, we were there to learn "support" in every sense of that word.

The first two days in camp passed like a whirlwind. It seemed like we spent about half that time moving in lines to get examined by doctors. We all had our feet checked for fungus, our vision checked, tonsils checked, reflexes checked, and our hearts and lungs checked. We were tested for color blindness. We had our hearing tested. We even had our teeth checked. We also learned what "Turn your head and cough" was all about, and many held themselves and joked about it the rest of the day we were put through that experience. One joker from Mississippi, mocking the high-pitched voice of the doctor who had tested us, kept going from soldier to soldier all day and asking "Want to turn your head and cough for me?" as those around him would howl with laughter. In the afternoon of the second day we even had an "equilibrium" check, which consisted of seeing how long we could walk back and forth on a raised beam before we fell off.

As a group, I think we did very well, especially considering how many had never had professional medical care before. Many of the men said it was the first time in their lives a doctor had examined them. The one area of great concern, however, had to do with our collective teeth. Tooth decay was rampant in our company, and I overheard one of the doctors telling Sergeant Ingram that dentists would have to be brought in—and soon—or we'd all be in big trouble. Funny, but my teeth weren't bothering me until I overheard that conversation. Then I was convinced I had gum disease and would probably lose all my teeth within six months. I also started getting a terrible toothache that I could feel all the way up to my left eye.

And, of course, there were more shots. Lots of shots. While the shots were being given, just like it always happened in the movies, several really tough looking guys fainted in line. Fainted dead away. Flopped to the floor. And the sight of those men fainting was the last straw for some who were already more than a little uneasy, so more would go down, like dominoes. A group of men behind me, offering up gallows humor, started yelling "Timber!" when a poor soul would start to fall. All I kept thinking about was if any of us ever got sick after all the inoculations we had, we'd deserve it.

When we weren't being given a good going-over by the doctors, we were escorted in small groups to the quartermaster to be issued our gear, which consisted of everything we'd need while in camp, from our clothes to our rifles. The fatigues, the army version of work clothes, issued to me were at least two sizes too big, but the corporal who gave them to me said smartly, "Eat double portions and you'll fit into them in no time." I didn't find it funny. Now I was going to look like Williams.

There were two barracks earmarked for our battalion, N-1 and N-2. I was shocked that rather than being assigned to each barracks based on some type of organized system, we were simply split into two groups the first day while we were waiting for noon chow. That put about sixty men in each barracks. Doc, Williams, and I were all standing together when the split took place so, fortunately, that kept us in the same group. We weren't going to be split up after all. For us, Barracks N-2 was our new army home.

I thought we were a pretty large group, but Sergeant Ingram said our battalion wasn't even half the size of a regular battalion. No one knew just how many more men would be joining us or when they might be showing up. For the time being, Sarge said we had to be one of the smallest battalions in the army. While he was explaining this to us, Williams piped in and suggested there weren't many of us because we were a special battalion. Sergeant Ingram reached out and playfully cuffed him on the side of the head as he said, "You guys were right. He isn't the sharpest knife in the drawer, is he?" We just shook our heads and frowned.

Somehow we had also managed to beat all the officers for our battalion to the base, so Sergeant Ingram was told to take charge of the men in our barracks. A white sergeant named Jackson, on loan from another battalion across the base, came over to watch over those in N-1 temporarily, but every chance he got he took off, leaving the men to fend for themselves. No one seemed all that interested in us, so we were all left pretty much alone when around the barracks.

The first time we entered our barracks the three of us gave a collective sigh of relief. Compared to the reclamation project we had lived in at Davis-Monthan, this place was like the Taj Mahal, especially when it came to sleeping conditions. At Davis-Monthan we had to sleep on cots. Here we had bunks, and I chose an upper because I figured I'd be able to sleep better above the general commotion of the barracks. In one motion I swung myself up into mine and landed with a thud. A quick check revealed the reason. We had boards instead of mattress springs. I complained to Doc, "Hard as concrete. I bet that floor's softer."

Doc replied, "I wouldn't complain if I were you. Look at Williams' mattress."

He pointed to a large slit near the head of the mattress where something like straw appeared to be sticking out. Upon closer inspection we discovered it was horsehair.

"And I always wondered what happened to Seabiscuit," Williams offered dryly.

Doc took the bunk below me, but not before giving it a thorough going over to make sure it wasn't booby-trapped or stuffed with anything worse than the remnants of a racehorse. The bunks might have been less than first-class, but I didn't care. I was just happy the three of us were able to stay together.

Like the barracks at Davis-Monthan, ours also had a recreation area with a pool table and pool cues. However, this pool table actually had a decent felt covering and the cues had tips. There was also a Ping-Pong table, complete with paddles and a box of new Ping-Pong balls. Four small tables were over along the west wall, and we assumed they were for games like checkers and cards. All in all, we were quite impressed.

I most enjoyed watching the men's reactions to the latrine area. About half the soldiers in our barracks were country boys who had never sat on a flush-commode before. "You mean you go to the bathroom inside the house?" several wide-eyed soldiers asked that first afternoon.

One baby-faced soldier who looked about fifteen, fresh off a farm in southern Georgia, had to have the mysteries of toilet paper explained to him. "Where's the catalog?" he asked while searching around the commode. A more experienced soldier standing next to him immediately gave him the nickname "Sears and Roebuck," alluding to a favorite catalog of outhouse users everywhere, a nickname that stuck to the awestruck soldier for the rest of the day. The experienced one continued, "Hey you, Sears and Roebuck, see that roll of white paper there on the wall? You won't have to worry about the shiny pages now!"—a comment that drew guffaws from others but at the same time also revealed that the experienced one wasn't all that much removed from an outhouse himself.

Mr. Experience just wouldn't leave that poor kid alone. He continued, "You don't have to use that nasty white paper if you don't want to. Didn't you get your sack of GI corncobs when you were at the quartermaster? I got mine. Good for at least fifty wipes a week."

Sears and Roebuck shrugged his shoulders and got as far as "I didn't know...." before the explosion of laughter around him told him he had been had.

Nothing like bathroom humor to draw men together.

The first day we were also put into temporary squads of fifteen men, and each squad was scheduled to take a turn cleaning and policing the barracks. The second afternoon, while my squad took a turn scrubbing the floors, the more I thought about our barracks, the more I couldn't get something out of my mind. I knew the building was fairly new because I could still smell the sweet odor of sap in the wooden rafters above me. It finally dawned on me it wasn't the condition of the barracks that bothered me. It was the geography. Just as it had been at Davis-Monthan, our barracks were nowhere near the other barracks in camp. As a matter of fact, we were in the very back of the camp as far away from the main gate as buildings could be located. It was evident from looking around the camp that new construction had been taking place for months, likely, I thought, in anticipation of support groups like ours being added. It appeared there were other places where these barracks could have been built, but they weren't.

I splashed some soapy water over toward Williams, who was singing quietly to himself as he scrubbed the floor. When I caught his attention I said, "I think we're guarding the mail again."

He wiped some suds from the side of his cheek and responded, "Oh yeah. When?"

No, he wasn't the sharpest knife in the drawer....

* * *

On the third day, at exactly 0530, we were jolted into what became our regular daily routine. Reveille sounded, and Sergeant Ingram marched back and forth through the barracks while banging two large frying pans together, which made enough noise to wake the dead. At that point we were instructed to fall out for a head count. Even though this was south Texas, the cool morning air stung my face as the count drifted down the line.

After the men in the other barracks were counted and it was determined all were present and accounted for, we were allowed to go back inside to finish getting dressed and get lined up for breakfast. Breakfast was at 0600, which meant we had very little time to get the sleep out of our eyes and get in uniform. We were marched in columns of twos to our mess, where we had just under half an hour to go through the chow line, find a place to sit, and wolf down our food.

After breakfast it was time to go back and finish cleaning up ourselves and the barracks before barracks inspection. If Sergeant Ingram found something wrong during his inspection, like a bed not made properly, a spot of dirt on the floor, a soldier's uniform not just exactly right, he'd shout, "OK you jugheads, we're going to do it again" as he stomped out of the barracks. That gave us exactly five minutes to fix the problem and inspect each other and the barracks again before he roared back in for a recheck. Every morning Sarge always found at least one thing not done properly, so "double checks" became a matter of routine. There were days when I didn't think we'd get out of the barracks before the war was over. One morning he shouted as we stood at attention by our bunks, "Oh no! I can't believe what I am seeing. Are you men just too stupid to see it? I'm going to go outside while you take care of it." Then he added, softly, as if he were whispering a secret, "And we're not going anywhere today until you find it, and fix it"—at which point he got right in the face of one of our younger men and shouted, "You hear me?"

We heard him all right, but we couldn't for the life of us figure out what he was seeing that we weren't. Finally Williams, of all people, pointed up to a burned-out lightbulb and said, "You think that's what's eatin' Sarge?"

We had no ladder, so Williams stood on the shoulders of Thompson, a giant of a man from Little Rock, and put in a new bulb. When Sarge finally came back in he didn't look right at the new bulb. All he said was, "Well, I guess you aren't as dumb as you all look. Now get outside on the double!" And we did. For the rest of the day I wondered if that bulb was the real culprit—or whether he was just trying to get us to work together as a team. In either case, we were starting to come together. A friendly rivalry was also starting to develop with the men in Barracks N-1, who always seemed to be outside waiting for us while we tried to find something else we had goofed up in the barracks. Their shouts and insults certainly didn't help as we tried to pass inspection.

* * *

Each morning after inspection, the real work of the day began. A parade ground designated just for us across from the barracks was our first stop. There we worked on marching, which was a complete and utter disaster at first. As a matter of fact, Sergeant Ingram, who finally out of necessity just took charge of the men in both barracks, got so disgusted with us so quickly I was afraid he was going to have a stroke. He really did try, starting out each session with the same instructions:

"Ok, even boneheads like you can learn to do this. It's very, very simple. Watch me again. You're going to learn the steps of your cadence count. Here we go. When I say the word 'forward,' that is what Uncle Sam calls a 'preparatory command.' That means you better stop your daydreaming and prepare for action. Then I'm going to add the word 'march,' which is called the 'command of execution.' And trust me on this—if you don't get this right, there just might be a few executions."

He wasn't smiling as he said this. And none of us laughed. Sarge took his marching seriously, like it was a part of his religious faith, and we all knew it.

He then continued, "Remember, when you hear 'march,' you start moving your *left* foot forward, so you really need to be concentrating. When this foot, your left foot, hits the ground, you shout 'one!' After that, you keep counting, out loud, each of the next steps, all the way up to four. Now you know the number four. It comes right after three. That's three toes plus one more. You can take your shoes off to help you count if you want."

The first day one soldier in our group actually started to do just that and Sarge screamed at him until the soldier cringed back into line. There may have been a few smiles, but the rest of us knew better than to laugh.

It was funny watching Sergeant Ingram try to build up steam for one of his tirades. He was a quiet man, soft-spoken by nature. He didn't exactly muster terror in our souls by his words alone, but his hand and arm gestures were really something to behold. When he'd scream at us, what he lost in volume he more than made up for in action. He'd wave his arms, as Doc described, "like a windmill in a hurricane." On top of that, he'd punctuate the arm motions by pointing and shaking fingers at us. At the end of the day I noticed his arms always hung loosely at his sides and he was always hoarse as a goose.

"Now watch me again," Sarge would continue. "See how easy this is?"

He'd then scream "Cadence count! Forward, march!" and start marching and shouting, "One, two, three, four—one, two, three, four."

Every once in a while he'd add a "hup" or a "hut" for variety when he came back to the number one: "Hup, two, three, four. Hut, two, three, four."

He'd continue counting and marching back and forth in front of us until he felt we were ready to give it a try. But we never seemed to be ready. For some reason, large pockets of our group, and not the same ones each day, couldn't get it through their heads that "march" and "one" were actually just parts of the same first step. So, they would quickly take a step forward with the left foot when "march" was called out, and step forward on the right foot when "one" was shouted. This would add an extra step and have them ending each marching set on the wrong foot. When Sarge would see this he'd scream and yell and jump around like a chicken with a leg cut off. It wasn't until the fourth day that we started getting the rhythm down. At the end of drill that morning, I think he was just about to compliment us when soldiers in the back of the formation got out of step and caused a pileup as they marched into those in front of them. Sarge covered his eyes and shouted, "That's the way to do it! Kill those sons of bitches in front of you! Walk right over them if they get in your way. You working for Hitler?"

The next morning we got it right, at least most of the time.

Sarge also lectured us over and over again about the different march commands and which were to be followed and which were not. Above all, we were told to ignore "wrong" commands and keep right on marching until the correct command was given. He gave the same example of this every morning, obviously hoping that repetition would stick to us.

"Now if you hear 'To the rear, march!'—you turn about and march the other direction. But if you hear 'Turn around'—what do you do? You better keep going or I'll chew your asses!"

He said this all had to become second nature to us, that we had to feel, almost instinctively, what was right and wrong. To help us learn the difference between the right and wrong commands, Sergeant Ingram got the idea that every chance we got we should all play the child's game Simon Says. In that game, each direction or command had to begin with "Simon Says," as in "Simon Says, touch your nose." As long as "Simon Says" was there, we had to do whatever it was that followed. However, if just the command part was given, without "Simon Says" included, we were to do nothing. Absolutely nothing. For three days, we tested each other at every opportunity.

In the mess: "Simon Says, pass the salt."

While having a smoke: "Simon Says, give me a light."

In the barracks at lights-out: "Simon Says, please shut the hell up and go to sleep!"

It was dumb, really dumb, but it also brought us together even more. We'd try every trick in the book to catch someone off guard. And when someone was caught, he'd get a playful—sometimes not so playful—punch on the arm or slap to the side of the head. Did it help us with our marching? I thought it was helping until the day Sergeant Ingram had us really moving around the parade ground. We finally had our cadence count down pat. The way we were calling out "Hup, two, three, four!" announced a pride that was building daily in our unit. And then disaster struck. Nearing the end of the boundary of the parade ground, where a large and rather deep puddle had formed during a late shower the previous evening, Sarge decided to test us. He barked, "OK, turn around!"

Half of us did. Half of us didn't. It was probably the thought of marching into the deep water that set off the wrong instinct in so many up front, but there was no excuse I could see for those in the middle of the group.

The scene looked like soldiers being mowed down by machine

gun fire. Arms, legs, and rifle slings all tangled together as the men squirmed around like flies trying to escape a spider web.

We were all expecting Sergeant Ingram to lower the boom on us. Instead, he calmly brushed his hands together like he was wiping off dust, turned slowly, and as men screamed at each other and yelped for help, walked back to the barracks. He didn't say a word.

He didn't have to.

* * *

After drill practice each day, we remained on the parade ground for calisthenics. I was surprised that so many of the men didn't know how to do the various exercises. Sergeant Ingram had those of us who did know fall out and show the others the ropes. Each day we did long sets of jumping jacks, push-ups, squat thrusts, leg lifts, sit-ups, and knee bends. Most days we did sets of twenty-five of each, although there were times when men would get confused and off the count while doing squat thrusts or get out of sync doing jumping jacks and Sergeant Ingram would scream for us to do twenty-five or fifty more until we all got it right.

Physical conditioning was a big part of our morning each day, but the army also had its sights set on improving our minds. Sarge put it more bluntly. He said, "You stupid idiots are going to school. And if you flunk out, we send you to the..." and here he paused for emphasis, "Marines." He said it like a man who just discovered he had stepped in vomit. It was supposed to be funny, but few saw the humor in it. As a matter of fact, most of the men took to the idea of taking classes like men being led to the guillotine.

It didn't take long to figure out why. The day before our classes were to start, Sergeant Ingram was asked to survey the men to determine their level of schooling. Evidently, our instructors thought that would be valuable information to have. He called us together after a long set of calisthenics and asked all those who had gone to school at least through the sixth grade to raise a hand. We all snuck looks around the group. There were at least half a dozen who didn't raise a hand.

He continued, "Now how many went through grade eight?"
Several hands went down.

"Through the tenth grade?"

At this point, a couple dozen more fell away.

"How many of you graduated from high school?"

Fewer than half the men kept their hands up. I looked over at Doc, who was staring down at the ground. He may have been the best mechanic in Kinloch as a direct result of dropping out of school, but I could tell not having a diploma still gnawed at him.

It was pretty obvious by how quiet the men had become that more than a few were embarrassed about revealing their school history, and Sergeant Ingram seemed to sense this. After jotting a few notes on a clipboard, he then said, "Men, if you want my opinion, you can all take the schooling you've had and throw it out the window. Doesn't mean a damn thing. Starting tomorrow, you all start at zero. The army will now tell you what you need to know, and you'll all get it at the same time. Stay awake and pay attention in your classes and you'll all be fine."

I didn't admit it to anyone, but I immediately loved going to the classes that were set up for us. And they were definitely set up for "us." We were never scheduled to attend classes with others on the base. In so many ways these classes reminded me of my time teaching at Sumner. While working as a substitute teacher, I never knew in advance which courses I'd be teaching on a given day. At Fort Bliss, we never knew from day to day which classes we'd have or in which order we'd have them; a new schedule was posted for us each morning. At Sumner, we had roughly five minutes between classes; the same was true here. Even the banging and clanging of trays at noon chow, our break between morning and afternoon classes, reminded me of the daily commotion in the cafeteria at Sumner. There were so many times when I closed my eyes during a class and felt like I was back home. The biggest difference now was that instead of being the teacher, I was again the pupil—and I loved every minute of it. But while there seemed to be so many similarities, there was one big difference: The teachers at Fort Bliss were white.

The classes we attended, each typically lasting an hour per session, covered a wide range of subjects, not all relating specifically to information about the army. We had classes on "social hygiene." In those classes we were taught the proper way to brush our teeth, which, according to the camp doctors, was instruction we all desperately needed. Instruction was also given on proper bathing techniques, foot care, hair care, eye care—basically how to avoid eyestrain—and even care of our uniforms.

Special emphasis was given to the area of foot care. Our instructor, a young lieutenant with ears that stuck out like flaps, told us our feet "were the foundation of the army." He actually had a small wooden model of a foot that he used during his presentations. He powdered it neatly and showed us how to rub and massage our feet at night to keep them in shape. I thought he looked like he was enjoying it all a little too much.

We also had a separate course on first aid. The instruction was little more than how to pour sulfa powder into a wound and then use gauze bandage to wrap the area. That instructor had us pair off and take turns wrapping each other's imaginary shrapnel wounds. Doc and Williams had been paired off, and when it was Doc's turn to wrap Williams' shoulder he used one arm to pin Williams' arms back as he kept the gauze going round and round until he completely mummified his whole upper body, including his mouth. Williams' cries for help were so muffled, no one other than those right next to him could make out any sounds at all. When the instructor came by, he saw just Williams' terrified eyes staring out of the gauze and immediately started lecturing Doc about not taking this subject seriously. He said, "Someday this could save your life. Snap to it!" And he tried to snap his fingers, but couldn't, as he motioned for Doc to give it another try. The men around Doc quickly scattered.

There were also several classes dealing with our rifles. One class taught us how to clean them properly. Another showed us how to take the rifle apart and assemble it again within specified time limits, something we practiced over and over and over again until we could do it, literally, in the dark. Still another related class was devoted to the "manual of arms." That class taught us the proper "presentation" of the weapon, which included handling and movement of the rifle when marching and at attention.

One of my favorite classes was "military discipline." In that class we learned about the order of the different ranks, from private to general, so we would know who outranked whom. We also learned whom to salute and when and where not to salute, a lecture which also explained why that sergeant at Davis-Monthan had chewed us out so badly when we saluted him. Until this class, I also did not have a clue that snapping to "attention" involved the movement of fifteen different muscles, each pointed out in one demonstration after another. The instructor of that class, an older sergeant whose left cheek was full of scars, took his time explaining how we were supposed to react upon meeting sergeants. He told us sergeants were not called "Sir" and did not receive salutes. He also took one whole class session to show us, to his satisfaction, how to snap to attention when we found ourselves in contact with an officer. We were then paired off and took turns saluting each other. It wasn't until after he was convinced we had learned enough to keep us out of the stockade that he turned us loose.

Each day our schedule was broken up by noon chow, but as soon as chow was over, it was back to the classroom, usually for three more classes in the afternoon. Afternoon instruction typically began with a class on the "articles of war." This taught us what to do in the event we got captured. We practiced over and over giving nothing but our name, rank, and serial number to each other. We were also told how to treat prisoners just in case we ended up with some of our own.

One afternoon toward the end of the first week, we had a class on military history, during which we learned about the history of Biggs Field. Most of us didn't realize it until that class, but, technically, we were actually stationed at Fort Bliss with "assignment to duty" at Biggs Field. In terms of geography, one was just a part of the other as far as we could tell. We were told Biggs Field had been named after a pilot who was shot down over France during the last war. Aviation was very primitive at that time, and pilots were thought of as some kind of combination of daredevil, pioneer, and hero. We were also told this Lieutenant Biggs, who was from El Paso, was a risk-taker, a pilot who would dive so low enemy soldiers could actually see and hear him laugh at them as he roared by. He was a favorite son of the town, and when he was killed the field was named in his honor.

The men had been quiet and respectful while listening to this history. It was what came next that changed the whole atmosphere of the room. Our instructor, Sergeant Thorn, a career soldier whose enthusiasm for the army was both sincere and contagious, told us that after our basic training, most of us would be given special training in communications, with emphasis on the areas of construction and maintenance of communication lines. Without a good communication network, he told us, both ground troops and our boys in the air couldn't do a damn thing, couldn't move an inch. Sergeant Thorn drove the importance of this work home when he said, "Men, if you want to know the plain, simple truth, you're going to be an extra set of eyes and ears for a hell of a lot of guys somewhere in this war. Without you, they'd be moving stone-blind."

He followed that up by telling us that Biggs Field was now one of the best training bases for pilots and crews learning to fly B-17s, the bombers, we were told over and over, that formed the heart and soul of the Army Air Corps. The minute this was mentioned, I noticed the men all around me sat up straighter and whispers of pride could be heard throughout the room.

Sergeant Thorn silenced our whispers with a sharp, "Quiet!" He then continued, beaming proudly himself, "Men, we in the Army Air Corps hold the fate of the war in our hands." He held his right fist out and squeezed it shut for emphasis. "Don't let anybody tell you any different. Airpower is going to win this war. And you and me—all of us—we're all going to be a big part of it."

He paused again and looked around the room to make sure he had the attention of all. Like a preacher building a frenzy in his flock, he leaned forward and continued, this time with even more bravado in his voice, "When we level Tokyo, Berlin, and Rome—and we will—it's going to be because of what all of us right here on the ground have done. Don't you ever forget that."

For a moment, we all sat there absolutely silent. Then a sudden explosion of cheers rang out around the room. Fists of pride were punched into the air. Men were shaking hands, slapping each other on the shoulders, and nodding in agreement with everything we had just heard. Sergeant Thorn joined us. At that moment, for the very first time, I felt a cohesiveness in our battalion that hadn't been there before. We still couldn't march worth a damn and we hadn't yet been assigned any specific duties at camp, but we were suddenly transformed. We were now men with a common mission in sight, and it felt good. Damn good.

But the jubilation didn't last long.

As quickly as our spirits had soared, they were brought crashing back down to earth.

When Sergeant Thorn finished telling us all about Biggs Field and how important we all were to the war effort, he suddenly shifted gears and said, "Now I also want you to know about the city of El Paso."

He said it matter-of-factly, like he was telling us what we were going to have for chow that evening.

At first he fidgeted and looked down at the floor, not making eye contact with us, but it didn't take him long to make his point. It was made crystal clear to us that El Paso had places where our battalion was, and was not, welcome to go. He didn't use the "S" word, "segregated," but we didn't have to be hit over the head with boards, not even Williams, who was staring at the floor and shaking his head. Our instructor told us there were rules, both written and unwritten, we were to follow if we wanted to keep out of trouble. He finally got to the bottom line and said, "Men, there are about a thousand Negroes living in El Paso, and I am sure they will help you find plenty to do when you're on leave." He also told us Sergeant Ingram would fill us in more on what would be called "appropriate conduct" while in town. Nothing else needed to be said. When class was dismissed, there were no more cheers, no more pats on the back.

We filed quietly out of the room and walked slowly back to the barracks.

* * *

Because we were in classes so much, the days passed by quickly. I really enjoyed being a student again and did my best to soak up all the information I could. I found something interesting in all the classes, but the most riveting class for the battalion at large was, without a doubt, the one devoted to the "birds and the bees."

By the shocked expressions in our group during the first class, it quickly became apparent that many had never been stung before. We were shown movies that had cartoon characters, one a dead-ringer for Daffy Duck, telling us about male and female reproductive organs, and specifically what happens when the two get together. It was so quiet most of the time in that class I was sure I could hear the soldier next to me blink. When it was finally time for questions, no one dared raise a hand. That didn't mean there weren't any questions. It just meant no one wanted to admit he was a tenderfoot in this arena.

The second class meeting was one I guessed many men would remember for the rest of their lives. During that second class we again saw movies, but this time there weren't any cartoon characters. We saw real pictures of real men who had contracted venereal disease. The pictures were enlarged for dramatic effect, but they didn't need to be. Open sores. Oozing pus. Scabs that appeared the size of nickels. It wasn't long before men, hands pressed to mouths, jumped up from their seats and were rushing for the door. The doctor in the film explaining all of this was an older, distinguished-looking gentleman who smoked one cigarette after another while looking sternly straight ahead. He was so focused it appeared he was talking just for our benefit.

At one point in the film he said sharply, like a father warning a son, "If you're one of the lucky ones, one day in the latrine you'll feel a tremendous burning sensation during urination. Or you might look down and see a yellowish discharge. Then you'll know VD has invaded your body." And here he sat down his cigarette, moved forward so that his face filled the entire screen, and continued, "But not everyone is so *lucky*. Some never exhibit symptoms. Some can go years without knowing they have it. If that happens... Well, let's just say you might suddenly find yourself going blind, deaf, or losing your ability to reason."

The soldier next to me leaned over and whispered, "That means 'insane' don't it?"

I nodded that it did. The soldier shook his head and quietly said, "Damn!"

Similar quiet exclamations could be heard all throughout the room.

The next part of the film was short and sweet—sort of a play in two acts. Two actors, one in a private's uniform, the other a woman who could only be described as a boozed-up bar floozy, were shown leaving a bar and walking across a busy street to a convenient motel. The woman kept curling a finger, beckoning the soldier to follow her. As they entered the motel room, the screen went black for a moment. As the screen went dark, so did our classroom, which unsettled many of the men. After just seeing the part about venereal disease, some probably thought they were already going blind. Act Two of this part of the film had the boozed-up floozy now about nine months pregnant and standing outside the fence at the soldier's camp. As the soldier marched back and forth during a stint of guard duty, the floozy screamed, "You did this! It's *your* responsibility to make things right!"

At this point, the doctor who had scared the snot out of us during his VD warning suddenly appeared back on the screen and said, "This could be you, soldier. Take precautions!"

The film ended with some pretty clear morals: We should consider everything off the base to be an annex of Sodom and Gomorrah. All women were potential harbingers of venereal disease and should be avoided at all costs. If we did have sex and didn't die from VD, it was certain the woman would get pregnant. Basically, we were told if the Germans or Japs didn't get us, our baser instincts probably would.

We had been in the classroom well over an hour, and many of us needed to rush right to the latrine as soon as we were excused. While relieving ourselves, Jenkins, a tall, skinny kid from Jonesboro, Arkansas, suddenly screamed, "Oh, god that hurts! I've got it! I got the VD!"—and he staggered back, crashing against the wall of the latrine. Several started to rush over to pick him up but slowed when they saw him smile and burst into laughter. The rest of us did, too. Well, all except one poor unfortunate soul we could hear losing his chow in the last stall of the latrine.

* * *

Even after evening chow, the work of the day wasn't finished. We were "allowed" to go back to the barracks, but it wasn't to goldbrick. We still had shoes to shine. Rifles to clean. Uniforms to check and mend if needed. The barracks also had to be cleaned, policed, and made ready for the next morning's inspection. In a great irony, our recreation area inside the barracks was stocked with diversions, but most nights by the time we finished our work we were so tired all we wanted to do was hit the sack. I could hear that pool table calling my name, but I was usually too exhausted to do anything about it. Once in a while a few hands of rummy would be played or a couple of insomniacs would make a halfhearted attempt to learn Ping-Pong, a game only a handful of us had ever even seen before. But lights-out, 10:00 P.M.—2200 army time—always seemed to come in a hurry, and I, for one, was always ready for it.

At first, sleeping in the same room with about sixty men took some getting used to. The snoring was the worst. Some men snored like buzz saws. Others sounded like the *rat-tat-tat* of jackhammers. Some snored in such a way that they actually whistled, sounding like trains fading off into the distance. And then there were the coughers. Croupy coughers. Wheezy coughers. Bark-like-a-dog coughers. One night the barracks sounded like a whooping cough ward at a hospital. That night Sergeant Ingram, who had a small room of his own behind the recreation area, had had enough. He turned on a switch that started huge ceiling fans swirling above us. They not only helped cool off the barracks and suck out the stuffiness, but their steady hum drowned out the coughing and snoring. From that night on, we begged to have those fans turned on at lights-out, even on cool evenings.

Finally the day would draw to a close. When I finally drifted off to sleep I slept like the dead. We all did. But for as long as the days seemed, the nights felt doubly short by comparison. All too soon, at 0530, Sergeant Ingram, banging and clanging his frying pans, would once again march through the barracks, rousting us for the work of the day.

Yes, we *were* in the army now, and it was a whole new world.

A world like none of us had ever known.

7

WONDERS

I had heard of "ninety-day wonders" before, but this was ridiculous....

Two weeks into our training at Fort Bliss, I was summoned to our battalion headquarters, which was finally operational now that some of our officers had arrived. We were right in the middle of a set of jumping jacks when a jeep pulled up to the parade ground. A sergeant I had never seen before got out and walked over to say something to Sergeant Ingram. Sergeant Ingram then looked around our group, obviously searching for someone, until he pointed right at me and said, "Perkins. Fall out—on the double!"

Without any explanation, I was instructed to get in the jeep. My mind was filled with a thousand thoughts, most of them bad, as we drove to headquarters. Maybe word had come that someone in the family was ill or had died. Maybe someone had turned Doc and me in for putting a "Kick Me" sign on Williams' back the day before in the chow line. Maybe I was being transferred to another base where I could use my chemistry training. The more I thought about the possibilities, the more I started to sweat. The sergeant saw how uncomfortable I was and said, "Easy, soldier. You're not being shot. At least not as far as I know."

That was a great comfort.

We pulled up in front of headquarters, and without saying a word he motioned for me to get out. He then quickly sped off. As soon as I walked into headquarters a lieutenant told me to sit in a chair in the corner by the window and wait. I picked up the new issue of *Life* and pretended to read a story, but I was so nervous and my hands were shaking so badly I couldn't have read that story if my life depended on it. I felt like a kid called to the principal's office. I didn't know what I had done, but I was guessing I didn't get an invitation to headquarters just to give me a breather from morning calisthenics.

A drop of sweat slid from my forehead down to my cheek just as the lieutenant came back over and said, "The colonel will see you now. This way."

Colonel Ellis was sitting behind his desk and didn't look up right away when I entered the room. The lieutenant announced me, "This is Perkins, Sir."

I snapped to attention. I also had the feeling I should have said something like "Private Perkins reporting as ordered..."—but my mouth was so dry I didn't have any spit.

After what seemed like an eternity, Colonel Ellis returned my salute and said, "At ease, soldier. Sit there."

He then continued, "I've been looking over your file, Perkins. Quite impressive, I must say. University of Iowa. Not a bad school. Not as good as mine, but still not bad."

He smiled and added, "I'm a Big Ten man myself. Wisconsin. Which reminds me, I'm still sore you Iowa boys beat my Badgers in football this year. Just dumb luck. That damn game cost me five bucks."

I grinned but didn't say anything. My heart was still pounding.

I looked down to see his lips moving as he read something silently to himself. "You'll have to help me here," he said. "What was the title of your master's degree thesis?"

"Action of Bromine on N-Hydroxylbenzaldehyde and Related Compounds, Sir."

"I'm not going to ask you what that all means. I know bromine, but that's as far as my chemistry goes. Journalism's my game. I *think* that's why I got shoved into the Signal Corps."

He put down my folder and said, "I bet odds are I could throw rocks out this window, and for every three soldiers I hit only two would have even gone through high school, if that many. And between us we've got as many degrees as a thermometer. If there's anybody else on this base other than us with master's degrees, I sure haven't met them. That makes us either really smart—or really stupid—because of where we've ended up. I still haven't made up my mind yet which it is."

I finally found the courage to speak. With as straight a face as I could muster, I said, "Why, enlisted men are dumb, and all officers are smart, Sir."

He looked back at me with a warm smile and laughed. "Yes, I think you'll do."

He didn't explain what "you'll do" meant, and I started to sweat even more.

"I see you're from St. Louis. Grow up there?"

"No, Sir. I was born in Macon, Missouri, but we moved to Des Moines when I was five. I moved to St. Louis two years ago."

He picked up my folder and studied it again. "So, I take it you moved there to teach at that high school, right?"

"Yes, Sir. Sumner High School."

He continued looking at the folder and said, "It looks like you taught several courses there, including mathematics and something called 'driver's training.' Is that also right?"

"Yes, Sir. I taught a dab of just about everything at one time or another."

"So, you're a good driver?"

I had to laugh. I remembered the last time I was asked this question—by the principal at Sumner. My response, a lie, had gotten me the job. But now, unlike that first time, I actually did know how to drive.

"Sorry, Sir," I said while still laughing. "Yes, I did teach my students to drive."

Following up on my laughter, he raised an eyebrow and asked, "Just what exactly did you teach them in that class, soldier?"

"Most of the time, how not to get hit, Sir."

He smiled. "I can only imagine. I'm just glad it was you and not me. I wouldn't have the patience for it. Or the stomach."

He then paused for a minute, stood up, and sat on the edge of his desk. His tone became more serious. "I'm particularly interested in your math and driving skills. I've got two things I want you to do. First, we need drivers. About twenty more. I need them to drive every type of vehicle we've got. Some will be assigned as drivers for officers on the base. Most of the others will fit in with our convoys. It takes more fuel than you can imagine to keep our birds in the air. You've probably noticed convoys coming and going around here at all times of the day and night to get that fuel here on time. Frankly, they wake me up at night. But the cargo they haul keeps us in business, so I can't crab too much."

As I listened to Colonel Ellis, I noticed he had an unconscious habit of pushing his glasses back up on his nose every minute or so, whether he needed to or not. He was also thin, almost painfully thin. His blonde hair was longer than regulation and was parted so irregularly on the side the part looked like a snake's path.

He pushed his glasses up again and continued, "By now you're probably wondering how you fit into all this. I won't keep you in suspense any longer. I've got a job for you. You're going to be a teacher again."

At this point he walked over to the window and motioned for me to follow him. "See that Quonset hut over there—the one back behind the parade ground? That's your new classroom. I'm sorry it's damn near in the woods. Hell, it *is* in the woods. But that's the best I can do for you. You can pick some men to help you get it in order, but I want it ready to go in two days. I don't care how you do it, but I also want you to go through your battalion and find twenty men to form your class, to be your pupils—to be our drivers. You choose them. Any questions so far?"

"No, Sir." Actually, I did have a few questions, but I thought it best to keep my mouth shut until he finished.

"Good. Then here's the rest of it. That Quonset hut isn't just going to be your classroom. It's also going to be the motor pool for your battalion. I'm guessing somebody in your group has worked as a mechanic. We'll promote him to corporal and put him in charge of keeping everything on the road."

I tried to hide my smile, but he caught it. "I take it you already know someone?"

I nodded.

"Talk to him tonight. Don't wait. We need these drivers fast, but more than that, we need the trucks roadworthy ASAP. We'll pull him from classes tomorrow and get him started right away. There are already some trucks over there that can be repaired, and I'll see that some decent ones are also brought over. While he's working on the trucks, the men you've chosen to be your drivers can be sent over to help get the rest of the hut ready to serve as your classroom."

He walked back to his desk and gently threw me a thick manual. "Study this as quickly as you can. It tells everything you'll need to know about the vehicles. It will also tell you the army way to drive—and that won't be like what you taught those kids back in St. Louis. You know what the army driving motto is, don't you? 'Drive like hell and you're sure to get there.' Think about that one for a minute."

Colonel Ellis sat back down and motioned for me to do the same. "At ten each day your drivers will be pulled from their regular classes so they can report to your motor pool. Except for the break at noon chow, you'll have them for as much of the rest of the day as you want."

He paused here, looked me right in the eye, and said, "I'll give you two days to get your classroom ready and then two weeks to get your drivers ready. Can you do it?"

"I'll do my best, Sir."

"I want your best—and them some. Those men *have* to be ready. We've got a group moving out, and if you don't get your men ready to replace some drivers, we're going to be screwed. I wish I could tell you more, but I can't. That's really all I can say. Just take my word for it. You've got to get them ready."

He looked at the calendar on his desk and said quietly, "Sixteen days, total. Then I want 'em ready."

"Yes, Sir," I replied. "Will do."

"OK, now to your next duty. You're good at math. Hell, you *taught* math. I need someone to help with the payroll and to help with the operation of this office. I'm surrounded by nothing but idiots. We've got only a skeleton crew for this battalion, and I've been told not to expect more help anytime soon, which doesn't surprise me. Frankly, I'll be shocked if anyone else ever shows up. So you're going to pitch in and help out. I know it's slicing off a pretty big piece of pie for you, as my grandma use to say, but you're also going to lend a hand in the mornings. You'll do payroll, cut papers, do inventory, and anything else

I can think of. Handle that, too?"

He didn't give me a chance to respond.

"Now there's one more thing. I'm putting you in charge of a lot of men. You're a teacher, so I know you can handle it. I've always felt the ability to lead is a gift, that either a man has this gift or he doesn't. The army doesn't feel the same way. The army feels leaders are *made*. That means I also have to send you to school. You're going to be a teacher during the day and a student at night. Most nights you'll be so tired by taps you'll feel like you could drop."

He paused here and poured two glasses of water, handing me one. I drank quickly and then asked, "What type of school will this be, Sir?"

He held his glass toward me as if to toast and said, "I'm sending you to noncom school. As soon as the papers are cut, you'll be Master Sergeant Perkins. Today you woke up a private—tomorrow a sergeant. That's this screwy army for you."

At first what he was saying really didn't register. "I beg your pardon, Sir?"

He said it again, and this time the full impact hit me.

"You're really not pulling my leg, Sir?" I asked. "Me, a sergeant? I just got here."

He continued, "The army has regs, and right now this is as high as you can be promoted because, well... well, just because."

Here he paused and looked down at the floor for a minute. I had a feeling I knew what he originally was going to say after "because," but I also knew it wasn't the time for me to say anything. I took a deep breath and blew it out slowly.

Colonel Ellis then looked up and added, smiling warmly this time, "Don't worry. You've got the education and the background. And don't forget, I'm considered a very good judge of horseflesh. I take great pride in my first impressions, and I think you'll be just fine."

"I don't know what to say, Sir. I'm shocked. I'm grateful—I think—but shocked. I'm really going to be a sergeant?" I asked again, still unsure if he wasn't just playing with me. I actually felt woozy, like I had felt when I opened the letter from my draft board.

He didn't answer my question. He paused and pushed his glasses back up his nose before continuing. "Oh, I just remembered something I was going to tell you. I'm also promoting Sergeant Ingram to battalion sergeant major so you don't outrank him. He'll still be top Sergeant. I *don't* want you to have to deal with all that, too. And one more thing. I don't know what happened to the other sergeant we were supposed to get, but he hasn't shown up yet. That means you and Ingram will have to work together to take care of the men in both barracks for the time being, maybe longer. I'm going to have Ingram move into N-1 tonight so he can keep an eye on things there. That's going to leave you in charge of your barracks while he's out. I want you two to work together on this. I'm counting on that. You understand so far?"

"Yes, Sir. I do. At least I think I do."

Here he lowered his voice before continuing, "Good. There's just one more thing I'd like to say right now. I guess I don't have to tell you there will be plenty of men who have served for years who will resent this—will resent you. This will come especially from outside our battalion."

He repeated it again, slowly, for emphasis, "Especially from outside our battalion."

His meaning was clear.

Then he continued, his voice even more quiet than before, "And one more thing. Always remember where we are. This is the South. You're going to outrank some men who feel you shouldn't even be here in the first place. Your stripes won't be the first thing those men see. I think you get where I'm going."

He paused. He was clearly uncomfortable continuing, so I spoke up.

"I understand, Sir. I understand. Thank you, Sir."

"At times it may not be pretty."

I paused before responding, choosing my words carefully.

"Sir," I said, "it never has been."

He stared out the window and nodded several times.

After that, neither of us said any more about the subject. We didn't need to. We understood each other.

A convoy of trucks rumbled by, the floor of the room vibrating under our feet.

* * *

It was already time for noon chow when I left headquarters. As I entered the mess, all eyes seemed to be on me. The looks all seemed to be asking, "OK, what did you do?"

Doc and Williams had saved me a spot next to them just in case I made it back in time to eat. I went through the line as quickly as I could, not really paying attention to the food being slopped onto my tray.

As soon as I sat down, Doc asked, "What's going on? We in trouble?" He was obviously wondering, as I had, about the "Kick Me" sign we had hung on Williams.

I was so nervous, so excited, I couldn't remember if Colonel Ellis had told me to keep quiet about all of this until the papers could be cut.

"I'll tell you later," I whispered. "But I'll tell you this much now: You won't believe it."

"You're shaking," Doc said, watching me unable to pick up peas with my fork. "Is it *that* bad?" He looked genuinely worried.

"It's not bad news. It's *big* news. Can't tell you now. Too many ears around."

Williams, who looked even more concerned than Doc, leaned over and asked, "Is this one of those 'Loose Lips Sink Ships' things?"

"I don't think so." And here I paused because I remembered Colonel Ellis saying the drivers had to be ready in nine days but he couldn't tell me all the reasons why. "I'll explain it all tonight. At least as much of it as I know. You're involved in this, too," I said patting Doc on the back.

"It is that 'Kick Me' sign, isn't it? Who stool-pigeoned us?"

I just laughed. "You'll have to wait and see."

* * *

That night after chow I asked Doc and Williams to walk with me across the parade ground over to what was to be Doc's motor pool and my classroom. Doc paused to light a smoke and then held his match over to me. After mine was lit I motioned for Williams to light his, too. He was still so concerned about that "three on a match" superstition he actually jumped back from the match as if he were about to be stuck with a hot poker.

"Didn't you hear what Albertson said the other night? He knew a guy back home who was third on a match who fell down the steps right after and broke both his legs!" Williams lit his own cigarette, inhaled deeply, and coughed so hard Doc started pounding him on the back.

"Yeah, and you're going to be 'first on a match' who choked to death."

Both asked question after question as we walked, but I just smiled and ignored them. When we got to the hut I started to walk in, but both of them stopped short.

"I'm not going in there," Williams said.

"Off-limits," Doc added.

"Not anymore, chums. This is *our* building now. It may not look like much tonight, but just you wait and see how this sow's ear turns into a silk purse—and faster than snot through a goose, too."

"What do you mean 'our place'?" Doc asked. "Don't tell me this is our new barracks. We went though this before at Davis-Monthan."

"It's nothing like that at all. If you two will just shut your traps for a minute I'll tell you all about it. Here, sit down a minute."

We sat on the ground outside the hut and finished our smokes. It would have been cruel to keep them in suspense any longer, so I started filling them in on the details. When I got to the point where I mentioned needing to find someone to be in charge of the motor pool I calmly asked, "Have you met anyone in the battalion who might be able to handle that? I've got to find somebody right away with some mechanical experience and I thought I'd ask for your opinions."

Doc took one last drag on his cigarette and started coughing just about as badly as Williams. "Well," I continued. "Know anybody?"

Doc stood up, towering over me. "If you don't give me this job, I'll pull your ribs out through your mouth—one at a time."

"And he would, too!" Williams chimed in.

I fell back and pretended to cringe away from him. "Well, in that case, I guess the job is yours, Corporal."

Doc pulled me up by my shirt and hugged me as he danced me

around like a rag doll. "I've been praying, but I never thought… Thanks, Perc. I won't let you down."

And then it hit him. "Say, what did you call me?"

I toyed with him again. "When? You mean when I called you a picklehead yesterday?"

He grabbed me again by the shirt, lifting me off the ground and dangling me at the waist as I kicked my feet in the air.

"Hey, put me down," I protested. "Is that any way to treat a superior in the army?"

The look in his eyes, a playful but 'I'll get you' look, told me I'd tortured him long enough.

"OK, OK. The head of our motor pool gets corporal stripes. Your papers will be cut tomorrow. As a matter of fact, I might as well tell you now. You'll be excused from classes tomorrow so you can come over here and get started."

Williams, who had been listening attentively to all this, asked, "Doc, a corporal? Holy mackerel—we might as well just throw in the towel. We've lost the war now!"

Doc was on him the minute the words came out of his mouth and playfully swung him around like a sack of flour. In midswing, Doc stopped, letting Williams fall back to the ground.

"Wait a minute," he said, looking puzzled. "Didn't I just hear you say you outranked me? Just what did you mean by that? And how come you get to make all these decisions?"

To this point I hadn't mentioned anything about my promotion. "Well, you know what they say—truth is stranger than fiction. Now I *know* that's true. Men, starting tomorrow you can address me as Sergeant Perkins. And I expect from now on to be treated with all the respect due someone of my rank and station."

To show me they intended to do just that, Doc ran over and grabbed me by the shoulders while Williams took my feet. Rocking me back and forth a few times, they finally flung me through the air and into the hut.

When I walked back out, covered with dirt, brushing myself off, I said, "Very funny. Very funny. That was some fine show of respect. You two just keep in mind I can now assign you to latrine duty if I feel like it. For the rest of your lives!"

Williams snapped to attention and gave me an exaggerated, sweeping salute, "Yes, Sir, Sergeant Perkins!"

At the same time Doc and I yelled at him, dragging out each word, "You don't salute sergeants!"

Both then shook my hand and congratulated me while asking questions about the promotion that I still didn't know the answers to. I just told them I was in the dark as much as anyone and would let them know details when I got them. We then each lit another smoke, Williams again jumping away when the match was offered to him, and entered the hut. The sky was overcast and the sun was starting to set, so it was already pretty dark inside. We found light switches, but when we flipped them nothing happened.

"Maybe the bulbs are just burned out," I said. "I sure hope that's all it is."

Even in the fading light Williams and I could see the grin on Doc's face as he looked around. There were half a dozen jeeps and three six-by-sixes in a row to the left. Doc raised the hood on the first jeep, poked around for a minute, and then shook his head. "It'll live, but I sure hope we've got some parts somewhere. I'm not a damn magician."

He then rolled up his sleeves and stepped on the bumper of a six-by-six next to the jeep, hoisting himself up so he could pop open the hood and lean in to check its engine.

"Not tonight, Doc." I grabbed the back of his pants and tugged. "We're really not supposed to be here yet. Tomorrow will come soon enough."

"Oh, you can't ask me to leave now. I've been dreaming of working on these ever since we got here. Can't I stay?"

The way he said "Can't I stay?" —the way he pleaded with me— was something right out of the mouth of a seven-year-old kid.

"No, you've got to help me back at the barracks. We've got a lot more work to do tonight. Don't worry—your trucks will still be here in the morning. I'll explain more on the way back. Now let's get out of here before we do get in trouble."

He wasn't happy about it, but he finally jumped down and ran to catch up to us. I finished telling them about my ideas for a driving school and asked them to help me choose my students when we got back to the barracks. As we walked back, I asked Williams if he'd like to be a driver. "No," he said. "I'm a cook. I've still got to hold out for that. But thanks for asking, Perc. That means a lot to me."

* * *

Back at the barracks we went straight to the recreation area and moved three tables together so we could each sit behind one. I got paper and pencils for each of us so we could rate each candidate, based on his previous driving experience, as we interviewed them. When we were ready, I stood up on my chair and called out, "May I have your attention everyone. Your attention please. I've got something important to say. Listen up."

The mood in the barracks was pretty quiet and subdued this particular evening. Men looked up from shining shoes, cleaning rifles, writing letters, reading magazines.

I continued, "I've been asked to get the ball rolling on something. I've got a job for some of you. It won't be easy, but it's a good job. An important job. It's something you'll be proud of—and others will be proud of you."

The men, their curiosity getting the best of them, slowly started moving up toward our tables.

I couldn't see who it was, but one of the men in the back called out, "Who died and made you Roosevelt?"

In the short time we had all been together, I had gotten to know a few of the men in the battalion, but other than the time spent with Doc and Williams, for the most part I had been keeping pretty much to myself and hadn't made any waves. So I really wasn't surprised by the question and couldn't blame the guy for asking it. However, the way Doc stood up and scanned the room after it was asked put an end to any other catcalls.

"Look," I said in response. "I didn't ask for this job, but now that I have been asked, I'm going to give it everything I've got and would appreciate your help. So listen up and listen good. Do you remember in class one day when our instructor said this war would be won in the air? Do you remember him saying we'd be a part of that—that they couldn't do anything in the air without what we did here on the ground?"

I paused, letting the rest of the men move in closer.

"Well now we have a chance to prove him right. Now we have a chance to show what this battalion can do, to show that we *can* help keep those birds in the air. And how do they stay in the air? Fuel. Lots of fuel. More fuel than any of us could ever imagine in our wildest dreams. And if that fuel doesn't get here, nothing gets off the ground. Nothing."

I paused, scanning the group, which was now moving even closer to our tables, and continued, "Starting tomorrow, this battalion is going to have its own motor pool—and we need drivers, drivers who will help bring this fuel to the base. We also need drivers to keep everything else moving around the base, too. You may not think so right now, but that's just as important. I'd rather have volunteers, but tonight, one way or the other, I've got to find twenty of you who'll be trained to be army drivers."

I expected a buzz and at least some show of excitement from the men, but most just stood there, staring blankly back at me. The barracks became absolutely quiet. It didn't take long to find out why.

I continued, "OK, I want everyone who knows how to drive to form three lines up here in front of us. Go ahead. Don't be shy. Move right on up."

No one moved.

"Don't be bashful. You'll take a class that will teach you the ropes. Step on up."

Still no one moved.

"I think I know what it is," Doc leaned over and whispered to me. "Watch this."

He then stood up and said, "Let me see a show of hands. How many of you know how to drive?"

Six hands went up.

Six.

I guess I shouldn't have been surprised. I hadn't learned how to drive until taking the job at Sumner. Our streetcar system in Des Moines was so good a person could go anywhere in town as easy as walking across the street. As a result, there really wasn't a need to have a car there, so most of the families I knew didn't own one. A ten-cent streetcar fare, with transfers included, was a lot cheaper than upkeep on a car.

I didn't know what the transportation system was like in other cities, but I thought at least some of the men came from places where having a car was a necessity. Well, it turned out *some* was right. Some six of them.

"What do we do now?" Doc asked.

I thought back to my days at Sumner. If I was in the science lab and needed students to help demonstrate an experiment, I always asked for volunteers first. It was usually the same kids who volunteered, so I'd have to recruit others and make them feel like they had also volunteered. And to make them feel this way there had to be an incentive. A carrot on a string. It was usually enough to say, "The volunteer who helps the most will get five extra points added to his grade on the next test. That's half a letter grade."

I could tell this group needed an incentive, needed a carrot. But this wasn't Sumner, and these weren't my regular students. So, I did the only thing I could think of to do under the circumstances. I leaned over to Doc and whispered, "Get ready. I'm going to tell a lie—and you're going to have to swear to it."

I then quickly addressed the men again, "Oh, I'm sorry. I forgot to tell you something. Those who sign up to be drivers won't have any more of those little ten-mile hikes with full packs. You won't have time for that anymore."

I leaned forward and added, "And I *heard* that the drivers will be given special chow, and extra helpings of it."

Well, that was all sort of true. I did actually "hear" that. I heard "myself" say it. It may have been stretching the truth more than just a little, but that moment, looking out at the group before me, I wasn't going to let it bother me any.

Doc just shook his head and quietly said, "Holy shit."

The carrot worked. The barracks immediately came alive, and that buzz I was anticipating became so loud it drowned out the ceiling fans.

I asked the six who had previous driving experience to stand in Doc's line so he could check them out. There wasn't any need for Williams to have his own line so I asked him to come sit next to me and write down names as I asked questions. It took me a while to figure it out, but I finally realized the men from farms would do just fine. Most had at least some experience driving farm equipment of one type or another, especially tractors. I figured if they could drive a tractor, they could drive a jeep. When that finally dawned on me, I stood up and shouted, "Those of you who grew up on a farm—come join my line."

After we had grilled everyone, we still had chosen only sixteen men. Colonel Ellis had said he preferred that I stay within my own barracks because the other half of our battalion in Barracks N-1 was being earmarked for something else down the road. I had no choice but to lower my sights and find men who at least had a semblance of coordination. My teaching would have to do the rest.

"OK, how many of you can ride a bicycle?"

Eager hands shot up throughout the room. At that point I figured it didn't matter all that much, so I took the first four men who rushed up to the table.

"You'll do," I said to each of them. "Give Williams your names."

We ended up with six who had driven cars, seven who had driven tractors, two who had driven wagons pulled by teams of horses, four who knew how to ride bicycles, and one who had once stolen a motorcycle. I figured he'd fit right in.

As I looked at the motley group standing before me, my thoughts wandered back to Mrs. Livinia Lucille Little teaching me how to drive back in Des Moines. I could still hear her yelling, "Puttin' on a hat! Puttin' on a hat! Jumpin' the fence! Jumpin' the fence."

I had a feeling I'd be yelling a lot more than that before I finished with this crowd.

8

PREPARATIONS

I was in the biggest hurry of my army life, and all I could do was "hurry up and wait" until the classroom section of the motor pool was ready before I could start teaching my "pilgrims." With their collective driving experience, pilgrims was definitely the word that came to mind.

Actually, circumstances may have forced me to wait, but there wasn't time to loaf. Flush with my new rank and with chevrons on my sleeves, I ordered the men around like, well, a high school teacher. I just didn't have the growl I thought a sergeant should have. I tried a few times to chew out men who appeared to be slacking, but I usually ended up laughing instead. I caught Jamieson, a kid I thought had real promise, washing the same window in the Quonset hut over and over as he dreamily stared through it at the rest of the camp. I got right in his face and shouted as authoritatively as I could, "Jamieson, just what the hell are you doing? There's not going to be any glass left at the rate you're going. You know what? You give me a pain!" We both just stared at each other a minute and ended up rolling our eyes and laughing at the unintentional pun.

Some authority figure I was.

Doc, resplendent in his new corporal stripes, on the other hand, was a natural-born leader. When he gave instructions, the men didn't have to be told twice. It wasn't just his physical presence that commanded attention. He was at home in our new motor pool, and the men saw that right away. If he said something needed to be done, they knew he was right and felt they would be letting him down if they didn't get right on the job.

He was also a hands-on leader. If he saw someone having a problem, he'd get right in there and say, "Give me that wrench. Let a *man* show you how this is done." The men would then gather around and watch as if they were looking at a surgeon performing a delicate operation. He really was "Doc" to all of them.

He also had his work cut out for him. No one else in our battalion had any mechanical experience to speak of, so he was on his own. We talked it over and decided, because of their inexperience, it made sense to have him teach our drivers as much about the vehicles as possible. We split the men into two groups, and while half worked getting the classroom area ready, the other group got a cram-course in engine basics from Doc. We then switched groups the next day.

We made a good team.

At the end of the second day my classroom was as ready as it was ever going to be. I had a blackboard brought over from battalion headquarters and found a couple dozen camp stools in the back of the hut that I put into rows in front of my desk. The stools weren't comfortable and were hard to keep upright on the uneven dirt floor, but they were better than sitting on the ground. But not by much. I also put a jeep hood on two sawhorses to make a desk. It actually worked quite well. It wasn't exactly like my classroom back in St. Louis, but it would do.

I knew there had to be some way to partition off the classroom from the rest of the goings-on in the hut or my students would never pay attention to a word I said. Williams came up with a simple but effective solution. It was rapidly becoming apparent he was a natural-born scrounger. He was so frail and innocent-looking, no one ever questioned him when they saw him walking around with something slung over his shoulder. He scrounged up some tall fence poles and planted them at equal distances around the classroom area. He then went to the laundry and "liberated" enough sheets to tie between each of the poles. He left just one opening, toward the front, for a door. The sheets didn't provide any sound insulation, but that wasn't their purpose. The idea was to block the view of the action going on in other parts of the hut. Out of sight, out of mind. The only time the sheets bothered anyone was when a stiff breeze would suddenly blow through. Then the sheets would swish and sway like Monday's wash.

Right away I decided if I was going to do this, I was going to do it right. This would be a real class, and it would have rules just like every other class I had ever taught. The first morning of class, after I had called the roll, I told the men what behavior I expected in the classroom. They were not to talk to their neighbors while I was talking. If they had something to say, they were to raise a hand and be acknowledged first. If they didn't understand or hear something, they were to raise a hand. No one was allowed to make fun of anyone else. I told them there were no stupid questions, just stupid people who didn't ask questions. To take the edge off a little, I made a dunce cap out of a newspaper and placed it on my desk. I told them, "If I catch you not paying attention, you are going to put this on and do a stint in the corner." They laughed and tried it on during breaks, but I never once actually had to use it.

There were times when I had to shout over hammers banging and jeeps being revved, but I was pleased by how seriously the men took to the instruction. For most of them, everything I said was new, so I paced the class slowly and asked them to repeat information every few minutes or so to make sure we were all still on the same road together.

I would have given anything for one of the manuals I had used in the driver's training class back at Sumner, but I was going to have to make do from memory. In each class session we went over everything from "rules of the road" to "identification of road signs." I drew the shape of each road sign on the blackboard and quizzed the men until I was sure they could identify them in their sleep. What I didn't know was whether they understood the "meaning" behind the signs. I had the sick feeling that signs like "Yield Right Of Way," "Narrow Bridge," and "One-Way" wouldn't mean much to them until they actually experienced those particular situations themselves. That had been my experience back in St. Louis, with nearly disastrous results. One of my students, a "straight-A" student on tests in class, darn near killed us all one day on Easton Avenue when we came to a "Yield Right Of Way" sign. Instead of yielding to oncoming traffic at that intersection, in her mind she decided the right thing to do was "Yield Right" and headed down the embankment off the right-hand shoulder just in time to avoid a truck that was bearing down on us. We all screamed

like kids going down a long slope on a roller coaster until the car finally came to a sudden stop, just inches from the edge of a large drainage ditch. That day I learned the meaning of one of Olivia's favorite
expressions: "Knowledge without experience is like money without a
place to spend it." And the pilgrims I now had before me were facing a
double-whammy: They were flat broke when it came to experience.

I knew they wouldn't encounter most of the signs we were going
over in class while they practiced driving on the base. What we needed
was our own driving course so they could practice what I was preach-
ing. The higher-ups didn't like the idea at first, but Colonel Ellis did
manage to get permission for us to paint lanes on the parade ground
so that we had our own miniature road system on which to practice.
Williams, using still more of his scrounged poles, made street signs
and positioned them at the intersections. On one stretch of road in
our make-believe city, I also had him make a "Narrow Bridge" section.
He found some old forty-gallon oil drums and lined them up on both
sides of the road to narrow the lanes at that spot. At different points
we also had "Stop" signs, "Yield Right of Way" signs, "One-Way" signs,
and even a "Railroad Crossing" sign. After the last of the signs went
up, Williams and I took a jeep around the course to check out his
handiwork. I was proud of him for taking charge of this. The course
was actually damn good. These weren't exactly the streets of downtown
St. Louis, but they would do.

On the other side of the hut in our motor pool, Doc was taking
care of the vehicles. It didn't take long for everyone to see firsthand
how he had earned his nickname. Within three days everything that
was going to run was up and running. He would have been finished
even sooner if he had had a decent supply of parts. Parts were scarce, so
when Williams took breaks from building the driving course he went
to the other side of the base to see what he could "find." Between those
parts and the ones Doc cannibalized from the hopeless cases parked
out back in our junkyard, we eventually had enough left over to start
our own parts supply room in the back of the hut.

My students were coming along fine, but I knew they could learn
only so much in the classroom. When I was satisfied the men had
soaked up enough of the textbook rules of the road, it was time to

move outside to meet the real world of driving. Figuring it would be the easiest to do, I decided to teach them to drive the jeeps first and save the six-by-sixes for last.

Instead of bringing the campstools outside with us, I had Doc and Williams get all the jeeps that ran and put them in a semicircle around my jeep-hood desk, which I brought outside. Then I told the men to climb in, four to a jeep. Those were their new classroom seats. We now had four jeeps that were ready to roll, so only one group of drivers had to be rotated in and out.

I first explained the physical act of driving. The most difficult part was trying to explain the delicate balance between the clutch and the gas pedal, the lifting up of one foot on the clutch as the other pushed down on the gas. I knew until that was actually practiced, my words wouldn't make a grain of sense to them at all. Same with the shift pattern of the transmission. I went over as much as I thought would help before letting them see everything in action. I had put at least one experienced driver in charge of each of the groups, so I asked them to get behind the wheel and drive the pilgrims around our new driving course so they could watch how it was all done.

When it was time to start the jeeps, I was more nervous than they all were. Like a man setting birds free from a cage, I wondered how they'd be able to fly. There was only one way to find out, so I said just one more thing.

"This is it, men. Make me proud of you."

And they did. The experienced drivers inched slowly and cautiously around the course, with their passengers studying every movement they made. Stops were made at the appropriate times, and none of them even came close to hitting our "Narrow Bridge."

Each pulled back to their original place in our outside classroom when they returned. The drivers all had serious, but proud, looks on their faces. Their passengers, on the other hand, had smiles, although nervous ones, from ear to ear.

I *was* proud of them. I motioned for them to shut their motors off, then said, "A very wise man once said, 'A journey of a thousand miles begins with one damn step.' Today we took that step. And you know what? I'm proud of you. Really proud."

I started clapping for them. Just then Doc walked out of the hut. I pointed to him, bowed slightly, and started clapping again and encouraged the men to do the same. Finally I had the men clap for each other. But the loudest applause, peppered with cheers and laughter, came for Williams, who was pulling a wagon filled with ice-cold Pepsi-Colas toward us across the streets of our make-believe city. He saw me giving him the eye and said, "Don't ask."

He handed a Pepsi to each man, and then one to me. We toasted each other.

"It's better than champagne," I said.

And it really was.

9

SURPRISES

President Roosevelt, in describing the morning of the sudden and shocking attack on Pearl Harbor, had called it "a date which will live in infamy."

Well, now I had one of those of my own.

The mornings in El Paso were beautiful. The air always seemed fresh and cool. As the sun came up the sky would become almost aquamarine. There were seldom any clouds, and those that did appear were quickly swept away. About half an hour after sunrise a warm, gentle breeze settled in, usually lasting for the rest of the day.

Such a morning dawned on our fifth day of driver's training, the first day my pilgrims who had never driven before were to take the wheel. This had actually been scheduled for the day before but had to be put off because of a ten-mile hike—for all of us. My drivers weren't happy about this and gave me constant reminders that I had said they would be exempt from these. All day I kept shrugging my shoulders while saying, in a shocked tone of voice, "Well, I *heard* we wouldn't have to do this anymore."

I hadn't eaten much breakfast, and by 0730 my stomach was already talking to me. Even back at Sumner, under the best of classroom conditions, I never knew what my driver's training students would do until they actually got behind the wheel and pulled away from the curb. My stomach was now also churning and burning because I had these same anxious thoughts, only more so. Just how much the men had learned in our Quonset hut classroom was yet to be seen. In addition, the pages of the calendar were turning fast. Too fast. The colonel wanted them to be ready in five more days.

When my students finally showed up that fifth session, fresh from another class on personal hygiene and dental care, they were wound up and raring to go, eager to prove they could put their classwork into practice. Several, probably sensing my nervousness, even came up to me as they entered the classroom and wished *me* luck for the day. I didn't even have to ask them to quiet down before calling the roll.

Our class session started normally enough. We went over the road signs and rules of the road again one last time and all seemed fine. When asked questions, the men were sharp and confident in their answers. Then we moved outside to the jeeps, which were again parked in a semicircle. I didn't bring my desk outside on this morning, so I paced back and forth in front of the jeeps as I gave final instructions.

"This is it, men." I said. "Everybody take a deep breath first and try to relax. Today we'll see what we're made of. Now a few last instructions."

And then it started.

Because most of our vehicles had been stored for months inside the dark hut or out back in the weeds, a recurring problem we had was finding all manner of insects and animals in them. One particular nuisance, which the men positively despised, was spiders. In particular, wolf spiders. They were everywhere in this part of Texas, and they were huge. Many were so hairy they appeared to be the size of baseballs. They weren't actually considered dangerous to humans, but the men were deathly afraid of getting what all across the base was being called an "El Paso asshole." A circular ring appeared around their bites, and for a day or two a milky, brown liquid oozed from the wound. It also didn't help that Brown, a city kid who was as tough as a ten-cent steak, had one crawl up his leg one night just after lights-out. He had leapt from his upper bunk so quickly his sheet and blanket went right along with him, making him appear like an apparition as he ran screaming through the barracks. His screams were so pitiful and so loud they woke nearly everyone over in N-1. The rest of that night more than a few men slept on "top" of their blankets.

After Brown's experience in the barracks, there was no way I could keep men from screaming and bolting when one was found in our vehicles. I'm not sure what it was on this particular day—maybe it was something in the atmosphere—but as soon as the men climbed into the jeeps, two crews immediately bailed out, like parachute jumpers from a plane. When they hit the ground they took off in different directions, screaming and yelping, "Spider! Spider!"

It was all I could do to get them back. I first had to take a broom and make exaggerated sweeping motions in the jeeps before they'd even come back near enough to take a look. It didn't help that one of our drivers, Clark, swore he had been bitten and was convinced he was going to die. It also didn't help that the men around him showed no sympathy at all. One asked if he could have his watch. Another asked if he could have his wife. All were selfishly grateful they had not been bitten—yet. The other groups all decided to hop out of their jeeps and do a "safety" inspection before they would get back in.

It was like herding cats.

And then the wasps and hornets showed up. We had our own little private war going on with mud daubers, hornets, and yellow jackets. The underside of dashboards were particularly popular places for their nests, especially among the wires. It was hard to see up under the dash, and when I suggested the men stick their hands up there to check for nests, one would have thought I had asked them to stick their hands into a roaring campfire. Most did a cursory "duck and wince" while making a hurried and halfhearted glance under there, but that didn't help solve our problem one bit.

The hornets were particularly bad. When hornets appeared, they stung people. The men started calling them "Texas tail gunners" and "Bee-99s." One afternoon while washing the seats in one of the jeeps, Sanders was stung three times on the leg before he could jump out. He soon started having trouble breathing, so one crew got some unexpected driving experience as they rushed him to the infirmary. He survived, but his leg blew up about twice the size of his other one. His new, slow gait, a direct result of the swelling, soon earned him the name "Elephant Boy." No one ever said serving in the army made for sympathetic men.

But the yellow jackets were the most dangerous of all. Their nests were in the ground, and they attacked silently and swiftly, like snipers. The men soon learned to walk to their vehicles as if they were traversing a minefield. If a man was unfortunate enough to step on one of their nests, he was soon swarmed—and the more he swatted, the more he'd get stung. I gave permission for the men to pour gasoline down the holes and try to burn them out, but this only seemed to make them worse.

It took some doing, but I finally convinced the men there were no more spiders in the jeeps. They gingerly climbed back in and sat down as if they were sitting on shards of broken glass.

"Come on now—that's enough of that," I scolded. "We've got work to do—trucks to drive."

And at just that moment the crew in the jeep on the far right ran screaming and swatting because one of them had accidentally kicked his leg up under the dash and knocked down a mud daubers' nest.

The rest of the men jumped from their jeeps too, just in case.

I was starting to feel like Frank Buck of *Bring 'Em Back Alive* fame.

It was time for a break, time to get their minds on something, anything, but critters that could bite or sting them. "Take five!" I ordered in as gruff a voice as I could forge. "Light 'em if you got 'em. Smoking lamp's lit."

And I added, but probably shouldn't have, "While you're at it, blow some of that cigarette smoke up under the dashboards. Wasps don't like smoke, so maybe that will drive some of them out."

I noticed that suggestion didn't get any takers.

And then, just when I thought I had seen it all, the coup de grace.

A mangy looking roan hound missing an eye wandered right through where the men were smoking. All were already so skittish the dog startled them. A few stepped back cautiously. Someone sharply scolded, "Bad dog!"

A wide-eyed soldier toward the edge of the group asked excitedly, "What'd he say?"

Someone else screamed, "He said 'mad dog'! Let's get out of here!"

And the curse words flew as they scattered again, crashing into and bouncing off of each other like cattle at the start of a stampede.

The poor dog took off running.

I stood there with my mouth open.

I was so frustrated I couldn't speak. We were burning valuable practice time, and I didn't know what to do about it. I certainly had never experienced anything like this back at Sumner. I lit a smoke and tried to take a few calming breaths. "It'll be OK," I said to myself. "It'll be OK."

Williams, who had just returned from "borrowing" a set of tires for one of the jeeps, came out of the hut and asked, "Perc, what in the heck is going on? From in there it sounds like you are beatin' hell out of these guys."

I had just started to speak when Davis stepped on a yellow jacket nest. He was a large man who had no chance of outrunning them, so he decided to stand his ground and fight it out. Bad decision. He looked like a heavyweight boxer trying to nail a swaying speedbag. His buddies finally pulled him into the nearest six-by-six and rolled up the windows. They all lit up cigarettes to protect themselves, and in a matter of seconds they could barely be seen through the smokescreen they created. All I could see were eyeballs in a fog.

I smacked Williams on the shoulder and then pointed back to the truck. "That's the problem. This is a damn combat zone. And I don't know what to do about it."

"I'll take care of it," Williams said. "Back these jeeps out of here. I know what to do."

"What are you going to do?"

"Don't ask."

I was learning not to.

* * *

The afternoon went downhill from there.

After our smoke break, the experienced drivers moved the jeeps away from the motor pool and, hopefully, away from anymore distractions. Those who had never driven before needed a wide-open space for practice before they tried out our new road system on the parade ground. The only other open space that was big enough for this was our baseball field, so that's where we reconvened.

"I'd like the experienced drivers to sit in the front passenger seat so they can help out the new ones. Each man should drive around the field for about five minutes. Then, stop and let the next guy take the wheel."

I then added, loudly, emphasizing each word, "And for goodness sakes don't run into anybody!"

I took one last look at the men, raised my hands toward the sky, and said, "Please, Lord, just don't let them kill each other."

The rest of the afternoon spiders and wasps were forgotten. The laws of physics became our new enemy. Particularly Newton's Third Law: "For every action, there is an equal and opposite reaction." I watched this Third Law in action, and I couldn't believe my eyes. Every action the men took seemed to produce an opposite reaction—at least opposite of the one desired.

First attempts to master the clutch resulted in what looked like bucking broncos all over the field. The jeep transmissions were geared so low it was nearly impossible for the men to kill the engines, and in some cases the bucking continued all across the field. They looked, for all the world, like rodeo riders. The passengers in each jeep held on for dear life until the jeeps picked up enough speed to stop the bucking and jerking.

But once they finally were up to speed, they had to shift gears. The sickening grinding of gears could be heard all across that baseball field. When gears weren't grinding, tires were spinning and squealing. Sideswipes also were common, but that didn't stop anyone. The jeeps could take it. I was learning why they were called the tanks of the road. Out-and-out collisions were few, but that was only because the men drove so slowly they had plenty of time to change course before disaster struck. And because the jeeps were so rugged, when a collision did occur, it was more a source of embarrassment for the men than anything.

Because we still had just four drivable jeeps, I added a six-by-six to the mix so the fifth crew didn't have to be rotated in and out of the other vehicles. Its cab could only hold four if the fourth person sat on a lap. I wanted everyone on the road at the same time, whether they were behind the wheel or were just passengers, so the six-by-six crew had to jam themselves in like sardines. By luck of the draw, they had the smallest man in the outfit, Johnny Tyler. Tyler, dripping wet, couldn't have weighed more than 110 pounds. He made Williams, by comparison, look positively fat. Tyler was also just over five feet tall. If I had passed him on the street I might have mistaken him for a kid in the sixth grade.

When the six-by-six stopped so that a new driver could be rotated behind the wheel, I ordered two men to climb in the back of the truck so I could sit comfortably in the cab with the other two of the crew. The new driver was Tyler. He was so short it looked at first as if he were looking *through* the steering wheel. He held his hands on the wheel in the position I had taught, at 10 and 2. In his case, that made his hands as high as his head.

I was about ready to suggest we find a box for him to sit on when he suddenly gunned the gas and the truck lunged forward. He didn't bother shifting as we picked up speed. The engine was straining and whining, begging him to shift to second gear. Halfway across the field, instead of shifting, however, he slammed on the brakes, catching us all off guard. I heard the men in back rolling around like firewood. I threw out my hands to brace myself against the dashboard, catching myself just in time to avoid a glass supper. As the truck skidded to a stop, two whiskey bottles—one half full and one empty—rolled out from under the seat, accompanied by a tube of lipstick, one pack of Lucky Strikes, and a single silk stocking.

"What the hell did you do that for!" I screamed at Tyler. As a teacher I had been trained to wait ten seconds before scolding a student, to allow time for the heat of the moment to cool. But after the other events of the day, I had had it.

"Are you trying to kill us! Are you so damn simple you can't tell one pedal from the other? What in the hell is the matter with you? If you can't do this, get out of here and let someone in who can. You got that, soldier?"

Tyler looked over at me and I noticed his lower lip was quivering. He hung his head and very slowly started reaching for the door handle.

Jenkins had been sitting in the middle and hit his head on the windshield. "I think my skull's broke, Sarge. Am I bleeding?"

Tears were now welling up in Tyler's eyes. He slowly shifted his body and opened the door so he could climb out of the truck, but I couldn't let him do it. At just that moment I realized it wasn't all his fault. It dawned on me I had never actually told them to press slowly and firmly on the brakes. In his inexperience, he probably just figured it was "all or nothing" when applying them. This was something else about driving that couldn't be explained fully until firsthand experience was thrown in. There was also a practical reason I couldn't let him go. I needed him, needed him to round out our roster of drivers. The sergeant in me started falling away as the teacher came back. I reached over and grabbed him by the shirt before he could get out of the truck.

"Where do you think you are going?" I asked. "Sit your ass back down and listen to me a minute."

He closed the door, but he still looked like a kid waiting for a whipping. I was afraid he was going to start crying, so I quickly added, calmly this time, " Look at me a minute. Sorry, Tyler, but you've got to do better. Hell, we've all got to do better, me included. We just don't have much time to get ready, and I'm truly sorry about that. Now, I want you to think about what just happened. Brakes can be tricky until you get used to 'em. I want you to try this again—only this time, gently on the brakes. Very, very gently. And how about shifting gears, too? OK?"

He nodded his head. I could see just the faintest hint of a smile, but the tension was still thick. Jenkins was still running his hand over his head, searching for blood. I had done a pretty good job of destroying any confidence Tyler had, so I had to do something. I picked up the half full whisky bottle and said, "And by the way, Tyler. For criminysakes, see if you can find a better place to hide your contraband next time, OK?"

Jenkins stopped searching for blood and howled.

Tyler, who was definitely one of the "unstung," smiled and started up the truck again. I hopped out and shouted back at them, "You don't need me anymore. Show them how it's done."

It took a good hour, but the men started to settle into a rhythm and a routine. Every five minutes, as instructed, they rotated in and out behind the wheel. Bucking clutch movements appeared less and less frequently. The gear grinding almost completely disappeared, with just an occasional crunch heard over the spinning of tires.

It was time for the men to hit—not literally, I prayed—the roads of our make-believe city. It was approaching evening chow, so I yelled for all to line up, in convoy formation, at the start of the course and park there. Williams had posted one of his signs there: "Entering Blood Alley."

The men looked tired and disappointed in their own efforts. I may not have been all that thrilled with their actions, but I had no complaints about their hearts.

Jenkins, now convinced he hadn't "broken" his head, spoke up. "Sarge, I'm really sorry. We're all sorry. We can do this. Give us another chance. I *know* we can do this."

A quiet chorus of "That's right" and "Yes, we can" followed.

"I know you can, men." I then checked my watch. "I tell you what let's do. It's about time to eat. Go get your bellies full—refuel yourselves—and then everybody meet back here at 1700 sharp. We'll start again and keep going, even after dark if we need to. These things have lights with blackout shields on them, and it wouldn't hurt to get some experience driving at night, too."

I paused for a minute and studied the group. They were anything but quitters.

"Now get out of here and get something to eat." Before they started to leave I added, "And stay away from Tyler. He's a bad influence!"

As they walked away I could hear Jenkins joking with the others about Tyler's hidden drinking habits.

Their laughter sounded so good.

* * *

When I got back to our road course at exactly 1700, the men were already in their vehicles. If nothing else, they were eager.

I again quickly went over the rules of "convoy formation" and explained how the course was laid out, but I couldn't stay to watch them practice. I had to get to the other side of the base for my non-com class. Doc wasn't happy about it because he still had vehicles to work on, but I asked him to take over in my absence. I had thought of asking him to take over anyway because all it took was one look at his icy stare to get the men back on task. His physical presence alone provided discipline. Actually, it might have provided fear, but at this point one was just as good as the other.

Running across the base, I could hear behind me the grinding gears, spinning tires, and honking horns of our convoy. I thought about it, but I didn't dare look back.

* * *

My noncom class ran late. I didn't get back to the barracks until after the men had already policed everything and were getting ready to knock off for the night. Our drivers were bonding quickly and were visiting quietly in the recreation area.

I had told the men not to acknowledge my entrance to the barracks unless an officer was present, but when I came into the building Jenkins, still rubbing his head, shouted, "At ease!" The men stopped what they were doing and immediately fell in line. I wasn't expecting this and was taken aback. I was genuinely touched. In a way I thought it was their way of saying they were sorry for the day's events.

"As you were!" I shouted, and then quickly added, looking over at the drivers, "Anyone killed tonight?"

Doc stepped forward and said, "I know a few who should have been."

The tortured expression on his face told me all I needed to know.

"Well, at least it looks like we all survived. And I don't see any bandages or anybody on crutches."

"Men, I want to say something. I'm probably not going to say this well, but I'll give it a shot. I've been spending a lot of time with our drivers lately, but I've noticed what the rest of you have been doing, too. The reports I've gotten from your instructors tell me you're really getting the hang of things in your classes. This battalion is really starting to shape up, and I'm proud of you all. We've all hit a few potholes along the way, but we're doing pretty damn good."

The drivers were still clustered together. "And now, a word about our jeep-jockeys. I'd like all of you to join me in congratulating them for surviving so far—and wish them well as they continue on."

I started clapping and was soon joined by everyone in the barracks. The drivers, embarrassed, sheepishly grinned and proudly waved to the others.

"You want to know why I am convinced those guys are going to make it? Because if somebody like Tyler can learn to drive, *anyone* can learn!"

Tyler, grinning from ear to ear, was playfully shoved back and forth between the men next to him as laughter and cheers filled the room.

I finally motioned for attention again. "Get good shuteye tonight. I want everybody bright eyed and bushy-tailed tomorrow. Finish up what you're doing and hit the rack. You don't have to wait for lights-out tonight."

They were so tired, they didn't.

And neither did I.

10

FENCES

The next afternoon, while Doc and I watched our drivers take another stab at the road course, Williams came running up, out of breath and drenched in sweat.

"That was a close shave," he gasped. "Another minute or two and I probably would have been caught with my hand in the cookie jar. Would have been dead meat."

He wiped his forehead with his sleeve and continued, "That sergeant was *mean!*"

"What the hell are you talking about?" Doc asked. "What close shave? What sergeant?"

Williams lit a cigarette as he tried to catch his breath, which made him only cough and wheeze even more. Doc took the cigarette out of Williams' mouth and threw it to the ground.

"Tell us what happened," I said.

"Close shave. Scared me to death."

He was so slight, when he breathed rapidly his chest appeared for all the world like an accordion sucking in and out air. When he finally gained his composure he relayed the whole story to us.

He had gone over to the motor pool by the airfield to look for the distributor caps Doc said he needed to resurrect a couple of our old six-by-sixes. When he got there he walked right inside and immediately initiated small talk with a young soldier fresh to camp who was cleaning a set of spark plugs.

Williams said, "He was the only one in there, so I figured I could take a look around for the distributor caps while we talked. He seemed so lonely. He talked about growing up in Los Angeles and how this was his first time away from home. I told him how much I missed St. Louis. Then he got all sad and said today's his mom's birthday and that he would have given anything to be back there with his family. He was a nice guy."

"So what happened?" Doc asked impatiently.

"He started putting the plugs back in, so while he did that I went over to the shelves by the door to see if the caps were there. Just then his sergeant came around the corner. He was looking down at some papers and didn't see me. I tried to get out of his way, but it was too late. He ran right into me—our legs got tangled—and we both went down."

Here Williams' eyes got wider and wider. "Wow, was he mad! He started shouting words that my dad won't even use. But funny thing, though, when he finally saw it was me and not that new kid, he just shut right up. I thought he looked kind of scared really."

He wiped more sweat from his forehead and defiantly lit up another cigarette before continuing his story. "You won't believe it, but then I did something kind of dumb."

Doc and I glanced quickly at each other as I said sarcastically, "Oh really?"

The sarcasm went right over his head. He was wound up and continued, "Before I knew it, I saluted him. Perc, I know you've told me a thousand times not to salute sergeants, but I didn't know what else to do. I was scared. I guess that really made him mad. He got this real mean look on his face and yelled at me, "Hey you—what the hell are you doing in here?"

"He didn't even give me a chance to say anything. You know what he did next? He picked up a wrench and started chasing me with it. I'm not lying. He kept shouting at me, 'Don't you ever come back here again!'"

He choked a last puff of his cigarette and dropped it to the ground. "You know what I think?" he continued. "Those guys must really have some valuable stuff in there because he sure ran me out in a hurry. Must have been worried I was going to steal something. I haven't seen anybody that mad in a long, long time. Chased me with a wrench!"

Doc and I burst out laughing.

"Good thing he didn't whack you with that wrench," Doc said.

"You don't weigh as much as a good sneeze. You'd still be flyin' through the air somewhere."

We continued laughing for a long time, not so much about the story, but about the way Williams told it. He was always so serious about everything, often missing the real import of what he was saying. But what he lacked in understanding he covered up with sincerity, even if it was misplaced at times.

I finally jumped in. "You need to be more careful next time. OK? I appreciate your efforts to keep us in supplies, but you aren't going to be much good to the battalion if they make you sit out the war in the stockade."

That night Doc told the story over and over to the men in barracks, giving special emphasis to the part about the sergeant chasing Williams with the wrench. At one point he rolled up a newspaper to represent the wrench and went running back and forth between the bunks as he illustrated how the sergeant had chased Williams. The men loved it. Each time he told the story, it got larger and larger, until he finally had the sergeant, a half dozen other men, *and* a pack of dogs chasing Williams all the way around the camp.

The last time Doc told the story—this time adding two MPs in a jeep chasing him, too—Williams interrupted him and corrected him, "Well, there weren't really any dogs."

And the men howled as they settled into their bunks.

* * *

The next morning at our battalion headquarters all hell broke loose.

I was typing in the front corner behind the door when a colonel and a sergeant I had never seen before came storming in. The colonel walked right up to the lieutenant and ordered, "Colonel Rogers to see Colonel Ellis. Tell him it's important. And tell him now, Lieutenant."

"Yes, Sir!" he responded and immediately knocked on Colonel Ellis's door.

I could hear Colonel Ellis say, "Enter." But before the lieutenant could announce them, the colonel and the sergeant barged into his office. The sergeant quickly closed the door behind them.

"What do you suppose that's all about?" the lieutenant asked.

"I don't know," I shrugged. "They're sure in a hurry about something."

The walls in headquarters were not designed for sound insulation, so it didn't take long for us to find out what was going on. The lieutenant and I moved our chairs over by the door so we could listen.

Colonel Rogers was so livid that his first words were difficult to make out. When he finally slowed down enough for us to understand him, I quickly felt a sick feeling growing inside my stomach.

He was there to talk about Williams.

Colonel Rogers was shouting. "I'm sick and tired of this, Ellis. I've had it. I'm not going to tolerate this anymore. I've seen your men all over this camp. Maybe you don't care, but I do."

Then, slowing down to emphasize every word, he continued, "They are supposed to stay where they belong."

Evidently they were all still standing because Colonel Ellis asked them to sit down. He then said, calmly, "I understand your concern, Rogers. I really do. But you need to remember something, too. We were brought here to build a support battalion, and to learn everything they need to know, the men are going to have to be part of this base."

Colonel Rogers butted in, "I don't give a rat's ass what they're here for. I don't want them around my men. They're lazy and they're shiftless. Hell, you know they don't belong here as much as I do."

"I don't agree," Colonel Ellis responded, this time sharply. "I'm with them every day and see what they can do. They may be a little rough around the edges, but they're going to be good soldiers, and we need them."

Growing angrier, Colonel Rogers said, "I've seen what they can do, too. Look at my sergeant's head. He's got a bump the size of an egg. One of your men knocked him down from behind in the motor pool yesterday and took off running. For no damn reason at all. None."

And then he got to the heart of the matter, "I'm telling you, those black sons a bitches don't belong here."

The room was suddenly very quiet. Colonel Ellis didn't say anything about that last remark. Instead, he said, calmly again, "Do you want to have charges filed against this man? If you do, I'll find him."

"No, goddammit. That's not the point. The point is, why was your man loafing in our motor pool? They just get in the way and cause trouble. I'm telling you, they're useless. And I don't want them around my men ever again. You got that?"

Colonel Ellis lowered his voice and said, "Just where do you suggest I tell them to go? They get to go to the Service Club just one night a week. They haven't even been issued any passes yet. Just where are they supposed to go? They're not prisoners, for godsakes."

"I don't care what you do with them, but I don't want them near my men anymore, and I mean that. I'll take this higher up if you can't control them. That's not a threat, Ellis. That's a fact—and a promise."

"I understand," Colonel Ellis responded, this time anger seeping into his voice. "I'm sure we'll be talking about this again soon."

At that point he called for the lieutenant. We quickly moved our chairs back before he knocked on Colonel Ellis's door and opened it.

"They're leaving now. Please show them out," Colonel Ellis said matter-of-factly.

Colonel Rogers and the sergeant, clearly miffed at being excused so abruptly, turned and headed out of the inner office. This time they saw me, and as they passed I heard Colonel Rogers mutter, "Son of a bitch…"

I looked back down at my typewriter and started typing again as fast as I could.

Just a few minutes after they left, Colonel Ellis asked me to step into his office.

"Perkins," he said. "I've got another job for you. Sit down. We're going to talk."

He knew I had heard what Colonel Rogers had to say. "I'm sorry about that, Perc. I really am. I want you to listen to me a minute. This is the South. Most of the men in this camp grew up with segregation as a natural part of their lives."

There it was. The "S" word. Segregation. That word had never been mentioned the whole time we had been at Fort Bliss, but now it was on the table, like a basket of spoiled fruit.

He offered me a cigarette. I shook my head no. Then he continued, "I told you once before there were going to be times when this wasn't pretty. Well, this is one of those times."

He pushed his glasses back up his nose and added, "This isn't just about Colonel Rogers and what he thinks. We *know* now how he thinks. This cuts a lot deeper than that. I'm betting most men on this base have never even talked to a Negro before. But you can bet they have *heard* a lot about them. I don't have to tell you that prejudice runs deep. You've lived it. I forget who it was, but somebody famous once said that prejudice, like a river, is mindless. It just rolls along without thinking about where it's going. And that's what we're dealing with now. I'm sorry. So sorry."

He put his hands together like he was praying and continued, "I was hoping it wouldn't come to this. I guess I was hoping the war would draw everyone closer together. Maybe it still will. I don't know. What I do know is I was given some strong 'suggestions' when I was assigned to be in command of this battalion, and because of what just happened, I'll probably have to follow those suggestions now."

He looked down and didn't say anything for a minute. I knew that was a bad sign, that the other shoe was about to fall.

Without looking up, he continued, "I was told to help turn the men of this battalion into first-rate support troops. That's being done. The next thing they told me was that all the men in the battalion would be Negroes. I grew up in the North like you did, so at first I wasn't sure what that would mean. I didn't have much time to think about it because I was *told* exactly what it meant. I wasn't exactly given orders, but the message came through loud and clear anyway. While the men were being trained for their duties, the battalion was to keep to itself as much as possible. There would be separate mess halls, separate barracks, separate training facilities, and separate recreation areas. Even told the latrines would be separate. I had heard about how segregated everything was in these Southern states, but I never saw it before to this extent myself. That is, until coming here."

He lit another cigarette off the one he was smoking and continued, "The first night the battalion got here, I called Sergeant Ingram in and explained some of this to him. Enough of it so he'd know what was going on. But I also told him not to put out a list of rules, or do's and don'ts. I was hoping I'd never have to."

Colonel Ellis was drawing small circles on a piece of paper as he talked, avoiding my eyes.

"I don't know what to do. We've got to do something now. I just don't know what it is. If Rogers goes over my head…"

I hadn't interrupted him to this point. He was a man, like many of us, still sorting out for himself the issue of race. I wasn't sure what all of his personal feelings were on the subject, but I could tell he at least wanted to set up a climate where conflict could be avoided wherever, and whenever, possible. Avoiding conflict was, at best, a stall tactic—one more way of avoiding the real issues. The real issues for me, and for many of the others, were these: Were we all part of the war effort, or weren't we? Were we all fighting for the same reasons—for the same purposes? Were we all men, or were some of us merely "support"? The bottom line seemed pretty clear: If we were truly being asked to be part of the war effort, if we were "all" fighting for the same reasons, and if we were "all" men, then shouldn't we be offered the same dignity and respect—and opportunities—as all soldiers?

In my mind, if we were going to win this war, we needed to be unified in every area, and especially in the army. There was no place for segregation in our armed forces. We weren't the Army, Navy, Marines, and Negroes. If we were truly to be "part" of the war, then we needed to be "part" of the war. It seemed just that simple to me.

But old habits and beliefs die hard, and this was the case not just within the ranks of the white soldiers. The majority of the men in the battalion had also grown up with segregation as a way of life and had never known anything different. It would never have occurred to them to walk into the "white" mess halls or recreation areas. From the time they were children, the world was completely black and white. No shades of gray. None. They just expected the army to be the same way and would have been shocked if it hadn't been.

But still another group of Negroes, and not just those from the Northern states, were, like Colonel Ellis, trying to walk an emotional tightrope, unsure of whether there was a safety net under them or not. In this group, there were two major schools of thought. On the one hand, they believed that hard work and perseverance would lead to better circumstances for themselves and their families. They felt they had the power, through their own actions, to knock down the fences of segregation. They saw the war, in so many ways, as a means to an end. When they heard we were fighting to preserve "our" way of life and "our" liberties and freedoms, they believed it literally and completely. "Ours." They also believed that a common enemy, the Axis powers, would, in a great irony because of the oppression they had caused all over the world, provide their freedom from racial discrimination and entrance into a way of life shared by all. From oppression to freedom. And defeat of the Axis might provide this because through their actions in helping defeat them, they would show themselves worthy of not segregated citizenship, but full and equal citizenship.

On the other hand, there were those who felt just the opposite, or, in the very best of moments, highly skeptical. The more of segregation they saw, and especially now in the army, the more their thoughts shifted in this direction. This group felt if they *weren't* going to be part of the war, and if they weren't going to be allowed to share the same liberties and freedoms won, then why fight at all? What was in it for them? What was the use of even trying to do well? They believed all would just go back to the way it was before the war started, that all would be returning to their segregated slices of life back in their hometowns. Those thoughts were hard to fight when the world, and the army in particular, still seemed to be so divided.

I wasn't entirely sure where I fit along this continuum of thoughts and emotions. All my life I had been the eternal optimist when it came to issues of race, but there were times when I didn't know if that was the real me—or if I was merely putting out an echo of the beliefs of my parents. My father was a teacher and a deeply religious man. My mother was a nurse. Growing up, what my father didn't touch on spiritually, my mother covered in the realm of the physical world. My father said we were all God's children; my mother said we "all bled red."

I was taught by both that, generally, we were all more alike than different. And this, according to my parents, was especially true in the area of race. I was also taught that both beauty and deed were not just skin-deep; rather, both had roots that ran all the way to the core of our souls. Differences, my parents said, were *created* by men, not inherently *in* men.

Growing up, there were times when I believed them and saw the world through their eyes. There were just as many times when I did not. I was born in Macon, Missouri, and spent my early years there. My father was a teacher for what was known in the town as the "colored school" of Macon. In his classes he preached the equality of all while teaching three miles away from the "white school" of Macon. Segregation was a way of life there, and nothing my father said could change that. We next moved to Des Moines, Iowa. While Des Moines was not a completely segregated city, I still attended a grammar school and a high school for Negroes.

On top of all this, as a child, even within my own race, I often heard comments about the color of my skin, which was very light in comparison to most of the other children in the neighborhood. All in my family were very light-skinned. As a matter of fact, my mother was often mistaken for being white. In grammar school, because of my fair skin, I was given the nickname "Whitewash" by Kenny Barclay. That is, I had the nickname until one day he called me that on the playground. The way he said it, in a sneering way, set me off, and I decked him with a quick right hook. The whipping I got from my father was worth it. I wasn't called "Whitewash" ever again. But I heard whispers and comments all throughout my childhood, not really understanding all the motivations behind them at the time.

When I went away to college at the University of Iowa, the classes there were open to all students of all races and walks of life. That was the first time I had ever been in a classroom where students of all colors sat side by side. The University of Iowa was one of just a handful of public universities in the country where this was allowed. But even at the university, while we were all taking classes together, students of different races could not live together. White students could live in the dormitories; colored students could not. Colored male students lived mostly in private homes in the area. Colored female students lived in a place called the Federated Home for Women. It was basically a dormitory given a fancy name. Equal in the classroom—not outside of it.

When I left the university I moved to St. Louis, a city that seemed to have everything, including, unfortunately, deeply rooted segregation.

Sumner High School was located in a section of the city called "the Ville." The Ville was the hub of the Negro community, and those who lived there did so with great pride. The Ville was, in many ways, a city in and of itself. Its residents seldom had to leave the Ville to find goods or services they needed. There were stores and businesses of all types, medical facilities, and one of the best school systems around. Children in the neighborhood could go all the way up the ladder of education, from elementary school through training after high school graduation.

The Ville was also one of the few places in St. Louis where Negroes could own their own homes. There were real estate covenants that prohibited this in most of the city, but this was not the case in the Ville and became one of the most important reasons why families moved there. There were no fences around the Ville, but local residents felt the streetcar lines that ran on the outer edges of the community served that purpose. They felt safe and secure inside those lines, unsure of themselves outside of them. After being used to being able to make use of most public facilities throughout Des Moines and Iowa City, it was quite a change to find those invisible fences in St. Louis.

And now, here at Fort Bliss, we were being asked to live in our own version of the Ville, and the geography was obviously starting to chafe both white and Negro soldiers alike.

I don't know how long Colonel Ellis and I sat there without speaking. We were both lost in our own thoughts about what had just taken place. He finally broke the silence.

"Perc, what do you think we should do?"

"I'll talk to the men tonight."

"I was going to ask you to."

Our conversation was over that quickly. Nothing else needed to be said. I got up, saluted him, turned, and walked out.

For the rest of the afternoon, I went through in my head at least a dozen speeches I could give, but as the time to talk to the men drew near, I still didn't know what to say or how to say it. I had gone into my classes before not fully prepared, but this wasn't Sumner, and these weren't my high school students. I wished I had more time to think about it, but I had been told to talk to the men immediately. There was only one thing I could do. I was going to speak from my heart—and hope and pray the right words would come.

Those who grew up with segregation as a way of life wouldn't be shocked. I was more concerned about those who were just starting to feel they *were* part of the war effort, those who felt their worlds were changing. Their egos were growing, but they were still fragile. This was a crossroads for many of them. They could continue what they saw as the path of belonging, but they could just as easily be sent packing back down the road of segregation and isolation.

So that I didn't have to give the information twice, I asked Colonel Ellis to send word that the men in Barracks N-1 were to report to our barracks at 1900 hours. All were to be present except those on guard duty or other special assignment. No other exceptions. They were also told that I, representing Colonel Ellis, would be speaking to them.

When all the men had finally assembled, the barracks was so full those toward the back couldn't see or hear well. I instructed them to spread out so that some were seated on the floor, others sat on the bunks, and still others spread out along the sidewalls.

I looked around the room one last time, cleared my throat, and started, keeping my voice as unemotional as I could. "You're probably wondering why you're all crammed in here tonight. It's because I've been asked to share some information with all of you. I'd like to begin by saying that change, when it happens, usually happens slowly. There are times when waiting for this change is agony, but the waiting is often necessary. People also have to get used to change, and that takes time."

I was already starting to lose them, to see confused looks across the barracks. I was also starting to sweat and my arms itched, which always happened when I was nervous.

"Men, I really believe we have a great opportunity to help win this war. Remember that day in class when we were told about all the training we were going to get? Remember how we were told part of that training was going to help keep our planes in the air? I can still remember the cheers that day, how proud we all were. I don't want you to lose that spirit, that enthusiasm. I *never* want you to lose it. We're being given a lot of jobs to do—important jobs—and I'm confident we'll do them well and to the best of our abilities."

My heart was still pounding a mile a minute, and my words were starting to match that pace. I took out my handkerchief and wiped my forehead to stall a little longer, then added, "But while all of this is taking place, change all around us is going to take place slowly. My hope is that it comes sooner than later, but however long it takes, there are going to be holes in the road in front of us."

I paused again here, scanning their faces, many of which were still blank, and then continued. "We've hit one of those holes now. I guess I don't have to tell you there are people who feel we shouldn't be here. And, at the same time, there are others who do. Those who feel we shouldn't be here have told those who feel we *should* be here that our presence isn't always welcome across the camp. I was told to bring this to your attention. Now listen to me carefully. I wasn't ordered to say this. But the message was still clear."

I could tell, finally, many knew where I was headed. Their eyes shifted from me to the floor. Others stared intently and silently, straining to hear every word.

My impulse was to tell them, "Men, we've been told, basically, that we smell. We smell black."

But I didn't. I couldn't.

I wasn't about to lie to them, but I also didn't feel I could take a chance at closing a door that would be almost impossible to reopen once it had been shut. I stalled as long as I could before continuing.

"Until the army figures out how it wants to use everyone, we're in sort of a state of limbo. It's all about that slow change I mentioned before. Time. Slow time. Possibly necessary time. Definitely necessary for some."

I paused one last time, then said, "For the time being, what we have is each other. If you've learned anything in the army so far, you have learned that the individual isn't as important as the group. That's the army way. And our group is important. We need to keep our focus on that. Yes, *I* think we're important as individuals, but we're in the army now."

I pointed to Williams, seated on the floor in front of me, and said, more sternly than I should have, "If you start singing that song right now I'll break your neck."

He knew exactly what I was talking about and weakly smiled up at me before looking back at the floor.

"We're in the army now, and we'll succeed, or fail, as a group. I want you to look to each other for support. I want you to look to Sergeant Ingram and me for support. I want you to look within yourselves for support. I want you to do this because when change comes, you'll be more ready for it. We're going to hit a few more holes in the road before all is said and done. You can count on that. But I want you to remember, always, that we'll climb back out of them, or go around them, together."

I then added, raising my voice to make sure all would hear me, "And one more thing. I expect you to be proud of yourselves and of each other…as I am of all of you. That's all I have to say. You're excused."

I then walked quickly to the side door, opened it, and stepped out into the cool night air. I could hear the men starting to talk to each other back inside as I slammed the door behind me. I reached into my pocket for a cigarette, but changed my mind. I didn't feel like smoking. I felt sick.

I had stopped short of telling them there were places where we could go and not go on the base. I didn't tell them we weren't supposed to mingle with the white soldiers. I didn't tell them there were parts of El Paso we weren't supposed to go into when off the base. I hadn't been ordered to say any of this. I had just been ordered to talk to them.

And I had.

I told them what I wanted them to hear, and I did my best to tell them what was in my heart. I knew some would get the message and share it with others. Some would still be confused, but at this point confusion was better than disillusion.

I was feeling a little of both. We were between floors on the up and down elevator of race. I felt like I was at the balance point of the fulcrum of change.

There was no way to know how much change was coming or how quickly it would appear.

For now, there were fences.

Lots of fences.

Of all types.

11

MESSAGES

We had finished evening chow and returned to the barracks when a jeep skidded to a halt outside. The driver gave the horn several blasts and shouted "Mail call!" as he threw a large duffel bag stuffed with letters and packages on the walk leading up to the barracks. Then he spun the jeep around and sped off, leaving a cloud of dust swirling in his wake.

As far as I was concerned, the mail couldn't have come at a better time. The men weren't exactly down, but the spirit that had been forged in the battalion suddenly seemed in danger of losing some of its punch. Some were still confused by what I had said and others were wandering dangerously close to the edge of disillusion. We definitely needed, and quickly, something that would help bring the men back together. I hoped the mail would provide a start.

I was used to seeing the men bolt and scatter when spiders or wasps were in the immediate area, but nothing I had seen to that point prepared me for the commotion that ensued when that bag of mail hit the ground. The men poured out of the barracks, trampling those unfortunates who tripped and fell to the ground. No one stopped to help them. They were pinned to the ground as others either stepped on or over them as they rushed to the mailbag. I just shook my head. I had never seen a group of men who ended up on the ground through tumbles and falls as much as these guys. At times, it was like watching bad circus performers.

Since arriving at camp we had been cut off from all news of home. To soldiers, mail call was the umbilical cord that connected us all to family, loved ones, and lives left behind. And it was obvious that connection was needed now more than ever.

When the men reached the mailbag, instead of ripping it open to get at its contents, they formed a circle around it and just stared at it, almost as if they were afraid it would disappear if they touched it. They became very quiet and still, and I could hear their breath coming in short gasps as they regained composure.

I had visions of someone making a grab for the bag and then the others piling on top to get at their own mail—something like a rugby scrum I had once seen.

"At ease, men!" I scowled in my best sergeant voice, which was becoming more of a growl with each passing day. "I'll handle this. Let me through."

I undid the knot on the cord holding the bag shut and reached in for a handful of letters. I called off the names on the letters one at a time, holding the letter up for the lucky soul to claim.

"Jenkins. Tyler. Williams. Jamieson. Albertson."

Each name brought the same response—"Yo!"—and I'd hand the letter over or pass it into the crowd to be routed to the soldier.

"Benson. Davidson. Clark. Perkins. Hey, that's me!" I shouted through the nervous laughter of the others waiting for their letters. I snuck a quick glance and saw it was from Olivia before stuffing the letter into my pocket. Then I distributed the others as quickly as I could.

Once in a while a soldier would get a second letter, and the group whistled or shouted its approval in response. When the last of the letters had been given out, I reached to the bottom of the bag and pulled up the small packages that had been sent. There were only half a dozen or so, so it didn't take long to find the owners. At the very bottom of the sack was a bundle of *Stars and Stripes* newspapers. There weren't enough to give one to each man, so I passed them out to those who didn't receive letters or packages. About a fourth of the men didn't receive anything. They were easy to spot because they were the ones walking around in small circles, eyes pointed to the ground, as the last of the names were called. I felt sorry for them. They looked so sad. I quietly walked through the group and handed each a paper. At least they would have something to read. I also figured since they were going to be the first to read the papers, they could pass the news along to the others and that would take their minds, at least temporarily, off not getting a letter from home.

Ten minutes earlier the men were trampling each other as they fought to get at the mail. Now they were sprawled out on the ground for a different reason—to relax and soak up news from home. As I scanned the group, I noticed some smiling broadly as they came to sections of letters that pleased them. Others slapped foreheads as something shocked or surprised them. Still others, in their loneliness and longing for those left behind, put their faces in their hands and quietly sobbed, trying not to let others see them. There were also more than a few belly laughs that rang through the group.

It didn't take long before the atmosphere turned again as men started reading letters aloud to others around them. "Listen to this," someone would say, and others would come over to hear the news, hanging on every word. Clark recounted how his father had fallen off a ladder and broken his arm in two places. Brown's sister sent short descriptions of all the movies she had seen over the past two months; it was like listening to "Coming Attractions" at the theater. Davis received word that a first cousin had been killed in an auto accident, and those around him did their best to console him.

We were all impressed when Jenkins read aloud that his brother had won a set of pretty decent tires in a crap game. Tires were impossible to get, not just because of rationing but because of a genuine shortage of rubber. The fact that his brother won some was cause for celebration throughout his whole family. As he read the letter, something occurred to me. I interrupted him and asked, "Jenkins, I didn't know you had a car. And while I'm thinking about it, you didn't volunteer to be a driver, either. How come?"

He responded, "Oh, we don't have a car."

"Then why is your family so excited about the tires?"

"Sarge, you have any idea how many meat ration stamps we can trade those tires for?"

I just nodded my head. Dumb me.

The letter that got the most attention was sent to poor Tyler, jeep driver extraordinaire, who was becoming something like our battalion mascot. He was liked by everybody, but we all had to admit that if something odd could happen, it would happen to Tyler. Some people just seemed to have that fate, and he was definitely one of them. He had been pacing back and forth as he read his letter, alternately raising his hands up the heavens and then asking in his high-pitched, scratchy voice, "Why me, God?" Jamieson finally snatched the letter away from him and held it high as he read it aloud to the group. Tyler was mortified and tried with all his might to get the letter back. He jumped up and down under Jamieson, like a dog trying to grab hold of a piece of meat.

Jamieson started reading, mimicking Tyler's voice, "My dearest, I'm afraid I have a little bad news for you. You don't have to worry any more about me taking care of your dog while you're away. It ran away last week, and I haven't seen it since."

Jamieson paused here and said, sarcasm dripping from his voice, "Oh, that's too bad!"

He then continued with the letter. "And remember that money you left with me to pay off the last installment on your radio? Well, I had to use it to buy flowers for Mrs. Gibson because your dog bit her before it ran off and she fell down and the poor thing has now taken to her bed."

Jamieson again paused, this time saying, mock empathy filling his voice, "What a dirty shame. That's so sad."

He continued again with the letter. "Mr. Gibson says he is going to sue you when you get back, but you know what an old windbag he can be."

With as much insincerity in his voice as I had ever heard, Jamieson then said, "I'm so sorry. What a tough break!"

Tyler was still jumping up and down, trying to snatch back his letter, as Jamieson stiff-armed him to hold him off and continued reading. "And then yesterday the man from the store came and took your radio away."

By this time a crowd had gathered around Jamieson, who was now laughing so hard he could barely continue reading. He scanned a little farther down the letter and his eyes lit up. He then raised his voice and continued. "But I feel worst of all about losing the ring you gave me. I took it off when I went dancing last week at a war bond dance so I wouldn't lose it, and wouldn't you know, I lost it! I thought it fell down a drain over by the refreshments. When I stuck my hand down the drain to see if it was there, I got stuck and couldn't pull my hand back out and they had to call the fire department. That's when I met Jim. He was the fireman who put grease on my arm so I could slide it back out. He was so nice about everything I just couldn't turn him down when he asked me to go to a movie with him the next day. You'd like him. He just lost his girlfriend, so I am going to go with him to another movie on Friday night to help ease his pain."

As the rest of us roared with laughter, Tyler finally gave up trying to get the letter back. He clutched his chest and pretended he had been shot—and then fell backward and flopped to the ground. He closed his eyes and let his head fall to the side. He looked dead.

Jamieson stopped laughing long enough to catch his breath, then read the last lines of the letter.

"I better sign off now. Remember I'm crazy about you, Poopsie. Please write and send me a souvenir of where you are. Sincerely, Belinda."

"Poopsie?" Jamieson shouted. "Poopsie?"

A chorus of "Poopsie! Poopsie! Poopsie!" filled the night air as Tyler's limp body was hoisted and carried into the barracks.

If he hadn't wished he was dead before, he sure must have then.

* * *

Doc, Williams, and I decided to slip away from the group and headed over to the motor pool. Our battalion was allowed use of the base Service Club just one night per week, Thursday night, so the motor pool became our main meeting place outside the barracks on other nights. Its importance as a place for the men to relax increased dramatically after "the talk" gave everyone a pretty good idea of how some felt about our presence around the base. In so many ways, "the pool" had now become our own Service Club.

All three of us had received a letter from home. We grabbed camp stools and leaned back against the building as we opened the envelopes. The coolness of the metal of the hut felt soothing against our aching backs and we let out a collective "Ahhhhhh…"

"Who's your letter from, Doc?" I asked.

He was already absorbed in his letter. Without looking up, he replied softly, "My mom."

"Who's yours from, Perc?" Williams asked.

"Olivia. How about yours?"

"My cousin, Alice. We've been close since we were kids."

"Close?" Doc mocked, suddenly putting down his letter. "Why you two invented the game of 'Doctor' didn't you? I heard you two had to be separated when you were about thirteen because you couldn't keep your hands off each other. It was all over Kinloch. Big scandal."

"That's not true," Williams shot back. But the way he avoided our eyes and the smile that started forming told another story. He added slowly, pausing after each word, "We are *cousins*—and that's all."

"Yeah," Doc continued. "Kissin' cousins—and then some! You know, you can go blind from that, and look at you. I've never seen thicker glasses in my life! You're blind as a bat."

I added in a serious tone, "It's also a well-known fact that fooling around with cousins will stunt your growth. And looking at you, well, I'm just guessing you've been a busy little beaver. Make that a *blind* beaver."

"Leave me alone you guys. I haven't done anything that I'm ashamed of. Story closed!"

I wanted to pick on him some more, but I was aching for news from Olivia. I carefully opened the flap of the envelope and removed the thin onionskin paper. Olivia's penmanship was beautiful. So beautiful, in fact, that it was often difficult to read, especially on the nearly transparent paper that everyone now had to use for writing letters. Her letter was dated the day after I left St. Louis.

October 3, 1943

My Dearest Perc,

As I watched your train leave last night I felt like parts of my heart and soul were going with you. Oh, my love, how I miss you already. I didn't sleep a wink last night. I tossed and turned and cuddled up to my pillow, hoping it would somehow magically turn into you. I just don't know how I am going to stand this being apart.

These last glorious weeks we spent together taught me that you are truly what is most important in my life. I love you with all my heart. That will always be true. Always. We may be hundreds of miles apart, but I know now my love for you will only continue to grow. I feel such a connection with you, and I feel this no matter what we are doing. Whether we are holding hands at the movies, walking to school together, or just sitting close and listening to the radio, I feel an electricity arc between us that tingles me all the way down to my toes.

I don't know when this will get to you. No matter when it does, know that my love will already be that much greater than when it was written. You are so deep in my heart. So deep.

Above all, remember this: I love you with all my heart—now and forever.

Olivia

I was already putting the letter back into the envelope and drifting off into thoughts of our last evening together when I was jolted back to the present. Doc leaned over toward Williams and swiftly grabbed his letter while saying, "You don't mind if I read this, do you?"

Williams went wild. That is, after his camp stool slipped out from under him, dropping him to the ground. He got up and jumped on top of Doc, knocking both of them to the ground. They looked like a couple of young wildcats wrestling with and pawing at each other. It was all a friendly row, but Williams, not even half Doc's size, was going to let the larger man know he was there. My brother and I used to fight the same way, and someone always ended up getting hurt. Before that could happen, I pulled them apart and said, "OK, kids. We don't have time to go to the infirmary, so cut it out before I whip both of you."

I also reached over and yanked the letter from Doc's hand and gave it back to Williams. The teacher in me knew I needed to offer a distraction, and fast, to keep them from going at it again. I quickly asked Doc, while strategically positioning myself between them, "What did you hear from your mom?"

I felt like we were playing musical chairs. I was now sitting on the stool in the middle so I could keep them apart. When we were all seated again and after everyone took a deep breath, Doc finally responded.

He took one last swipe at Williams and then turned to me and said, "It's mostly just family news. My sister got some award in school for winning the talent show. She plays the piano and is pretty darn good at it. Oh, and right after we left, my dad's victory garden came through with enough tomatoes to feed darn near the entire neighborhood. He did a second crop of them this year. I didn't think they'd grow because the weather was getting cooler, but they did. I've never seen anyone so proud of tomatoes. They're like his children. I can still see him crawling around on his hands and knees, pulling the grass and weeds between the plants. And if he ever saw one little bug anywhere in the garden, he'd be out there giving everything a good dusting. Last year because of how hot it got they were stunted and he took it hard. Really hard. But according to Mom, this year they were the biggest yet, and Dad was constantly singing his tomato song. I bet he drove everyone nuts."

"Tomato song? What's that?" I asked.

"Oh, a few years ago he made up this cornball song to the tune of that one I think is called "Bicycle Built for Two." You know, 'Tomato, Tomato, give me your flavor, too. I'm half crazy, all for a taste of you.' He's got about a dozen more verses he's made up. And his singing! His voice sounds like a dog with its tail caught in a screen door. Drives us all crazy. I'd give anything to be back there now because I miss that old coot."

I turned to Williams and asked, "How about you? Seriously, now. What news did your cousin send along?"

Doc jumped in with, "She probably said she's knocked up!"—and Williams came rushing at him again. This time I got the worst of it. One of them accidentally poked me in the eye, and my right foot got a pretty good stomping.

When I finally got them back to neutral corners I said, "Hey, I'm not the enemy here. Look at me. You guys are killing me. Give it a rest, OK?"

Williams gave Doc a cold stare and then said to me, "OK, Perc.

Sorry about that. If that lummox will leave me alone I'll quit."

"Lummox? Why you little…"

This time I let them fight, but not before I moved completely out of the way. They rolled around on the ground and beat on each other until Williams sunk his teeth into Doc's arm. Doc let out a scream that scared Williams so bad he stopped to see if Doc was really OK.

Doc sat up and rubbed his arm. "Damn, that hurt! Perc, now we're going to have to quarantine him. If I start foaming at the mouth, promise me you'll shoot him."

They didn't bother getting back on their stools. They both just sat there on the ground in front of me, still poking at each other. "What's the news from Olivia? Things OK?"

"It was just a short note. She wrote it right after we left St. Louis, so there wasn't much time for any new news. She just wanted me to know she was still there."

"Still there," I said again, looking off in the distance at the lights of the barracks.

"You really miss her, don't you?" Doc asked sincerely.

"It's hard to put into words," I said. "Yeah, I really miss her, but it is more than that. It isn't just that I miss *her*. I miss *us*. I miss the time we used to spend together. Does that make any sense at all? The last year and a half have been the best of my life because of her. The very best. Hands down. She's the only woman I've ever met who can make me laugh all the time. Sometimes at the stupidest things. We went to the movies right before I left, and she said something about the newsreel that got me laughing so hard I thought I was going to choke to death. And everything's just beautiful to her. She isn't a 'goody-two-shoes.' That's not what I'm saying. She just finds something good in everything, and that makes me feel good when I'm with her."

I wasn't sure I should say it, but I also added, "And she makes me feel like I'm important. Like what I do makes a difference. Like there's nothing I can't do."

I then lowered my voice and continued, smiling, "I'd also be lying if I didn't say the way she kisses me revs my motor. There is that, too."

Williams cupped one ear and leaned forward as he said, "Are those wedding bells I'm hearing? You hear 'em, Doc?"

Doc looked right at me and asked, "Well, Perc. Is that so?"

"I won't kid you guys. I've been thinking a lot about that lately, but I know this is a rotten time to be considering it. Who knows where we'll be a month from now? Heck, even a week from now. And we'd be apart for who knows how long no matter where we get sent. How fair would this be to her? She certainly can't traipse around the country and follow me. And even if we do get stationed in the States, she's got a job she loves in St. Louis, and her family is there. I don't know—this gets more and more complicated the more I think about it. I just don't know what to do."

Doc cut in and said, "You want my advice? Who knows where any of us will end up. I say you two should go ahead and tie the knot the first chance you get. Right now, the army can tell us what to do in every way except for what's right here—in our hearts. And it's plain yours is pretty full right now, so I say go for it."

Williams added, "I never, ever, thought I'd encourage anyone to get hitched, but even I can tell how bad you've got it. I guess I'm with Doc. I say go for it, too."

"Thanks, guys," I said. "That means a lot to me. It really does. I don't have it all sorted out in my own mind yet and I've still got a lot of things to work out, but I really do appreciate what you just said. For a couple of nincompoops you two aren't half bad."

"Just don't think about it too long," Doc said. "If you're going to do something about this, you really better try to do it sooner rather than later."

Williams, who had been nodding in agreement while Doc was talking, suddenly looked up and shouted, "Nincompoops? Nincompoops?"

The next thing I knew they charged me and wrestled me to the ground. I didn't fight it. I knew there was no use.

* * *

After another nearly sleepless night of tossing and turning, by the next morning I was completely and absolutely miserable. No matter what I started to do, my thoughts kept returning to Olivia. I chewed out the men over and over for losing concentration while doing their work, and here I was, now the worst offender of the lot. We all got orders to drop what we were doing and report to the obstacle course first thing, and while there I slipped while climbing the rope wall and ended up as tangled as a fly struggling in a cobweb. At headquarters I added the same column of figures four times before I finally came up with the right total. At noon chow I sat down to eat and realized I had forgotten a fork. Yes, I was smitten. And bad.

Halfway through the afternoon, while watching the men drive in perfect convoy formation around and around our make-believe road system, I sat down against a tree and closed my eyes, daydreaming about the walks I used to take with Olivia around the Ville. The sudden honking of horns ended the dreams. The men still weren't sure of the "Yield Right Of Way" protocol, and two jeeps had arrived at that intersection at the same time, neither willing to give ground to the other.

"Hey, Sarge!" one group yelled. "Tell them to back off. We've got the right of way."

"Figure it out yourselves," I snapped back, not really interested right then in whether they crashed into each other or not.

The driver of that jeep just shrugged his shoulders and, with a sweeping motion of his arm, motioned for the other jeep to move on through the intersection.

I yelled over at them, "You're on your own. Try not to kill each other until I get back."

I took one last look back and saw blank stares following me as I headed over to the motor pool.

Doc was so far down into the engine compartment of a six-by-six that all I could see was one leg sticking out.

"Don't get up," I said while patting him on the leg to let him know I was there. I walked around the truck a few times, mustering steam. I finally said, "I can't take it anymore. You were right last night, Doc. I'm going to ask her. As soon as I can."

Without saying a word, Doc climbed back out of the engine compartment and stuck out his hand. His usual firm handshake was tempered somewhat by a thick layer of grease, but he smiled broadly and said, "Williams is going to be so sick." Then he quickly added, "Oh, and by the way, congratulations."

"Thanks—but why is Williams going to be sick?"

"Because last night I bet him five bucks you'd decide to propose within two days. Perc, my friend, you didn't let me down."

"Very funny," I said. "Very funny."

"No, I'm happy for you. I really am. Olivia sounds wonderful. I wish you two all the happiness in the world. I mean that."

I thanked him, then said, "Now all I've got to do is get her down here or get back to St. Louis."

"You know what scuttlebutt is saying, don't you? We're getting leave as soon as our basic training is over. That's not that far off. If it really happens, you can do it when you go home then."

"How come scuttlebutt knows more than I do? I'm the one who works in headquarters, and I haven't even heard anything about leaves."

"If you hold your horses for a little while it'll all work out."

"Thanks, Doc," I said, shaking his hand again. "Thanks."

* * *

I would never have been called the most romantic guy in the world. I always had to struggle to let my feelings be known, especially when it came to members of the opposite sex. But I really put my foot in it one day the previous spring when I had been joking around with Olivia about what I thought it would be like to be married to her. During that talk I had promised if I ever got to the point of proposing, I would do it in such a way that she would never forget it. She said she would expect nothing less—that she wanted to hear bells ringing and angels singing.

That was all swirling around in my mind the next afternoon when I saw it: the Pepsi-Cola trailer.

I had heard the men talking about it for days, but I hadn't gone over yet to see it myself. The Pepsi-Cola Company, to help support those in the service, was sending trailers equipped with recording booths around to bases all over the country. The men went into these recording booths and for twenty-five cents could sing a song or make a recording of a letter on a slightly smaller version of a regular record. These could be mailed to sweethearts or family members back home.

I wasn't sure exactly how romantic Olivia would consider it—and I sincerely doubted any singing angels would be involved—but an idea came to me. I could make my proposal by way of the Pepsi-Cola Company. At least, I figured, it would be something she'd never forget.

I immediately rounded up Doc and Williams because I had specific ideas about how I wanted to do this. Olivia's favorite song was "As Time Goes By," from *Casablanca*. Every time we heard that song on the radio she would snuggle up to me and sing it softly in my ear. I decided that song, which had become "our" song, would be perfect background for the proposal and asked Doc and Williams to help me sing it to her.

When I explained my plan to them, I was actually surprised they thought it was a good idea. Both instantly agreed to help. I told them to meet me after chow at the Pepsi-Cola trailer, which was parked outside the Service Club. Since this was a Thursday, our night to use the club, the timing was perfect.

After what seemed like the longest afternoon of my life, the time to head over to the trailer finally arrived. When the three of us got there, a line was already forming, but Doc started shoving men out of the way as he shouted, "Make way for your sergeant! What's the matter with you?" He was smiling when he said it, but the men still shrank away just to make sure he wasn't going to whack them. I bowed smartly to the men and headed inside.

The recording specialist greeted us, introducing himself as Mr. Simmons. He was a white-haired, grandfatherly looking man with small, round glasses that rested at the tip of his nose. He looked like pictures of Ben Franklin I had seen in schoolbooks. He quickly went through the procedure for making the record, emphasizing over and over that we would have exactly two minutes total, not a second more. He had a soft, gentle voice that was often difficult to pick up. I was pretty nervous, so that also might have had something to do with it, too. I explained to him that I wanted Doc and Williams to sing with me for the first part of the recording, and then I'd end with a message to someone back home. He said that would be fine if we could all cram ourselves into the booth. It was a tight squeeze, but we managed. I instructed them that I would count to three, and at that time we would all start singing. On Mr. Simmon's signal, I quickly counted and we cut loose.

It wasn't exactly "three-part harmony"—it was more like "three-part horrifying"—but we got the job done. Doc's voice was very nice, very bass, and carried us through. Williams voice was a little high and he kept singing the wrong words. I was so nervous I think I croaked the words more than I sang them.

When we finished the first two verses, I motioned for them to stop singing and stay quiet as I said, "By the way, my love, I'd like to ask you something: Will you marry me? Will you be my wife, now and forever?"

I had more I wanted to say, but Williams horned in, "For goodness sakes say yes so he'll shut up about you."

Doc leaned toward the microphone and added, "He's pitiful, but he's all yours if you want him."

Mr. Simmons was starting to make a slashing motion across his throat and held up both hands, sliding down one finger at a time to show the seconds ticking down. I added as fast as I could, "I love you, Olivia. I…"

Then the recording machine stopped. Mr. Simmon's said, "I've been doing this for a month now, and that's the first proposal I've heard. I hope she says yes, young man."

"Thank you, sir," I replied, my voice still shaking. "That's very kind of you."

He motioned for us to stand to the side while he picked up the record and tested it to make sure the recording was fine. It was. He slid it into a special mailing envelope that had a beautiful red and blue Pepsi-Cola logo on it and handed it to me.

"Be careful with this," he said. "The envelope is pretty stiff cardboard, but try to make sure you don't accidentally bend it before you get it in the mail."

He then shook my hand and said, "Good luck, soldier" as he quickly, and firmly, ushered us out of the trailer so others could get in.

It was done. Now all that remained was mailing it.

"You can still change your mind," Doc said, sensing my nervousness as we left the trailer.

"Not on your life," I replied. "This is the best thing I'll ever do."

Williams chimed in, "You're getting married. This is probably the *last* thing you will ever get to do!"

While they both laughed, I just stared at the record.

* * *

Later that night after I put the record in with the outgoing mail, Williams and I sat outside the barracks and had a last smoke before lights-out. He still wasn't used to smoking and coughed and wheezed like an old Duesenberg.

Doc had drawn late-night guard duty, and we could see him off in the distance, marching back and forth in front of the auxiliary gate. The gate had to be guarded all the time even though it was used only when the front entrance of the base flooded, which happened quite often after the sudden Texas rainstorms.

As Williams gagged and sputtered, I asked, "You've known Doc a long time. What was he like when you two were growing up?"

Williams lit another cigarette off the one he had just finished and responded, "I actually hated him when I first met him. He was a bully. A bad one. We were all afraid to be around him because he would sock guys for no reason and was always stealing our lunches. That's really how I met him. He took my lunch away from me one day, and when I said something he knocked me right on my butt. That was in the fourth grade, I think."

"So what changed him?"

"I'm not completely sure, but one thing happened that year I've never forgotten, and I don't think he ever has, either. He got just what he deserved, and after it happened, it just seemed like he was never the same. Thank goodness!"

"Well, what happened?" I asked.

"I can remember like it was yesterday. One Friday that spring some kid threw up in the hall right after lunch. All us kids started playing 'Jump Over The Throw-Up.' You know, that's where everybody takes a turn jumping over it. When it was my turn to jump, Doc came runnin' over to see what he was missing. He elbowed me out of the way and decided it was his turn next. Well, and you should have seen this, he rocked his arms back and forth and jumped—and didn't quite make it over. Those already-been-chewed string beans stuck right to the seat of his pants. It was great. Everybody started laughing and pointing fingers at him and started making gagging sounds. Doc screamed for everybody to shut up, but someone started shouting, 'Taylor's in the puke!' He got so mad he just ran off down the hall."

Williams coughed again but kept going. "Doc didn't come back to class until late that day. I remember our teacher didn't ask where he'd been. She was probably sorry he came back at all. We sure were. Roxanne Brown—boy, I had a crush on her even then—was the first to notice the smell and started gagging. It wasn't long before all of us were doing the same. Our teacher walked to the back of the room and said, 'Children, what is that smell?' Someone yelled out, 'It's Taylor!' Somebody else yelled, 'Taylor's in the puke!' She picked Doc up by the back of his shirt and ran his ass out to the hall. He didn't even fight it. He knew he was whipped. I remember we all clapped."

"Then what happened?" I asked.

Williams flicked the ash off his cigarette and continued, "We were really hoping Doc would leave us alone after that, but I'm telling you it sure didn't work out that way. Doc came back to school on Monday all full of himself again and punched two people right in the eye when they said something. But you know, he was never the same after that. Slowly but surely, he got more and more quiet as the years went by. He still picked on us once in a while, but he also started to protect us when kids from other neighborhoods would come around looking for trouble. Whenever we'd say 'thanks' he'd just turn around and walk away. We didn't become friends until years after that, and then it was only because he dated my next door neighbor for a while and just got used to seeing me around."

I put my hand on his shoulder and said, "That's the most I have heard you say in the whole time I've known you. Thanks for telling me that. I won't say anything to him. I promise."

I then added, "All things considered, he's a pretty good guy now, isn't he?"

He just smiled and took another puff of his Lucky, choking once again.

We sat there in silence, finishing our cigarettes. Both of us watched Doc, rifle held to his shoulder, eyes focused straight ahead, marching slowly back and forth in front of the gate. As I watched him, I could just picture him as a kid. Back then, people didn't break the rules in his territory.

Some things never change.

12

CHALLENGES

The rain started on Wednesday and continued all through Friday. It wasn't a heavy rain, just steady. The main gate flooded again, so the auxiliary gate behind our barracks became the main checkpoint in and out of Fort Bliss. When the men weren't busy with classes or other duties, they sat inside the barracks where they could look out the windows at the constant coming and going of vehicles. Other than the fact that the noise kept us from sleeping at times, it was a refreshing change of pace.

After chow on the second night of rain, the men lined up two deep to watch a gasoline convoy, followed by a general supply convoy, come onto the base. Jenkins said, "This is great! Just like a movie!" To me, it was a pretty dull movie, but at least it gave the men something to do on an otherwise dreary night.

The rain didn't put a crimp on our regular daily activities, however. We still fell out for drill and calisthenics early each morning. Sergeant Ingram could have spared us this experience if he had wanted to, but he kept saying every time someone complained, "You don't think it's going to rain overseas?" The men responded like a bunch of grammar school kids, stomping and jumping up and down in the deep puddles that were everywhere. Those still attending classes also kept up with that, and our drivers continued to practice every afternoon. For our drivers, the rain posed problems I hadn't anticipated. Most had never driven in rain, and it took two pretty good crashes on our course before it dawned on me the drivers couldn't see where they were going because they didn't know to use the wiper blades. They still had a few things to learn, but it was also nearing time for them to fly on their own. I was alternately cautiously optimistic and downright queasy thinking about it.

Then, Friday night around midnight the rain stopped just as suddenly as it had started. By morning, steam rose from the ground as its warmth reigned again. As the sun came out there was even a slight trace of fog. When the men fell out for the morning count, I could barely see those standing at the end of the rows.

We still hadn't been issued any passes to go into town, which really didn't surprise too many after "the talk" had been given. What entertainment we had, we had to create for ourselves. The main diversion for all of us had become baseball. And this was Saturday: baseball day. There were no classes for us. The trucks were parked back at the motor pool. The rain had stopped. The fog was lifting. The men were chomping at the bit to get to the field.

There were two fields at Bliss, ours and the one for the rest of the base. The other field flooded every time the main gate flooded. Ours was far enough back in the camp that it did not. As a matter of fact, because of the sandy soil in this part of Texas, our field, which was on higher ground than the other, dried almost as quickly as the drops hit the ground.

As soon as we finished breakfast on Saturday morning I could see men already over there checking the field to make sure it was playable. The excited looks on their faces as they came running back to the barracks told everyone it was, and the men cheered the messengers and patted them on the back like they had personally been responsible for drying the field.

We didn't have much in the way of baseball equipment, but it didn't matter to the men. They were just happy to be playing and getting away from our regular routine. Before "the talk," Williams had "borrowed" a half dozen gloves from the other side of the base. We also had two bats. One was in good shape, almost new. It was shorter and lighter than most would have liked, but we made do with it. The other was just the right size and heft for most, but it also had a nasty crack on the handle. It had been taped so many times that the handle's diameter was difficult to hold onto while swinging it. More often than not, if contact with the ball wasn't made, the bat would slip out of the batter's hands and go sailing across the diamond. That was one way to keep the infielders on their toes. Plus, the ball just didn't seem to travel all that far when hit with what we called "Old Cracky."

We also didn't have regular bases for our field. Williams had scrounged lids to some forty-gallon oil drums, and Doc had taken his cutting torch and cut square bases out of the round lids. When we first used them they were so slippery base runners actually fell down if they stepped directly on them while running the bases. We also couldn't figure out a way to keep them anchored in place, so we came to an agreement that a runner just had to be "close" to the base when rounding it.

We weren't lacking for players. There was such a backlog of those who wanted to get into a game and there were so many fights over who should be playing at any given time that I finally had to come up with a type of lottery system to make this somewhat fair. I put all their names in a box and would draw out the names of the lucky players, nine to a team. This "fairness" also meant that something else had to be sacrificed: The teams weren't put together taking into account any special skill level or particular experience of the players. One day a team ended up being composed of four men who said they were catchers and five who said they were outfielders. None had ever pitched before, not even in playground games when they were kids. They argued so much about who should play where that I finally stepped in and said, "You—third base. You—first base. You—left field" and continued until they all had positions. One of the catchers pitched, and that team never even got up to bat. Final score: 29 to 0.

Games were played not by innings, but by the clock. In fairness to those waiting to play, games could go no more than forty minutes, regardless of how many innings had been played. At the end of that time, the team ahead was declared the winner. This quickly led to teams with the lead late in games learning to use every stall tactic in the book to drag out the time until they could be declared the winners. One late afternoon I watched a team with a two-run lead all rush over to help their third baseman, Albertson, who had fallen down when he let a ground ball hit him in the stomach. He put on a performance that rivaled any deathbed scene I had ever seen in the movies. He rolled around in agony on the infield dirt, twitching and kicking his legs out. He kept moaning, "I think it broke my liver." I was about to send someone for help when I saw Albertson, when he thought no one was looking, take his cigarettes out of his back pocket and transfer them to his shirt pocket. No need of his smokes getting hurt. I went over, picked him up by the back of his pants and his shirt collar, and heaved him over into foul territory, which "did" injure his cigarettes.

These stall tactics got to be ridiculous. Men suddenly had dust blow in their eyes and they acted like they were stone blind until enough time was eaten off the clock. There were also so many "sudden" sprained ankles that it looked like hospital ward teams playing. I finally called the men together one day and told them the story of the "boy who cried wolf," but it didn't do a bit of good. When Jamieson had the ball go off the tip of his glove and conk him on the head while his team was ahead, the other members of his team came over and just stood around looking at his limp body, figuring he was still faking. It wasn't until someone noticed blood trickling down his forehead and into his left eye that he got any help.

Something had to be done, but I couldn't figure out what. It was Doc who actually came up with a perfect solution. Drawing upon his experience with Indian ball, he suggested that three teams play at the same time, rotating in and out of the field like the three of us had done while playing back at Davis-Monthan. It was a genius solution because instead of stalling, teams started hurrying as quickly as they could to get as many times at-bat as possible. It did produce some odd scores, like 6 to 3 to 2, but it also kept the games moving right along.

On this particular morning three teams were really slugging it out with each other. The St. Louis Browns had a five-run lead over the New York Yankees and a two-run lead over the Birmingham Barons. After the Browns had gone out, the Yankees were the next team up to bat. While the teams changed positions on the field, I heard some commotion behind me and turned to see another team walking over toward us, gloves and bats in hand.

"You guys going to use the field this morning?" the tallest of the group asked Tyler, who was sitting nearest the backstop. He turned and was stunned by the white faces staring down at him. He was speechless and looked over to me as if asking for help.

I walked over and said, "We've got a pretty fair game going on. Want to watch?"

The men of all three teams had stopped all activity and were straining to listen to what I was saying. I motioned for them to resume play, and they did. But every chance the men got they still looked over my direction.

The tall soldier, the spokesman for his group, introduced himself as Wharton. He looked at my stripes but didn't say anything.

"Our field's flooded pretty good," he said. "One joker pulled a raft off one of the 17s and paddled around the field until he got caught."

The others muffled laughter.

"And we're not much at water polo, so we thought we'd come over to see if this field was being used."

It was apparent they had no intention of leaving. They could also see the men running on and off the field as teams changed positions, so they sure as heck knew the field was "being used." This was our field, and I wasn't going to let them run us off.

"That game is just about over," I said, motioning to the field.

I don't know what came over me, but before I thought about what I was saying I heard it coming out of my mouth, "If you want, we could fit you into the next game."

The minute I said it I started sweating, remembering "the talk" and thinking of potential consequences for what I was suggesting. If we got caught, I knew we'd never hear the end of it.

Wharton turned around and looked at his men before responding, "Think that's a good idea?"

"It is if you want to play," I said in my best sergeant growl.

There it was. I had thrown down the gauntlet. We weren't going to give up the field. If they wanted to play, they'd play with us.

I heard someone behind me say, "Are you crazy?"

I was also already starting to regret opening my big mouth, but I had made the offer and didn't think I should take it back, especially not with the Browns, who were rotating out of the current game, now standing behind me.

Sweat was starting to soak through my uniform. I had to think fast.

"I tell you what we can do. I'll get a truck over here and have it parked behind the backstop. If anyone comes along, we'll say we flagged you down and asked you to show us how to fix it. We'll also post some lookouts."

Then I added, "That is, *if* you want to play today."

Wharton circled his men and they talked for a minute. I couldn't see who it was, but one of his group said, "Let's just get out of here." Another shut him up by saying, "And do what? Go swimming? I want to play ball."

Finally Wharton turned back to me and said, "OK, we'll play."

Someone behind me suggested, "We'll also give you Tyler. That'll make the teams about even." That drew laugher from the men. I ignored it.

I then said to Wharton, "Believe me, you don't want to know what kind of game we've got going now, but when it's over we'll play a regular game. Just two teams. Yours and ours. OK?"

Wharton toed the dirt for a minute, glanced back at his men one more time, and said only, "OK."

I could hear our men quietly saying, "All right! Let's go!"

With that settled, I shifted to growled, "Tyler. Go get a truck and park it right here. Pop the hood and pretend you're fixing it."

I also whispered to him, "Tell Doc we need him right now. And I mean *now*. Understand?" His eyes lit up as he caught my meaning.

I then pointed to four other men and told them to position themselves at equal distances down the main road so they could form a "yelling chain" in case anyone started coming our direction from the main part of the base. It wasn't a foolproof plan, but it was the best I could come up with under the circumstances.

After the Barons made the third out of their inning, the players rushed off the field, eager to make way for the next game. I knew there would be a fight over who got to play against our visitors, so I took it upon myself to select the team. I had played with and watched the men enough to know the better players. Eager eyes were focused on me as I scanned the group.

When they had all gathered around me, I said, "I know you'd all

like to play. I'm going to pick the team myself, so if you have any complaints, complain to me later."

I also said, "And I'm going to play, for the obvious reasons." I said
this as seriously as I could while looking over at Wharton's team.

As quickly as I could, I chose all our players but one, saving a spot
for Doc, and assigned them to positions, also adding as I did, "If you
can work it out with someone else to switch positions, that's fine with
me. But no arguing about this. None."

I kept looking over my shoulder in the direction of the motor
pool, hoping that Tyler would get Doc and the truck here in a hurry. I
couldn't imagine a team without him batting cleanup and playing first
base. There wasn't a position he couldn't play, and play well. But he was
especially good at first base where he had an uncanny knack of digging
errant throws out of the dirt. And with our infielders, we'd need that
to have a chance.

I put myself at third base. I was what most would call a "good
field, no hit" player. My defense wouldn't hurt us, and with the hitters
on the team, I figured they could more than cover up for me.

Our guests were getting antsy to play. I noticed they, too, were
constantly looking back over their shoulders toward their part of the
base. I wasn't the only one questioning the wisdom of all this.

"Come on, Doc," I said to myself. "Hurry up. Hurry up!"

It was time for a stall tactic, a distraction until Doc arrived.

I called over Albertson, of "broken liver" fame, and told him we
needed to stall until Doc showed up. With a broad grin, he said, "Leave
it to me." I suddenly had the feeling I was creating a monster.

Albertson went over near the field and started playing soft-toss
with Jenkins, making it look like they were loosening up their arms.
They started close to each other and steadily moved back after each
throw.

I was watching them out of the corner of my eye as I started going
over our own special ground rules of our field with our visitors, who
called themselves the Pirates, an appropriate name, they said, because
three of them were from Pittsburgh. I explained about having only to
be "near" a base because of the slippery metal. I also pointed out that
the right field foul line wasn't straight because of two storage buildings

that stuck out onto the field. A ball hitting either of them inside the regular foul line would still be considered in fair territory, and the ball would still be in play. The last, and most important, ground rule involved a row of dilapidated outhouses, remnants of a past era at Fort Bliss, along the back fence in center field. A batter driving the ball into one of the outhouses would be granted a ground-rule double and any runners on base would be allowed to advance two bases. We came up with this rule because the outhouses were loaded with huge wasp nests, and extreme caution had to be used when retrieving a ball.

Just as I finished the ground rules, Albertson let a toss glance off his glove and hit him on the head. He went down like he had been shot and rolled back and forth in the dirt as he pressed both hands to his left temple. Men instinctively ran over to him to offer help. Those up front saw him wink at them as his moans got louder and louder, and to their credit, they played right along.

"Ohhhhhhh… I think I broke my skull. Am I bleeding? Ohhh. Ohhhhh."

One of the Pirates ran over and said, "Let me through. I've had medic training."

"Oh, he'll be fine in a minute," I said while rushing over to Albertson. I then ordered, "I'll take a look. Everybody back up and give him some air!"

I knelt down next to him and said, "Let me take a look at this, soldier."

I lifted his hands away from his temple as his moans and groans got louder and louder. "You're lucky," I said. "An inch lower and you would have lost an eye or had a fractured skull. But I don't see any blood and it isn't starting to swell too bad—yet. I think you'll be all right in a few minutes. Let's carry him over there and put him in the shade next to the tree."

Albertson got more attention than a soldier being carried home from battle on his shield. The men lifted him gently and carried him into the shade, where they offered him a drink from a canteen. Others started fanning him.

At last I could see the truck coming up the road from the motor pool, so I said to everyone, "Show's over. He'll be fine. Let's get on with the game."

Doc jumped out of the truck before it stopped and ran over to me. "What's going on here? You nuts, Perc?"

"Nuttier than a fruitcake," I said dryly. "You're going to play first. Get out there."

He was so stunned he didn't reply. He just shook his head and trotted toward the field.

I then went over to Wharton and said, "Since we're the home team, you can bat first. Let us throw the ball around a minute and we'll get going."

"Oh, and one more thing," I added. "Williams here is going to umpire for both teams. He'll show no favoritism. If he does, I'll have him on KP for the rest of his life."

The Pirates looked at Williams' thick glasses and just shook their heads.

I turned to the men and said, "OK, let's take the field."

Doc threw a few grounders to those of us playing the infield. The outfielders played long-toss to loosen their arms. Brown was pitching for us, and he completed the last of his warm-up tosses, finally motioning that he was ready to go.

Williams shouted, "Play ball!" The Pirates' first hitter, a lefty, stepped to the plate. Brown stepped off the mound and motioned the outfielders to shift more toward the right-field line. When they had repositioned themselves, Brown went into his windup and fired the first pitch.

"Strike one!" Williams shouted as the ball popped into Davis's mitt. The lefty didn't complain. He took a few more practice swings, stepped back into the batter's box, and dug in. Brown wound up and fired again. The crack of ball against bat rang out as the batter lined the ball right back at Brown, who stuck out his glove and caught it out of self-defense more than anything. He just smiled broadly at the stunned batter, who had started running with the crack of the bat, and pretended to mop his brow with his bare hand. Brown then tossed the ball to me, and I started the traditional "around the horn" throws between infielders after an out was made.

Watching the men—on both teams—was like watching spectators

at a tennis match following the path of the ball from one side of the court to the other. Between every pitch, most eyes took a quick glance down the road toward the main part of the base before focusing again on the game. Back and forth. Back and forth.

The game was on.

Their second batter looked familiar to me, but I couldn't quite place him. On Brown's 2-0 pitch he sent a rocket that carried to the right-field wall, the high barbed-wire fence that ran along the boundary of the base. The ball actually looked like it was still going up as it hit and bounced back on the playing field. He stopped at second base with an easy double. It suddenly dawned on me who he was when I heard one of his teammates yell, "Way to go, Candy!" I had seen his picture many times in the *St. Louis Globe-Democrat*. He was Tony Canducci, a prep player from St. Louis University High School, who had been recruited by every college in the Midwest. In the newspapers he was called "Candy," not just because of his last name, but because he had one of the sweetest swings the reporters had ever seen for a player his age. As I looked over at him again, I knew we were in trouble. Big trouble.

He wasn't at second base for long. Their next batter, another lefty, lined the next pitch into right field and Canducci scored easily. I walked over to the mound as soon as Canducci scored and patted Brown on the rump.

"Let's go!" I said. "These guys are just like anybody else. They're not the real Pirates, for criminy sakes. Just pitch to the catcher's mitt. You've got good stuff."

Brown was visibly nervous, fidgeting and tugging at his shirt collar, which probably felt to him at this point about three sizes too small. The first three batters had all drilled the ball. He wasn't exactly fooling them with his pitches.

"You've got a great curveball, Brown," I continued. "Mix it in. Come on—you can do this."

As I left the mound I added, "Your fly's undone."

It wasn't, but the look on Brown's face after he realized he had been had was priceless. He smiled and said, "OK, Sarge. We'll get 'em now."

His next pitch, a sharp breaking curve that didn't quite break enough, plunked the batter right in the middle of the back. It knocked the wind out of him, and he went down in a heap. Everyone rushed to the plate to make sure he was OK. Brown kept repeating over and over, "I'm sorry. I didn't mean it."

When we all saw the batter was going to be OK, a collective sigh of relief was let out. He got up, dusted himself off, and trotted to first base. They now had runners on first and second with only one out.

The situation looked bad, but I needn't have worried. Hitting that batter was the best thing Brown could have done. The Pirates didn't dig in at the plate anymore. The batters started looking like they had a "foot in the bucket," which meant they started bailing out of the batter's box as soon as he threw the ball because they were afraid of being the next one to get hit. Brown struck out the next batter, who took a feeble swing at a sweeping curve. The next batter grounded to second. We were behind 1-0, but it was a moral victory. We could have been blown out, and that would have been devastating to the men.

I set our batting order quickly. Jenkins led off, followed by Albertson and Jamieson. Doc batted cleanup. Davis, Sanders, and Clark followed. I'd bat eighth, and Brown would hit in the traditional pitcher's spot, ninth.

Jenkins stepped up to the plate and dug in. Three quick swings later he was headed back, shaking his head. "He's fast," he said. "Real fast. Reeeaaaalllll fast."

Their pitcher was a slightly built man who threw bullets. His name was Baxter. He double-pumped his windup and kicked his leg high, winding up like a spring and building leverage, before releasing the ball. He threw hard, but his pitches were also straight as a string. They had no movement at all. If we could stay close to them, he would tire, and if he lost any zip off his fastball, he'd be hittable.

Albertson, up next, made contact but grounded weakly to third. Jamieson, batting third, caught everyone off guard when he bunted down the first base line and beat the throw for a hit. The men, who had been quiet to this point, came to life, especially as they saw Doc pick up a bat and walk toward the plate. He took a few practice swings but then suddenly stopped and studied the bat. He dropped it and walked over to where the Pirates were standing. "You mind if I use one of these?" he asked as he picked up a bat from the half dozen they had brought with them. They were so stunned by his request it looked like they didn't know what to say. Finally Wharton said, "Sure, go ahead. Be my guest."

With that, Doc walked back to the plate and dug in. Williams, trying his best to appear like an umpire, shouted, "Play ball!"

The men were shouting, "Let's go, Doc!" "Murder that ball!"

The first pitch brushed him back, drawing "Ooohhs" from the crowd watching. Williams yelled, "Ball one!"

Doc stepped out, took a few practice swings, and dug back in a little closer to the plate, his body language saying, "Is that all you've got?" The next pitch was right down the middle and Doc jumped on it. He made such solid contact and hit the ball so hard there was no doubt from the second the ball hit the bat that it was gone. The only way to describe it was a "blast." Instead of cheering, the men just stood there, gawking, as they followed the flight of the ball. It soared so far over the fence out in left field that no one even thought of climbing it and going after the ball. Instead, one of the Pirates picked up another one of their baseballs and tossed it out to the pitcher. We were up 2-1, and judging by the reaction of the men, who were now cheering wildly, one would have thought we had just won the World Series.

The men didn't get much of a chance to drag out their jubilation. Davis, the next batter, grounded to the shortstop and the inning was over. But we had taken the lead and the men cheered each other on as they took the field.

The score remained the same until the fourth inning when Brown suddenly became wild and walked two in a row. After the walks, what should have been a single to left scored two runs as Sanders slipped on the wet outfield grass and let the ball get by him and bounce all the way to the fence. The batter ended up on third. We got out of the inning without any more damage, but they were now ahead, 3-2.

The game almost ended at that score when our "yelling chain" sounded the alarm as the Pirates were taking the field. Instead of dropping their equipment and running over to look like they were helping us repair the truck, as we had planned, for some reason they all climbed in the back to hide. In the process, each tripped over a napping Tyler as they climbed aboard, which resulted in a mass pileup. The "yelling chain" lookouts had done what they were instructed to do, but it turned out to be something of a false alarm when the jeep that had been coming our direction suddenly veered to the right and headed down the service road toward the main runway. They never got anywhere near close enough to see us.

When the jeep was finally out of sight, I went over and kidded Wharton, who was still sprawled out on top of Tyler, "Hey, thanks for helping us fix the truck. That was pretty sharp. I'm impressed."

Embarrassed, Wharton sheepishly replied, "It seemed like a good idea at the time."

I patted him on the back and said, "I know what you mean. When I heard the yelling I think I pissed myself."

Wharton smiled, "Me, too."

Williams, still puffing out his skinny chest and roaring like a major league umpire, scolded everyone, "Well, are we playing ball or hide-and-seek? Come on. Let's play ball!"

From that point on the game's tempo picked up and the innings flew by. There were plenty of hits, but neither team could plate a runner. In the sixth Clark golfed a low pitch, sending the ball crashing into one of the outhouses. Ground-rule double. He eventually got as far as third base, but we couldn't get him home. The Pirates had their share of base hits, but our defense was good. Very good. The closest they came to scoring was in the top of the seventh when, with a runner on first, their third baseman, Anderson, drilled a low inside fastball down the first base line for a hit. Jamieson, playing right, had been shading him to pull the ball, so he raced over and snared it before it could get by him. The man on first had started running with the crack of the bat, and their third base coach was waving him home from the time he rounded second base. However, Jamieson got to the ball so quickly and fired the ball so accurately home to Davis that the runner was out by ten feet. He didn't even bother to slide. He just pulled up and let Davis softly tag him. Anderson was standing on second, hands on hips, shaking his head. Their next batter grounded weakly to me, so we went to the eighth with the Pirates still hanging on to their 3-2 lead.

Brown was up first for us in the eighth. He was a good, all-around athlete who knew more than just pitching. He could also handle a bat. On a 3-2 pitch, he lined a single right up the middle. Albertson then grounded to the first baseman, but the ball was hit so slowly they had no chance for a double play. That put Brown on second with one out. Jamieson was up next. Their pitcher, as I suspected and hoped, was losing the pop on his fastball with each passing inning. Jamieson just managed to get a piece of an 0-2 pitch and grounded a three-hopper to the third baseman, who had the ball pop out of his glove for an error. Brown had to stay at second, but that put two men on with Doc coming up to the plate. The men, in unison, clapped their hands as they shouted encouragement. We couldn't have asked for a better chance to take the lead, and the men knew it. Doc slowly strolled over to the batter's box and dug in.

The Pirates' catcher called "Time!" and hustled out to the mound to talk to the pitcher about how they wanted to pitch to Doc. The rest of their infield joined them. When Williams thought they had taken enough time, he did what umpires had been doing since the game was invented and walked to the mound to tell them to break it up.

As Doc dug back in, their catcher stood up and held his right arm out to the side, indicating they were going to walk Doc intentionally. The men booed this strategy loudly and passionately. Someone back behind the backstop yelled, "What's the matter? Chicken?"

It was an unconventional move and went against "the book," the time-honored traditions of baseball. First and second base were occupied. Walking Doc would load the bases and put the potential go-ahead run in scoring position. Their strategy may have been against "the book," but I don't think there was a man there who wouldn't have decided to do the same thing if presented with the same situation. After ball four, Doc jogged to first, the other runners moving up a base. The bases were loaded. There was one out. We were behind by one run. Davis was up.

Davis was the physical stereotype of the catcher. He was large, pudgy, and slow. The Pirates were probably hoping he would hit a ground ball that could be turned into an easy double play to end the inning. However, Davis, like most catchers, also had power when he made good contact.

I called "Time!" myself and motioned Davis to come over to me. I cupped my hand close to my mouth so the Pirates couldn't hear what I was saying and whispered, "You don't have to get a hit. If you can hit any kind of fly ball, Brown will be able to tag up and score. He runs like a rabbit. But if you hit a groundball..." I didn't finish the sentence. Davis knew what I was trying to say. He just nodded and walked back to the plate.

The Pirates were really getting on him, trying to rattle him. Their shortstop yelled, "Come on, Fats. Let's see ya swing that pork chop. Oh, sorry, that's a bat—I thought you were still eating!"

Davis stepped out of the batter's box and glared at him. He stepped back in and held the bat high as he waited for the pitch. It was right down the middle. He didn't swing. "Strike one!" Williams called out.

Davis stepped back out and picked up a handful of dirt and rubbed his hands together, soaking up the sweat on his palms. He stepped back in and stared out at the pitcher as he took one last practice swing before setting himself for the pitch. The crack of the ball on his bat sounded so beautiful. He drilled a low line drive that looked like it was going to make it between first and second. I started to cheer until I saw Canducci racing over to try to catch up to it. Canducci was just about in front of the ball when it must have hit a rock or something in the field. Whatever it hit, the ball bounced almost directly sideways and down the right field line. Two runs scored before the ball could be thrown back in. Doc was standing on third. Davis had held up at first.

The Pirates, led by Canducci, threw down their gloves in disgust. It was a bad break, to be sure, but it was their bad break. Our men were going wild, jumping up and down and hugging each other. We were ahead, 4-3.

In all the time I had known the men, I had never seen them this happy, this together. For a moment, as I watched them, I considered asking Albertson to come up with another of his stall-tactics to try to get the game to end right there, with us ahead. But before I could give it serious thought, Sanders drilled the first pitch to him on a line to the first baseman. Davis had taken only a short lead, but he was doubled off. Double play. Inning over. But we were ahead, 4-3, and the men took the field like, well, men charging into battle. And to them it was a battle. Of many types. With three more outs the battle would be won.

I was halfway to my position at third when it hit me. We were winning. That was good. And, it suddenly occurred to me, that was bad.

Potentially very bad.

I started to sweat again.

I also started thinking again about "the talk"—and everything that talk had implied. I saw the face of Colonel Rogers as he stormed out of headquarters. I saw Colonel Ellis's face as he tried to explain to me "our" place on the base. I saw the men eating in a separate mess hall. I saw them working at our own motor pool. I saw them in our own barracks.

And more than anything, I saw them in the worst kind of trouble if we won this game. If we lost, the Pirates would probably go back to their side of the camp and talk about it in hushed tones for a day or two until they forgot about it. If we won, on the other hand, they would likely stew about it and argue about it until word got out to the rest of the camp. And if word got out, we'd be cooked.

"Why did I get us into this?" I asked myself as I watched Brown take the last of his warm-up throws. "How stupid could I be?"

I was feeling suddenly sick to my stomach and beads of sweat trickled down into my eyes. This was all my fault. We were on the verge of what one of my old college history professors had called a "Pyrrhic victory," a victory where an individual battle was won, but in winning the battle, the rest of the war was lost. It looked like we stood a good chance of winning the game, but if we did, we risked losing everything else we had built to this point. We could lose the motor pool. We could lose the upcoming driving assignments. We could risk losing every achievement we had made since coming on base.

I felt like I was going to throw up.

Then it dawned on me that maybe the Pirates would mount a rally. Maybe they would take the lead again. I felt even more sick when their first batter in the ninth popped out easily to Doc at first base. Two more outs to go. The cheers of the men became muffled in my ears as pictures of our days on the base crashed together in my head.

Their left fielder lined a sharp single over a diving Albertson at second base. Brown was tiring. He was pitching now with more heart than skill. I should have gone over and settled him down, but I couldn't move. My legs were shaking. I had never felt anything like this before. I could hear Doc shouting encouragement to him, but he sounded like he was yelling from inside a long tunnel.

Their next batter, their shortstop, topped the ball to the right of the mound. I should have charged in, but I broke late, causing Brown to have to field the ball. He got to it and threw as quickly as he could, but the runner beat it out by a step. The tying run was now on second and the go-ahead run on first. When the play was over, Brown walked a few feet past the mound over toward third and asked, "You OK, Sarge?"

My legs felt weaker with every step, but I made it to the mound. Doc came over from first and joined us. Davis also came out from behind the plate. When we were all together Doc punched his fist into his glove and said, "Two more outs! Let's get 'em!"

It should have been me who said it, but Doc asked Brown, "Are you OK?" Then he turned to me and asked, "Are *you* OK?"

"I'm fine," I lied. "Just nervous."

"Who isn't?" Doc shot back. "My hands were shaking so bad I damn near dropped that easy pop-up."

Brown, who had been watching the next batter take practice swings, asked, "We walk this guy, right?"

The next batter was Canducci.

I stared long and hard at Canducci while avoiding Doc's and Brown's eyes. "No," I said as calmly as I could. "That would load the bases and put the potential go-ahead run in scoring position. And their next hitter isn't any slouch, either."

"You've got to be kidding," Doc whined. "This is their best hitter. We walk this guy and take our chances."

"No," I said, a little too sternly. "We get him out and the game's good as over. Brown can do it. We'll get him out and shut them down."

Williams, attempting to be fair, started toward us while yelling, "OK, let's break this gabfest up!"

Doc took one last look at me, a disgusted look. In the same situation earlier in the game, the Pirates had walked Doc to get at Davis. Davis had come through, but it was still the right thing to do. No one could second-guess them on that.

Brown asked one more time, "We walk this guy, right?"

"Pitch to him. Keep it low. You get him out, and the game is as good as over."

I then turned and headed back to my position.

"OK," Brown called after me. "If you say so."

His first pitch to Canducci, a sharp breaking curve, bounced in front of the plate. Williams called out, "Ball one!"

The air was filled with shouts of encouragement from both sides of the field.

The next pitch was low, but Canducci got a piece of it, pulling it foul down the right-field line and over the auxiliary buildings. Brown looked over to me, his eyes saying, "That was close!" I shouted over to him, "Bear down now! Bear down!"

The count was a ball and a strike.

The next pitch was high and inside. Ball two.

The shouts from the men on both sides became louder and louder.

Brown rubbed up the ball and looked in for Davis's sign. His next pitch was low and out of the strike zone, but Canducci reached down and clubbed it into right center field. Both outfielders ran toward it, but it bounced between them and rolled to the fence, just barely missing the row of outhouses. Both runners scored. Canducci made it easily to third as the throw came back to the infield.

They had taken the lead.

The Pirates were pounding each other on the back and whooping it up. Canducci stood on the third base bag right next to me and yelled to his teammates, "Nothing to it!" as he bowed toward them.

Our men looked like they had just had the breath sucked out of them. One minute they had been bouncing around like rubber balls. The next minute they were standing motionless, watching the celebration build on the other side of the field.

"It's OK," I shouted over to Brown. "Game's not over yet."

I said it, but I knew it wasn't true.

Their next batter grounded back to Brown. He looked Canducci back to third before flipping the ball to Doc for the out. Brown, reaching back for what little energy he had left, struck out the next man and the inning was over. But the damage had been done.

The Pirates took the field with renewed spirit. Their pitcher, catching his second wind, struck out Clark on three pitches. I struck out on four. Brown, who had pitched his heart out, grounded to Canducci and the game was over just that quick.

The Pirates met near Canducci at second base and congratulated each other. Then, they headed over toward us. Wharton again spoke for the group.

"You guys are pretty good. We've played a few other teams since being down here, and I'd have to say you're the best we've played so far."

He pointed at Doc and said, "Especially you. You want to play for us?"

He was kidding, and the men on both sides laughed, somewhat nervously at first before warm, genuine laughter flowed. Doc thanked him and added, "You guys aren't bad either. Especially *that* guy," he said pointing to Canducci. "Want to play for us?" Both teams erupted in laughter again.

I was taken aback by what I saw happen when the laughter subsided. Following Wharton's lead, each Pirate first shook Doc's hand and then continued down the row shaking the hands of every man on our team.

"Let's do this again sometime. We want a rematch," Doc shouted as they started heading back down the road toward the other side of the base. Wharton waved back to us as if to say, "You're on!"

After they had gone, Brown said, "You know what, they were pretty nice guys."

"And pretty damn good ballplayers," Jamieson added.

Davis said, "If I had just gotten under that pitch a little more I'd have driven it out of here and we'd have won."

"Just a game," Clark said while patting Davis on the back. "And, hey, you were great, especially for a fat guy."

Davis playfully picked him up and flung him into the rest of the team. "Fat, eh? I'll show you fat!" He pulled up his shirt and started chasing Clark toward first base as the others egged him on.

Albertson added, "Hell, we were all great. We'll get those guys next time."

A few of the men looked at me as if asking me to say something, but I didn't know what to say. Out of the corner of my eye I caught Doc's cold stare. I kept quiet and watched the others alternately teasing and then bragging on each other.

Williams, who had disappeared at the end of the game, came walking over to the group. He took some playful ribbing from the men for calling the game fairly. Sanders said, "You *could* have called a few more balls, I think. That pitch you called me out on was a foot outside!"

Brown, who pitched a heck of a game, then teased, "Geez, we'd have won by a mile if your glasses weren't so damn thick. First time I ever pitched with a real blind ump behind the plate."

"Say, where you been? Where'd you go?" Doc asked, rescuing him from the ribbing.

"Men," Williams said proudly. "We won't have to play with junk anymore."

"What do you mean?" Doc asked.

He yelled in the direction of the truck, "Tyler—show 'em."

Tyler threw back the tarp covering the back of the truck. The men howled at what they saw.

Williams had stolen their bats.

* * *

The men picked up the rest of our gear and headed down the road toward the barracks. I hung back, telling them I'd get the bases and join them later. I actually wanted some time to be alone, time to think about what I'd just done. However, before the group had gotten very far, Doc turned around and jogged back to the field.

He picked up home plate and met me at third, where I had just picked up the last of the bases.

"I was wrong," I said as he handed me home plate.

"Yes you were," he said.

"I was afraid of what would happen if we won. I should have had Brown pitch around Canducci. I should have, but I didn't. I had him pitch to him on purpose. I was *hoping* he'd get a hit. We lost, and it's my fault."

Doc looked at me disgustedly and said, "I knew what you were doing. You were wrong. Dead wrong. You may have done what your heart said was right, but that doesn't make it right. You were still wrong." Then, coldly, he added, "I'm disappointed in you. I never thought you'd do something like this."

"I just thought it would be best if we didn't win. I really did. I was afraid word would get out...."

Doc cut me off and said, practically shouting, "You really don't understand, do you?" He then took a deep breath and softened his voice a little as he added, "They didn't lose. They won. Look at them."

We watched the men marching down the road, still laughing and slapping each other on the back. There was a happiness, a joy, in their gait I had never seen before.

Doc then added, "'You' are the one who lost today. You lost part of your soul, and you should be ashamed of yourself. You're the one I feel sorry for—not them."

I responded, "We played a hell of a game. We could have beat 'em. We *should* have beat 'em. I blew the game."

I paused before adding, "I'm going to tell them."

"You do and I'll break your neck," Doc responded. "You can't take this away from them. Playing this game was a huge victory for them. Look at 'em," he said, pointing down the road.

He then added, "You of all people should know better. Today's a day they will never forget. Never. And you don't have the right to take it away from them. You did what you thought was right. Most guys wouldn't do that much." Here he paused, stared at me coldly again, and said, "You were wrong, but *they'll* get over it. The big question is, can you?"

He took the bases from my hands and started walking toward the barracks. As he got to the edge of the road he called back, "I'm going to a victory supper. You going to join us?"

I stood there and watched him walk down the road. His words

still rang in my ears: "You should be ashamed of yourself."
I was.

13

PASSES

If there was an opposite of a Pyrrhic victory, I was witnessing it unfold right before my eyes. Yes, the men had lost a battle, but they acted like they had just won the war. The atmosphere of the whole battalion changed after our team—regarded now as a troop of conquering heroes—had marched back from that baseball game. By looking at them, one would never have known they were on the short end of the final score. When they came back into the barracks, laughter and pride came in with them, and the gloom of recent days started lifting almost immediately. They replayed the game pitch-by-pitch so many times practically everyone in the outfit could pick up the story in midsentence and not miss a beat, and that seemed to bring them together even more. Doc had been right. They had won.

I, on the other hand, was feeling as lost as I had ever been in my life.

I had been moping around battalion headquarters for several days, avoiding everyone as much as possible while trying to sort things out for myself. My shame quickly turned to anger, and I was having a hard time getting rid of it. Doc was also right about something else. I *should* have known better, and that thought was also gnawing at me night and day.

Clouding my thoughts was the fact that I still wasn't sure I was entirely wrong. I was stewing more about whether there might have been something else I could have done the day of the game. There *must* have been something else, but I just couldn't think of it no matter how much or how hard I tried. I finally just came to the conclusion that I was wrong—dead wrong—any way it was sliced.

Colonel Ellis had left me alone most of the week, but his curiosity finally got the best of him.

"What's bothering you, Perc?" he asked. "You've been low as a post. You missing your girl?"

"No, Sir," I replied. "I've just had a lot on my mind lately. Well, actually I do miss Olivia, but that's not it. That's not..."

"Well, what is it?" he asked while pulling up a chair next to me.

I didn't want to share too much with him. So far, it appeared news of the game had not leaked around the base. Either that or I was right that it wouldn't be considered a big deal given the outcome of the game. I was still holding on to that thought, hoping and praying that I was at least partly right in my actions.

I finally said, choosing my words carefully, "Colonel, you ever do something you know is wrong but feel under the circumstances it's the only thing to do?"

Colonel Ellis smiled. "Every single day, Perc. I'm an officer. I do what the army wants, whether I happen to think it's right or not. *Every* day. Most of the time I don't have the luxury to put my own personal two cents worth in before giving orders."

He then added, "What did you do that you think was so terrible?"

"I let my men down. I thought I was helping them, protecting them, but now I know what I did was wrong. I didn't see it at the time, but it's all I can think about now."

I could tell by the way he rested his chin in his hand and leaned forward that he wanted me to tell him everything, but I didn't. I had already made one horrible mistake; I wasn't going to turn it into two.

When he saw I wasn't going to open up, he suddenly leaned back and asked, "Did you follow your heart in making your decision?"

"Yes, Sir, I did. But what was in my heart was wrong. As wrong as could be."

"Then my advice is to let it go. Forget about it. We can't protect our men from everything all the time. It just isn't possible. And we shouldn't even if we could. We're trained to follow orders as closely as we can, no matter how we feel about them ourselves. In all other matters, we're human beings first, and, like the army..."

Here he paused and looked around to make sure no one else was listening. He then continued, whispering, "Like the army, we're not always going to be right. But I'll deny it if you ever tell anyone I said that," he added, laughing.

"And one more thing," he continued, more seriously this time. "The men aren't going to like everything we ask them to do, and they often don't know it is all just for their own good. Well, at least we usually think it's for their own good. There's no way they can see the larger picture. I'm not saying *we* always see it, but at least we usually have a higher perch in the tree. So, my advice? Go easy on yourself. If you keep following your heart, you're going to be right more often than you'll be wrong."

"Thank you, Sir," I replied. "I sure hope you're right. You have no idea how much I hope you're right."

Then I added, "I'm starting to think there really isn't that much difference between being a sergeant and being a teacher. I guess we teach them as much as we can, and then we have to set them loose and see if they can fly on their own. I just hope I teach them the right things before they take off."

I paused again, then added, "I guess what bothers me most is when we're wrong—when we give them the wrong tools—it affects so many people. The men trust us, and when we make mistakes…"

Colonel Ellis interrupted me, "That's just it, Perc. We *are* going to make mistakes. Like I said before, we're only human. Humans make mistakes."

"If that's the case, Sir, then I'm feeling really human this morning. *Really* human."

Colonel Ellis slapped me on the shoulder. "Join the club," he said as he smiled and got up and headed for his office.

When he got to his door he suddenly dropped the batch of papers he was carrying, spilling them all over that part of the room.

"Damn I'm clumsy!" he shouted. And then he smiled again.

He had done it on purpose, and I appreciated it. I went over and helped him retrieve the papers.

I was still miserable, but the old saying was right. Misery does love company.

At least now I had company.

* * *

Talking to Colonel Ellis had helped, but I was still feeling pretty low until the next morning when he called me into his office. "Close the door behind you," he said as he motioned for me to sit in the chair in front of his desk. His voice was quiet, serious.

By the tone of his voice and the drawn look on his face, I was bracing myself for bad news. I started sweating again as I began to wonder if he had finally heard about the baseball game.

"Perc, I've got something important to talk over with you. Our battalion has been on this base a long, long time, and I know it's getting to everybody. What do men in prison call it? Being 'stir-crazy'? I imagine you and the men feel just like that. I know I do at times."

He picked up a pencil and twirled it around his fingers as he continued, "Now we can finally do something about that. But I don't want this to end up a damn disaster. I don't want this to have the opposite effect of what it's supposed to do."

I could tell he was really struggling for the right words, so I decided to try to make it easier for him.

"I see you're concerned, Sir. What is it? How can I help?"

"I'm not sure 'concerned' is the right word here, Perc. I think 'scared to death' is probably more like it."

He stood up and walked slowly back and forth behind his desk. Finally he blurted out, "I've got a stack of passes over there. The men in your barracks are going to get their first leave. The other barracks will go next weekend if everything works out OK, but I want you to go first."

I instantly felt an enormous wave of relief wash over me. Passes! As far as I was concerned, that was cause for celebration, not concern.

"That's great news!" I shouted, too loudly. "Sorry, Sir. It's just that the men have been looking forward to this more than you can imagine. And me, too."

"That's what's worrying me," he said. "I know they deserve to get off this base. Lord knows they deserve it. I guess I'm just worried about…"

He didn't need to finish the sentence. I knew then, by the way he was pacing and staring down at the floor, what he was thinking about. "Oh…" was all I replied.

I then added, "I have already had a long talk with the men, Sir. And I'll talk to them again before they leave the base. I don't think you'll have much to worry about."

"I wish I had your confidence. What I'm really worried about is, where are they going to go when they do get off the base?"

It had already been made abundantly clear that our battalion wouldn't be all that welcome in El Paso. El Paso was a segregated town, as were most towns in this part of the state. Also, the colored community there was very small. I heard there were about a thousand black faces in the town, which actually sounded like a lot to me. But in proportion to the rest of the town, it wasn't. From what I had been told, the colored community also wasn't set up for the type of entertainment soldiers with money burning holes in their pockets would enjoy. Supposedly, there was exactly one bar in that section of town, one movie theater, and three restaurants, one of which closed each day after the lunch crowd cleared out. It hardly sounded like the Sodom and Gomorrah described to us in our "Health and Hygiene" classes.

Colonel Ellis picked up the stack of passes and handed them to me, adding, "I'm going to put you in charge of these, but there's one other thing I want you to think about first before you fill in the names. I'll let you use your own judgment to make the final decision on this: Should we be giving out so many all at once? Maybe we should rotate passes so the first men out can find places for the rest to go other nights. What do you think?"

"That's not a bad idea, but we do have a wild card here, Sir," I said. "I've been thinking about this for a long time now. Some of the men are going to want to go into El Paso, but don't forget we're really not that far from Mexico. Juarez is just over the border, so if we can grant permission for the men to go there, I think most of the problems you're thinking about will take care of themselves."

He stopped pacing and plopped down in his chair. "I'll be damned. That's a great idea! Why didn't I think of that? Of course we'll allow Mexico. Hell, yes!"

He came around the desk and shook my hand like it was a pump handle.

"Viva, Mexico!" I said.

"You're damn right," he said. "Viva, Mexico!"

* * *

I immediately started putting together a plan to get the men, who were wound up now to the point of exploding, off the base as quickly as possible. I felt like I was putting together a battle plan. I decided I would go ahead and ask Sergeant Ingram to be in charge of a small "scouting party" that we'd send into El Paso. I couldn't order them, but the rest getting passes would be "strongly encouraged" to come with me down to the town of Juarez, which I had heard through the grapevine was the favorite of our servicemen.

I called the men together on Thursday evening so I could deliver the news.

A low rumble started through the assembled crowd as the men began speculating about what was coming next. Scuttlebutt had indeed been at work.

I didn't tease them. As quickly as I could get their attention I said, "Men, I've got some great news for you, some news you've been waiting for for a long time. Starting tomorrow, many of you are going to be issued passes!"

The cheers were almost deafening. Shouts of "It's about time!" and "Told you so!" followed.

"Hold on!" I said, trying to get their attention again. "I said *many* of you will get passes. Obviously we can't send everyone off the base at one time. Some will need to stay here to take care of things. I've prepared two lists, Group Able and Group Baker. These lists will be posted on the bulletin boards just inside the barracks. Those in Group Able should report immediately to Sergeant Ingram over at the Service Club. Those in Group Baker should stay right where you are. I'll be in charge of your group.

I continued, "None of you have had passes before, so Sergeant Ingram and I are going to go over some ground rules with you. There aren't many, but I want them followed to the letter."

I paused for emphasis here and repeated, "To the letter. Got that?

If any of you knotheads step out of line, this will be your last pass. If you screw up, I'll do my best to see you spend the rest of this war on the base. Do you understand me?"

Most nodded, but I could tell that more than a few had already drifted off into thoughts of what they were going to do once set free. And I couldn't blame them.

"That's all I have to say right now. The lists of names are already being put up, so go ahead and see if your name is on one of them. If it isn't and you're one of those who will be staying behind to help run things, don't worry. You'll get a turn next time. Remember, if you're in Group Able, go see Sergeant Ingram. Those in Baker come right back here. Now take off!"

Earlier in the day, Sergeant Ingram and I had put together a list of "do's and don'ts" we'd each share with the men who were getting passes. Sergeant Ingram actually had the tougher job, and I was well aware of it. In addition to the "do's and don'ts" list, he was also going to be giving his own version of "the talk" to the men in his group and would be telling them where they would and would not be, welcome in El Paso. I didn't envy his task.

When all the men in my group had reassembled, I tried to make my instructions as brief as possible.

"Your passes will begin at 1700 tomorrow. This isn't an order, but I'd like to ask those of you in this group to do something for me and the battalion. I'd like you to tag along with me to Mexico."

The men first actually looked dumbfounded. Then, they started cheering again.

I continued, "Don't get me wrong. I want you to have fun. But I also want you to consider this a reconnaissance mission—sort of a mission of exploration and discovery if you will. I have heard that Juarez is one of the most popular towns with servicemen, and I want us to find out why. I also want you to check it out for future groups that will go there. For those of you who are going, I want you to keep alert, watch your money, and don't get into trouble. OK?"

Judging by the excited looks on their faces, I was guessing it was OK with them, so I added, "I have already made arrangements for transportation for all of you who want to go with the group. You are to assemble outside the barracks at exactly 1700, and trucks will drive you down there and, if you don't get lost or arrested, will bring you back. We're going to convoy down so that our drivers can get some more practice driving six-bys at night. *You're* going to be their cargo."

A few men laughed, but most of them groaned. One joker in the back shouted, "We'll all be killed!"

When they settled down, I started in on the "do's and don'ts" list.

"Now everybody pay attention. When we get to the border, you are all going to have to pay a tax of one cent for every dollar you're bringing into Mexico. That doesn't sound like much, but it's part of the rules and must be followed. If you are bringing in ten dollars, you'll owe a dime. Don't hide your money to try to get out of paying a few cents. It isn't worth it. If you get caught, you get to spend the night in a Mexican jail or will be sent back here to face someone on the base. Trust me, neither would be pleasant. Next, I understand there are a few places in town where we aren't exactly welcome, not so much because of how the Mexicans feel, but because of other soldiers who will be down there. I'm not happy about that, but this probably isn't the time to stick a hand into a beehive, if you get my meaning. I'll be giving you the list of the places I'm talking about. Also, Colonel Ellis advises that you probably shouldn't drink the water. So, drink lots of beer instead."

This last statement was met with an explosion of cheers.

"Finally, you are going down there as representatives of the United States Army Air Corps. I want you to act like it. Be proud, be smart, and be strong."

After scanning the group I asked, "Any questions?"

I was sure there were, but I had taught high school long enough to know that whether it was students or soldiers standing in front of me, they weren't going to ask questions in front of their friends lest they appear dumb.

"OK, then we'll meet outside the barracks tomorrow night. Until then, carry on."

* * *

The next evening the men were so excited they started assembling outside the barracks about an hour early. When the trucks pulled up, many immediately jumped right in just to make sure they would get a seat. Then they groaned as I ordered them back out and made them wait for the rest of the group so I could quickly go over the main rules one last time. I knew most weren't listening to a thing I said, but I went through the motions anyway.

As I finished the last of my advice, Doc pulled up in the jeep we were going to use as the lead vehicle to make sure no one got lost on the way down to Juarez. Williams and Tyler were in the backseat.

"What the hell?" more than a few men called out while pointing to Williams and Tyler. "How come they get to ride in that?"

I agreed with them until Doc said, "Tyler here says he speaks a little Spanish. I figured we'd need him when we hit the border. Knucklehead here insisted he come with us because he could take charge of the entrance tax and make sure no one gets pinched." He then shrugged his shoulders and said, "I think we're stuck with them."

Looking at Williams and Tyler in the backseat, I then added, sarcastically and loud enough for the rest of the men to hear, "This is great. I finally get to go to Mexico and I'm going with the Rover Boys."

That seemed to take the edge off the situation. The men just shook their heads and as they reentered the trucks gave me looks that said, "Lucky you…"

Williams and Tyler just sat there in the back of the jeep, arms folded, grinning like idiots.

The trip down to Juarez was uneventful except for a running commentary on Mexican women given by Williams and Tyler.

"I can't wait to get me one of them 'sisteritas'," Tyler said.

"I think you mean "señoritas," I corrected, but they were so full of steam they kept talking right over my voice.

""Me, too," Williams added, rubbing his hands together. "I hear those babes are hot as firecrackers."

Tyler practically stood up in the jeep as he responded, "Hot? I'm burning up just thinking about them!"

Doc looked over at me as he shook his head and raised a hand to cover a smile. The thought of Tyler, one of the unstung, talking so boldly about finding passion and romance with a "sisterita" was so funny, so ridiculous, I darn near drove us off the road. I did have to admit, however, that I admired his apparent confidence.

Doc was explaining the magical love potion "Spanish fly" to them just as the border checkpoint came into view. Just a drop of Spanish fly placed into a woman's drink would, according to rumor, cause her to lose every speck of inhibition she might have. Tyler was practically screaming to Doc that he had to help him find some of it when the border guards motioned for us to stop.

The border crossing went smoothly. I guess I had scared the men so badly about the possibility of having to spend the night in a Mexican jail they had their cash in their hands as Williams moved from truck to truck and helped them figure out the "entrance tax" each owed. The whole "entrance tax" idea seemed silly to me, but I was just glad no one got hauled off for trying to hide some money to get out of paying a few cents. I didn't ask how it had happened, but somehow between Tyler's Spanish and Williams' conniving, Williams ended up making a dollar for himself by the time all the calculations had been done with the guards. It might have had something to do with the American cigars Williams gave to each of them, but the guards seemed satisfied—and even happy—as they waved us on through.

We then drove ahead slowly and cautiously until we got to what looked like the north edge of the downtown area of the city. I had Doc pull our jeep to the side of the road so I could motion for the others to pull up and stop behind us. Even with the map of Juarez Williams had scrounged I didn't exactly know where we were going, but I knew we couldn't block the main street with our trucks and figured this was as good a spot as any to park our convoy. Crowds were milling around in the street just a few blocks ahead of us, so it looked like we were close enough to the action yet far enough away in case we needed to make a quick exit—a thought that kept swimming around inside my head.

I hated to do it, but I knew I had to assign guards to keep an eye on our trucks. I had heard of military vehicles suddenly disappearing in Mexico, and we had fought so hard to get the trucks I wasn't going to let anything happen to them if I could help it. I assigned the guards, who whined mightily when they were chosen, assuring them that they would be relieved in a couple of hours.

To the rest of the men I gave one final set of instructions.

"Remember what I said back at the base. I want you to have fun, but I also don't want anyone to do anything stupid. You've got your lists of places to avoid. As far as I'm concerned, everything else is fair game. Now go enjoy yourselves—but be back here by 0100. Those not in the trucks by that time will be left here for the Mexican authorities to take care of—and believe me, you *don't* want to face that."

"Now, get the hell out of here!"

They scattered like scalded dogs, each racing the other into the main part of the town. Doc came up to me and asked, "What do you want to do, Perc? Any ideas?"

Before I could respond, a sudden and loud cough caught my attention. I looked over at Williams and Tyler, who were itching to set off in search of true love, or lust, or both.

"You two get out of here—but be back by one," I said, motioning them out of the jeep. "And don't bring any 'sisteritas' back with you!"

"Thanks, Perc," Williams replied. "Come on. Let's go!" he said as he yanked on Tyler's uniform sleeve. They were gone before I could issue any other warnings to them.

"Heaven help the women of Mexico, " Doc said, looking up at the stars. "I just hope those two little snots don't get into trouble. Think we should go with them?"

"Are you kidding me?" I replied. "No way. I plan to enjoy my first night off that damn base. You can go with them if you want. Really—that'd be fine with me. I've already got plans of my own."

"No, I think we better let them run until they wind themselves down, and I just don't have the energy to keep up with 'em tonight," he said, shaking his head again. "What are your plans? What are you going to do?"

"All my life I've heard about Mexican food but have never had any. This might sound pretty tame to you, but I'd like to find a place to eat. You're welcome to join me if you want, but I'd understand if you'd rather do something else—like chasing skirts maybe?"

"If you don't mind, I'm starved. I'd like to tag along with you a while. You sure that's OK?"

I had been hoping Doc and I could spend some time together. Since the day of the baseball game, he hadn't said one word about it. Even so, I could tell he was still very disappointed in me. And I couldn't blame him. I also knew he'd never forget that day, but I was hoping he'd at least be able to forgive me a little. I didn't especially want to talk to him more about my logic, or lack thereof, the day of the game. I was just hoping for some time when the two of us could visit like we used to.

I turned to him and said, "I'm glad to have the company. Let's see," I said, looking around. "Sounds like the most noise is off in that direction. Let's walk over that way and see what we can come up with."

We headed toward the main part of town, passing bars and restaurants what seemed like about every twenty feet or so. Right away I noticed several places that were on the list of those we were supposed to avoid. Judging by how filthy most of them looked, I wouldn't have gone in them anyway.

The closer to the center of the business district we got, the more a general commotion surrounded us. We rounded a corner and, suddenly, servicemen were everywhere. The streets were so crowded it was like walking down the midway of a huge carnival. At the entrance of practically every bar on the main street, a man or woman stood outside, like a carnival barker, and in broken English tried to convince those passing by that their establishment was the best in town. Every once in a while we'd also see one of our men, but they ducked or did an about-face when they saw us, probably afraid we'd send them back to relieve those watching the trucks.

Doc finally pointed across the street to a place called Casa Azul— Blue House. It looked clean enough, so we made our way through the mob in the middle of the street and walked in. We were immediately met by a young waitress who started to usher us toward the back of the restaurant. I stopped her and asked if we could sit at one of the tables by the front window so we could watch the action outside as we ate. At first she said no, but she relented when I said we'd leave and go to another place if we couldn't eat there.

"You think we're supposed to sit in the back?" Doc asked after we had been seated.

"No, I don't think so," I said. "I think they just try to fill up the back first so people walking by will see empty seats and come in. It's just smart business."

It hadn't dawned on me that the waitress might have wanted us in the back for another reason. Now I wasn't so sure, but I wasn't going to let it bother me. I had been so nervous about getting the men ready for the trip I skipped chow back at the base, and my stomach was really roaring. More than anything, I was ready to eat, anxious to finally sample some Mexican food.

When our waitress came back to take our order, I said, "I tell you what. Bring us a big platter with a sampling of all the foods you'd recommend. We'd like to try them all. And please bring us each a beer. Doesn't matter what kind—whatever's coldest."

The waitress's English was excellent. She said, "I'll put together a nice meal for you boys. Don't worry, I'll take good care of you. Two beers, frosty, coming right up."

"Your English is incredible," I said as she reached for our menus. "You learn it from the servicemen who come down here?"

She responded, "Houston. I grew up in Houston, sweetie." And with that, she twirled around and headed back toward the kitchen.

"Well, how about that, sweetie?" Doc teased when she was no longer within earshot.

I tried to look mean and glared at him and shook my head.

He just laughed.

While we waited for the food, Doc and I were glued to the action on the street outside. I had made fun of the men for saying that watching gasoline trucks coming onto the base was like watching a movie. But now, looking out at the street, I really did feel like I was watching a movie—and a wild one at that. The street was absolutely packed with soldiers and young women of all sizes, shapes, and descriptions—usually with the soldiers following close behind trying to muster enough courage to go up and talk to them. What I didn't see were people I would call "locals." Doc was probably right when he said they were very likely the only ones with enough sense to stay away from this part of town.

Suddenly Doc reached over and poked me on the arm. "Well I'll be damned," he said. "Would you take a look at that?"

Every once in a while there was enough of a gap in the crowd moving up and down the street that we could see Williams and Tyler standing next to two women on the sidewalk directly across from us. It was obvious they were trying to talk the young women into sticking with them. It was equally obvious the women weren't budging. One had very long, jet-black hair who kept swishing it in Williams face, and he kept raising his hand to brush it back. She kept scratching her head, again and again, like it was a nervous habit. She finally leaned over to whisper something in Williams' ear, and they both broke out laughing. Tyler was trying to make time with the other woman, who was almost as short and skinny as he was. She had her hair piled up on top of her head in something of a bun and was wearing a flowered blue dress that stood out from anything else going by in the crowd.

Just as our food came, we noticed that all four of them, arm in arm, were headed into the bar behind them.

Doc just shook his head, "Can you believe it? I can't, and I just saw it. I can't believe they got girls that fast."

"Yes," I replied, "I think 'fast' is the important word here. I'm betting both of those girls are very 'fast.'"

Doc started to say something else, but our thoughts immediately jumped from Williams and Tyler to the spread of food set in front of us. It was incredible. I had never seen anything like it before. Our waitress did her best to give us the names of everything and took the time to describe each item for us, but after she left Doc asked, "What in the world did she just say?"

"I don't know," I replied. "Once she got past tortillas and beans, I was lost. Let's just dig in and we'll make up our own names for everything as we go along."

I don't remember ever laughing so hard while eating a meal.

"Cosmoline," Doc said after sampling some beans in a heavy sauce, making reference to the heavy grease the army used to prevent rust on weapons and vehicles.

"Turpentine," I said after eating some of a sticky tomato and onion dish.

Doc pushed a multicolored rice and vegetable dish around his plate before taking a bite. "Definitely old socks. Either that or dog hair."

To listen to us, one would have thought the food was right out of the trash pile. As a matter of fact, it was all so horrible we both ended up using soft tortilla shells to sop up every bit of the food and sauce we had been given. Those plates were so clean we joked they could have been reused without being washed. At least we hoped we were joking. Every time a waitress would enter or leave the kitchen the swinging doors would sway open long enough for us to get a pretty good view inside. I was glad I hadn't seen the bowels of the kitchen before we sat down to eat.

When our waitress came back, we each ordered another beer and decided to nurse them while watching the mass of bodies milling around outside. Doc turned unusually quiet for him, so I asked if anything was bothering him.

"No," he said. "Nothing's wrong. Believe it or not, I was just thinking about St. Louis."

"St. Louis? You miss being home?"

He studied me and took a long gulp of his beer before answering. "Not even Williams knows about this," he said, leaning forward. "So please don't say anything. I'm missing somebody back there."

Doc didn't let his guard down very often, so I wasn't about to tease him. "What's her name?" I asked.

"Judy. Judy Robinson. I met her about two months before Uncle Sam got me. Perc, I just can't get her out of my mind."

It was rare to catch Doc in a reflective mood. He always tried his best to present an exterior tough as carpet tacks.

"Where'd you meet her?" I asked, hoping he would continue.

"That's the funny thing. You'll never believe this, but I met her one day when *my* car broke down. I needed to call my uncle to come give me a tow, so I walked up to the nearest house and knocked on the door to see if they had a phone. The door opened, and there she was. The minute I saw her I forgot what I was there for. I think I scared her at first because she started closing the door when I didn't say anything. I grabbed the door and shouted 'Phone!' That's all that would come out of my mouth. 'Phone!' We wrestled over the door for a minute until I convinced her I wasn't some kind of crook or fiend. It took some persuading, but she finally let me in. After I called, we went back out on the porch and talked while we waited for my uncle to show. I just couldn't take my eyes off her. She was so pretty."

"Did you ask her out?"

"Just when I was getting ready to, my uncle pulled up. I didn't see her again for about a week. Like a dope, I didn't even get her phone number, so I couldn't even call her. One day I couldn't stand it anymore and just got in my car and drove over there. I knocked on the door, and when she opened it I told her my car had broken down and I needed to use her phone. She started laughing and invited me in. I finally got enough guts to ask her on a date, and we ended up going out three times before I had to leave. And now I miss her so bad I think I'm about to lose my mind. It isn't so bad during the day, but at night she is all I can think about. I just feel so, well, I don't know..."

He downed the last of his beer and just sat there shaking his head.

"I think I know what you mean," I said. Then I added, "I wondered why you didn't go with Williams and Tyler. So this is why you aren't chasing skirts tonight."

Without looking up he said, "This is why I am not chasing skirts."

"I'm really pathetic," he continued.

"My friend," I said, "We both are."

I looked back out the window at the crowd, but everything became sort of a blur. My thoughts, too, were back in St. Louis. We *were* pathetic.

And we wouldn't have traded that for anything.

* * *

After leaving Casa Azul, Doc and I spent the rest of the evening walking around and seeing the sights. We stopped at an old cathedral that had a series of beautiful stained glass windows, each representing a biblical scene. We hadn't seen anything like that before, so we went in to look around. We walked through a market area where farmers were selling fruits and vegetables. At first I thought it was odd they were out so late at night, but then it dawned on me this was the only time they could sell their goods to the servicemen who were visiting their town. As my dad would have said, they were "cuttin' cotton while the weather was dry." We also walked through a park area where there was an enormous statue of a soldier, but we never did figure out who it was.

After that we decided to walk the length of the main street before calling it a night. The street was so crowded it took us nearly fifteen minutes to weave our way up those five blocks. I was like a man trying to get back into a baseball stadium after the game was over. It wasn't any better when we turned around and headed back. When we again passed Casa Azul, Doc suggested we stop for one last beer—one for the road. We arrived as our original table was being cleared off, so we again sat there and watched the crowd.

After finishing our beer, Doc and I had had our fill of Juarez, so we decided to go back to the trucks to relieve some of the men standing guard. We knew they'd be thrilled at the prospect of getting in a little more of the town before we all had to head back. We also ran into Albertson and Jamieson and made them go with us. They had struck out in their attempts to find love, so they didn't put up much of a squawk.

One o'clock came around all too quickly for most. As the men trickled back, Doc and I asked them how they had spent their evenings. Most gave pretty tame accounts. A few had gone dancing at a nightclub, but for the most part, it seemed the rest had just grabbed a bite to eat, seen the sights, and bought souvenirs.

Even our battalion Romeos, Williams and Tyler, came back just under the wire, but they weren't happy about it. They started bragging immediately to anyone who would listen about the "good time" their sisteritas had shown them. According to Williams, his new girlfriend had "more arms than an octopus"—and she knew how to use every one of them. Tyler said his girl's lips tasted like prunes. I shuddered, until I realized he thought that tasting like prunes was a good thing. Doc told him she probably tasted that way because she hadn't brushed her teeth in weeks. It quickly became obvious they weren't going to shut up, so Doc grabbed each by the back of the shirt and ushered them to the first truck behind the jeep and commanded, "You're not riding with us. Get your skinny asses in there before I stuff socks in your mouths." Looking like they had been insulted, they turned up their noses and climbed in—and then starting telling everyone in that truck their story all over again.

At ten minutes past one, only Davis was missing. I had said we wouldn't stick around for stragglers, but I went ahead and sent Albertson and Jamieson back into town to look for him. It wasn't five minutes later that the three of them came running back like they were being chased by wolves. Davis was a big man, so it was quite a sight to see him rumbling along. He had been ahead in a crap game and was afraid of what would happen to him if he left being so much ahead. Albertson and Jamieson had seen the game going on in an alley between two bars and saw Davis still shooting the dice. Thinking quickly, Albertson, who was gaining my respect more and more each day, sized up the situation. He then ran into the alley while yelling, "MPs! MPs! Everybody run!" They took the opportunity of the confusion to grab Davis and haul him out of there.

"I'm sorry, Sarge," Davis said as he stood gasping for breath in front of me. "I thought they were going to cut my throat if I left!"

"That's OK," I responded. "*If* you buy us all a beer next week with some of your winnings we'll forget about it."

"Consider it done. I'd have been a goner if they hadn't come for me."

I didn't chew him out because I had the feeling he was right.

The inspection at the border checkpoint and the drive back to the base went like clockwork, uneventful. For the most part, the men were quiet. They hadn't had as much to drink as I guessed they would. Most were just plain tuckered out. So was I. The only real excitement came when Davis stuck his head out of the truck he was riding in and threw up. It could have been booze, the food, or nerves jostled in that crap game—or a combination of all three—that set him off. He hadn't quite made it to the back of the truck before getting sick, and the other men really gave him a hard time about it as they all stuck their heads out of the truck, gasping for air.

The Mexican trip, as I had hoped, had been just what the doctor ordered. Still, I started feeling more than a little sad as we drove back to the base. The men had all had a good time and enjoyed themselves tremendously, but it seemed so wrong and so pathetic to me that we had to cross the border into another country for this to happen. With the exception of a few bars and restaurants, the men had pretty much been free to come and go as they pleased in Juarez, to explore the city without having to follow a line of fences.

In Mexico, the only color that mattered was green, the color of our money.

The same couldn't be said back in El Paso.

And the closer we got back to Fort Bliss, the more this sunk in.

I had the feeling the same thought had occurred to more than a few of the men. The trucks were awfully quiet.

Awfully quiet.

* * *

For two days after we got back, all Williams and Tyler could talk about were the "sisteritas" they had been with in Mexico. They were the envy of the battalion until late the afternoon of that second day, when both realized they had a serious problem. Their heads itched so badly they had scratched them until they were bleeding. By evening chow they were in agony. I had never seen humans or beasts as miserable in all my life.

Sam Burgesh, one of our cooks who had become close to Williams, finally came over to our table in the mess hall and asked me what was going on. Tyler was scratching his head with his fork when Sam leaned down and said he'd take a look. He inspected the area and suddenly jumped back, laughing and saying, "Son, you've got yourself a good case of head lice!"

The men sitting around us got up and scattered, leaving their trays behind.

As I looked at Williams and Tyler, I immediately thought of Williams' girlfriend down in Juarez and how she had constantly scratched her head as she brushed her hair over his shoulders. The thought made me shiver.

I put down my fork, spit out the food I was chewing, and said, "OK you two. Let's get down to the motor pool. Now. We'll figure something out."

I started to grab them by their shirts but backed off—just in case. The rest of the men continued to back away, leaving a clear runway down the center of the mess hall as we exited.

Burgesh volunteered to go along with us because he said he had seen cases of lice before many times—that it wasn't that big a deal at all—and that he could cure them. When we got to the motor pool, he talked Williams and Tyler into covering their heads with globs of axle grease to "...suffocate them little buggers." It didn't work. Within minutes they were more miserable than ever because the grease started dripping down into their eyes and ears. Doc, who had also tagged along, more to help torture them than to offer help, suggested they set their hair on fire so he could stab the little critters with a screwdriver as they jumped up and down. They found no humor in that, especially when Doc fired up a welding torch. Burgesh also got them to wrap their heads with rags while he doused them with Pepsi-Cola, a bad move considering the axle grease then started foaming, too.

"Come on, guys," Williams implored. "This isn't funny. I'm scared."

Tyler looked like he was crying, but with all the grease in his eyes it was hard to tell.

Burgesh finally came up with what he said was a surefire solution to the problem. He took some long, rubber tubing, cut it in half, and attached each piece to the exhaust pipe of a jeep. He then put helmets on Williams and Tyler and ran the tubing underneath them to create a gas chamber. He started the jeeps while explaining that the fumes would drive them out. That didn't get rid of the lice, but it did make all of us feel more than a little sleepy. I shut the jeeps off because I knew we'd all soon be dead if I didn't.

"Well, I think we've 'exhausted' our ideas," I said, dryly, when I rejoined the group. I thought that was funny. None of the others even smiled. As a matter of fact, they all cussed at me, even Tyler.

"OK. Let's go," I finally said to them. "Doc, you get back to the mess hall and take charge while I take these two to the infirmary."

I made Williams and Tyler stand in the back of the jeep as I drove them, helmets on heads and grease dripping from their chins, to the Infirmary. They held on for dear life and scratched the whole way there.

The doctor was sympathetic, but he also started laughing uncontrollably when I explained all the "home remedies" we had tried, especially the gas chamber. After cleaning them up, he lathered some special cream into their hair and ordered them to return each morning for the next week for additional treatments. I quickly told the doc about Williams' girlfriend and how she had swished and swayed her hair all over him, so he also insisted they stay away from their new girlfriends for at least two weeks.

"No more sisteritas for me," Williams groaned on the drive back to the barracks.

"Me, either," Tyler added. "They might be like firecrackers, but they're too buggy!"

When we got back to the barracks, word had already spread and the men were waiting to greet us. They were all down on their hands and knees when we pulled up, looking for all the world like a herd of cows, and started scratching their heads on the ground. I had never seen anything like it in my life. Even Williams and Tyler howled. They jumped out of the jeep and started chasing the men, who scattered, still worried at the prospect of catching their lice. I laughed until I thought I was going to be sick.

Doc, coming from the direction of headquarters, rushed up, out of breath, and said, "I took a phone message for you, Perc. It was Olivia." He paused, breathing hard.

"Well, what was it?" I asked. "What'd she say? What'd she say?"

Doc smiled. "It was a bad connection, but I think I heard her right," he teased. "She said to tell you just one thing."

He paused again. "Well, what was it?" I demanded.

"She said 'Yes'."

"Yes?"

"Yes!"

I jumped out of the jeep and hugged Doc. "Yes?" I asked again.

"Yes, dammit," he said. "Yes!"

I backed up and sat back down in the jeep. "Yes!" I said to myself.

"You *are* pathetic," Doc said, shaking his head and heading for the barracks.

That I was.

14

HOMECOMINGS

(THE VILLE)

The rest of basic training passed quickly, one day running into the next. Our drivers also began their new duties right on schedule and, as it turned out, I needn't have worried so much about them. They were doing so well both on and off the base the whole battalion was just about to burst with pride. Meanwhile, scuttlebutt had it that our battalion wasn't going anywhere until after the first of the year, so the men were hopeful we'd be granted leave over at least part of the holidays. No one wanted this more than I did. Olivia's one-word telephone message was all I could think about, and I couldn't wait to get back home so we could finally get married. There were also times when I panicked, when I wondered if her message hadn't been misunderstood—if she hadn't been saying "Yes" to some question posed by the operator, like, "Would you care to add another twenty-five cents for three additional minutes?" All sorts of reasons for her to say "Yes" ran through my mind. We also hadn't had any mail since the night of her call, so I was starting to feel way out in left field.

We were lined up outside the infirmary for our haircuts when word came. Doc and I were about a dozen spots from the door when Sergeant Ingram came over. The first thing he said to me was, "If I were you, I'd get out of line."

"What do you mean?" I asked. "Why?"

"Just take my word for it."

He removed his cap to reveal a head full of bald spots and patches of scraped skin.

"White barber," he said matter-of-factly.

The men within hearing range started to bolt, but I ordered them back into line.

Sergeant Ingram then said he wanted to talk to me in private. I told Doc to hold my place in line while Ingram and I walked a few more steps away from the group.

"I just got back from HQ," he said. "I'll be damned, but this time scuttlebutt was right. We *are* getting leave."

His voice was rising and he was getting just a little bit too excited, so I grabbed him by the arm and pulled him even farther away from the group.

"When? When's it coming? How soon?"

"Colonel Ellis said he'd have more of the details tomorrow morning. All he said was it looked like we would be going home within the week!"

"Quiet down!" I said, trying not to act too excited myself. "Let's not tell the men until we're absolutely sure. This isn't the time to get their motors running and then turn off the key. Let's keep this between the two of us for now. OK?"

Sergeant Ingram nodded. I shook his hand warmly and said, "Thanks. I was praying for this."

"Me, too," he said. "Me, too."

* * *

As excited as I was about the prospect of getting leave, there was still one fly in the ointment that was really worrying me. When I asked Olivia to marry me, I did so fully aware of the fact that we'd have to keep our marriage a secret from all but our closest friends and relatives. The St. Louis Board of Education had a rule that had been in place for well over fifty years which clearly stated that female teachers could not be married. It was a ridiculous rule, one that seemed right out of the Dark Ages, but it was also one that if violated could mean the firing of the teacher involved. I had heard that not all school districts in St. Louis were still following it to the letter and that it would probably be rescinded soon everywhere because of the teacher shortage being produced by the war. But Sumner, unfortunately, was one of the places keeping the rule firmly in place. Teaching was Olivia's life.

At this point, losing her job was "not" an option. We were now playing with fire, and I did not want her to be consumed by the flames.

One evening the previous summer she told me about the rule when I tried to get a little too amorous on her back porch. I thought she was just pulling my leg and said as much. We were sitting out on the steps enjoying the cool evening air and each other's kisses when she suddenly got up and said she could prove it. A few minutes later she came back out with a folder in her hand. She handed me the folder and said, "Read page twenty-three if you don't believe me."

I read it, and I was shocked. I handed the folder back to her and said, "You've got to be kidding."

She ripped out that page and handed it to me. "Keep this," she said. "As a reminder."

"A reminder of what?" I asked, pretending not to get her point.

She sat back down, put her arms around me, and said, coyly, "The next time you want to get too romantic, remember you could end up with two things. A son or daughter—and an unemployed wife."

"Thanks a lot," I replied as sarcastically as I could. "You sure know how to put a guy in the mood."

I was being played with, but I didn't protest too much. She tightened her arms around me a little more and said, "I'll show you how much I'm worried about that." And with that, she kissed me so deeply I lost my balance and darn near got killed falling off the porch railing.

Then I decided two could play that game.

When I regained my balance, I said, "Great. This is what we'll do. We'll run off and get married and have, oh, two or three kids right away. You'll get fired, so we'll be poor as church mice. I'll be so overcome with your kisses I'll always be falling down steps or over railings. I'll always be so injured I won't be able to work, so we'll all starve to death. Sounds good to me. How about you?"

"Perfect!" she shot back. "Except I don't want you to get injured too much or I'll never be able to have those kids. Come on back over here—away from the railing—and I'll show you what I mean."

I knew exactly what she meant. Exactly. I walked over, put my arms around her, and hugged her as tightly as I could.

* * *

I opened my footlocker and pulled out the small White Owl cigar box where I kept my personal belongings. There, folded neatly, was the sheet of paper Olivia had torn from the folder that night. Page twenty-three. I read it over and over again:

Article VII.—MARRIAGE OF FEMALE TEACHERS.

"Your committee would recommend that hereafter the marriage of a female teacher shall be considered an equivalent to her resignation, and shall be treated as such."

Official Proceedings of the
St. Louis Public Schools, Vol. IV.

I had known women who quit their teaching jobs after getting married, but I had assumed they left of their own accord to start families. It had never dawned on me that they might not have had a choice in the matter. That same night we joked about getting married, Olivia told me about two of her colleagues who left the school shortly after tying the knot. One moved to Chicago because her new husband worked there. That made sense to me, and I didn't give it another thought. The other woman left her teaching position about a year before I came to Sumner. Olivia said this woman just came to school one Monday morning and announced she had gotten married the previous weekend and would be quitting her job. Just barely seven months later she had a "very" premature baby boy. No one ever said anything out loud about the timing of her resignation.

As I sat there reading and rereading the St. Louis Board of Education rule, I wondered how long it would be enforced with the war going on. Sumner had already lost half a dozen teachers, both men and women, to the war effort. At some point, teachers were going to become quite scarce, and when that happened it seemed to me those in charge would have to be a little more flexible in interpretation of the rules. All I knew was in the meantime I didn't want anything to jeopardize Olivia's work at Sumner. Teaching was in her heart and soul so deeply that nothing or no one would ever be able to pry it out. She was a natural-born teacher, one who loved and respected her students as if they were her own children. To Olivia, there were no bad kids, only what she called bad "circumstances."

I asked her to explain what she had meant by that, and she said, "These kids are born good, with good hearts and good minds. Many of them are lucky to be born into families where love and affection make them grow strong and tall. Others aren't as lucky. 'Circumstances' in their families take them off in another direction. It doesn't mean they aren't good kids. It means they just don't have the same opportunities to grow because their families are suffering in one way or the other."

She continued when she saw me raise an eyebrow, "Think of it this way. See those yellow dianthus over there by the fence. With the right rain and sunshine, they will continue to produce the most beautiful flowers all summer long. For dianthus, rain and sunshine are God's love. But imagine what would happen without that rain and sunshine. They would wither and die. They'd never bloom. As teachers, we try to give our students that rain and sunshine every single day in our classrooms, but it isn't always enough if the 'circumstances' at home don't match what goes on at school. Sometimes there isn't any rain or sunshine at home, and then even the very best of kids lose their way. That is what makes our jobs so important. At least, that is what makes my job so important to me. Does that make any sense at all?"

It did. The students were her dianthus. She was their rain and sunshine and I didn't want anything, especially not our love, to end that.

We were going to have to tread carefully to keep our marriage a well-guarded secret. That was going to take some doing but we didn't have any other choice. I wanted to shout our love to the heavens, to let everyone know how happy we were, but that just couldn't be done because of the risks involved. We'd tell our parents, siblings, and a few dear friends. But other than those, our lips would have to be sealed until the rule was suspended or abolished. It just didn't seem fair. Not fair at all.

* * *

Two days later, Colonel Ellis passed down the official word.

We were going home.

A skeleton crew had to stay behind to help take care of matters at the barracks. They were not happy about drawing the short straws, but someone had to do it. Colonel Ellis and I tried to choose those who did not have as many family ties back home, but it was still tough making out the leave list. Those who had been granted leave were told they could take off the following Monday. Just as my high school students acted rowdy a few minutes before the bell would ring to signal the end of a class period, from the minute the list was posted the men could not keep their minds on anything else but going home. I couldn't blame them. I made a few halfhearted attempts at chewing out those who didn't clean their part of the barracks or who drifted off during classes, but it was a lost cause to think I was going to have their undivided attention anytime before Monday. The men were going to all parts of the country, and there were train and bus reservations to be made. I helped as much as I could with this from headquarters, but all other available phones were kept busy by men making their travel plans.

On the Sunday night before the leave period was to begin, I was ordered to call everyone together for one last piece of instruction. I decided to speak to them during evening chow since they were already a captive audience. I asked Burgesh to bang on one of the trays to get their attention.

"Listen up, men." I said. "This is serious, so I want you to pay attention to me."

I could hear a few men saying, "Oh, no..." in a tone that said they were hoping their leaves weren't being canceled.

I quickly continued, "Now listen to me. You're still getting leave. But, there is one thing all of you must understand, and I mean completely, before I'll let your butts off the base."

When it appeared I had their complete attention, I continued. "In a sense, this is your graduation dinner. Graduation from basic training. I don't need to tell you again how proud I am of all of you. You know that. And when you get home, your families are going to be proud of you, too. And rightly so. Finishing basic is a tremendous accomplishment. As soon as you get back to the base, those of you who haven't already started it will be given more training, this time for a specific job you're going to be asked to do from here on out. We already have a pretty good group of drivers. Some of you will learn specific jobs to help keep our bombers and other planes in the air. We're a Signal Construction Battalion, so that means some of you are going to communications school—and just about all of us will get at least some training in that. Others will be taught construction of all types. Probably everything from hangars to outhouses. Some of you will even learn how to build airstrips. There will be other jobs I haven't been told about yet. Whatever you're asked to do, I know you'll do it with the same dedication and pride you've shown all along."

I paused to get their attention again and added, "You all know the reasons our battalion is here, but no one else can know. And I mean *no one*. When you get home, you can tell your families you are stationed here at Fort Bliss. You can tell them you are part of the 449th Signal Construction Battalion. You can tell them everything you want to about basic training. Well, maybe not about your trips to Mexico."

A few men laughed. Others just smiled. I could tell from the looks on their faces they understood the seriousness of my words, so I continued.

"Tell them all you think appropriate about your time in basic training. But, do *not* tell them about the bomber group here. Tell them nothing about how many planes you've seen, the types of planes that are here, how many men you think are on the base, how often you notice planes taking off and landing, and especially do not say word one about what the base looks like. Not a single word. All of you have seen the posters around the base that say, "They May Be Listening." Well, 'they' just may be. None of you would want anything you said to someone to be the cause of sabotage here on the base or give information to the enemy that could be used against us when we finally do get overseas. Everybody got that?"

Heads nodded all through the group. Albertson, never one to be bashful, had a question and raised his hand. "Hey Sarge. Does that mean I can't tell my dad about how many head lice Tyler's got? Would that be considered a military secret?"

"That would be fine," I said over the laughter that followed. "I'd rather you talk about Tyler's head than how many planes we've got here. As a matter of fact, when people start pressing you for information about what it's like here—and believe me they will—why don't all of you just bring Tyler up in the conversation to distract them. I think that would be a good idea."

I pointed to Tyler and said, "I told you you'd be an important part of this outfit!"

Albertson reached over and pretended to smash a group of lice on Tyler's shoulder. Others around him stepped back in mock horror.

"Any other questions?" I asked.

There weren't. "OK, here's the drill. Those of you getting leave should report to the barracks right now and get your belongings ready to go. That is, if you haven't already. Some of you packed the minute you saw your name on the 'Go' list. I'll have your paperwork ready for you in about an hour. After I get finished over at headquarters, I'll bring the papers back with me to the barracks. I'll set up shop at a table in the recreation area. You can line up as soon as I get there, and I'll go through the paperwork with you as you pick it up. Everybody understand?"

They said they did, but I knew most of them were already miles away in their thoughts.

So was I.

* * *

The train ride back to St. Louis seemed like it took forever. Like most of the men on the train, I was so excited to be going home I couldn't sit still. I caught myself pacing up and down my car just to be doing something.

Doc finally said to me, "Good grief, Perc. You going to walk all the way back to St. Louis? Think you'll beat the train?"

I stopped my pacing and laughed. He was right. But I was wound up tighter than a Big Ben clock.

"I guess I'm just a little anxious," I replied.

"A little?" Doc shot back. "You look like a guy waitin' for a hanging. Sit down. You're making *me* tired."

He then added, whispering, "Is it the wedding? That what's bothering you?"

"It's more than that. It just hit me this morning how long it has been since we've been home. I can't wait to see some old friends I've been thinking about lately. And I miss the Ville. That may sound funny, but it really is my home now. I also miss Sumner and want to know what's going on with everyone. I've just got a lot on my mind."

"And Olivia?" Doc asked.

"I can't hide it, huh? Oh, I'm not questioning whether I'm ready to get married or anything like that. There's something else you don't know about."

I hadn't told him anything about the Board of Education rule, so I sat back down and went through it, at the same time trying to convince both Doc and myself that what I was about to do was right.

When I finished, he said, "That's some risk, my friend. You sure now's the time to do this? What if you two get caught? What if she loses her job? Wouldn't it be better just to wait until they get rid of that stupid rule?"

"I've gone over everything so many times I'm not sure of anything anymore. I know I love her more than anything in this world. I know getting married is the *right* thing to do. I just don't know if it is the *smart* thing to do. What would you do?"

"I honestly don't know. It's plain how you feel about her, but I just don't know...."

He stared out the window before continuing, "A few months back I'd have said you'd lost your marbles. Now I think I know how you feel. For the first time in my life, I understand at least part of this."

He stuck out his hand and shook mine, firmly. "Just let me know what I can do to help. I hope you know that, Perc. Anything, anytime."

"Well, there is one thing." I said. "I've wanted to ask you this for a long time but I wanted to sort through the rest of this before I brought it up. I'm going to need a best man. I'd be honored if you'd stand with me."

"I'd be proud to," he said. "You just say when and I'll be there."

"Thanks, Doc. I can't tell you what that means to me. I..."

He interrupted me and said, "And there's one more thing I didn't want to mention before. I may be asking you to do the same thing for me one of these days. I'm still thinking about it, but there may be another one of these before too long."

"I had a feeling that's what was keeping you so quiet this past week. I'll just give you the same advice you gave me the night we made the record to send to Olivia. If you care about her that much, then follow your heart. Whatever you decide to do, I hope you also know I'll always be there for you and help any way I can."

"I know that, Perc. Thanks. I guess I know what I want to do, but I don't even know if she'll have me. What if I ask her and she says 'No?' She sure would if she's smart."

Before I could say anything else, Williams came walking back toward us. That ended our conversation quickly. He had been in a crap game two cars up and was now counting his money as he swayed back and forth with the rhythm of the train.

"Look at this!" he said. "What a roll! Tonight I feel like the luckiest man in the world."

Doc and I looked at each other and smiled. I said, "Oh, I wouldn't say you're the luckiest man in the world tonight. I'd say all of us are pretty damn lucky. Wouldn't you, Doc?"

He just smiled again and grabbed Williams' money.

*　*　*

In addition to all the big towns like Amarillo and Oklahoma City and Tulsa, our train seemed to stop at every whistle stop along the line. Doc, staring out the window most of the trip, again got his headache "the size of St. Louis." After all the stops and train changes, we finally made it back to Union Station early in the evening of the second day. Union Station, as it had been when we left, was again a sea of humanity. Men in uniform, surrounded by their wet-eyed families, were everywhere. As I passed several young soldiers obviously leaving home for the first time, I thought of the night I left and wished each a quiet "good luck" as I walked by them.

There was no one there to meet us because we hadn't known the exact timetable for the trip. We all tried to get through to St. Louis the night before we left to at least let everyone know we were coming, but for some reason the operator couldn't put our calls through. As we left the station, we knew we were going to be surprising the daylights out of a lot of people when they saw us.

Even though it was about a mile and a half from the station, we decided the smartest thing to do was walk west on Market Street to catch the northbound Grand Avenue streetcar. The evening air was cold in St. Louis, so different from El Paso. Almost immediately, as a light breeze started picking up, I was sorry I didn't think to bring a heavier coat. Even though blackout restrictions had pretty much been lifted for St. Louis, the city was still as dark as I had ever seen it. We didn't talk as we walked. I looked at my traveling companions, and it was pretty obvious they, too, were anxious to get the rest of the way home. The last part of a journey always seems the longest, and this time was no exception.

We shared the streetcar for several miles as we passed familiar streets—Lindell and Delmar and Page. The distinct sound of the trolley bell was music to our ears as we drew nearer homes and loved ones. Doc and I suddenly realized we had forgotten to exchange phone numbers. He gave me his parents' number, and I gave him Olivia's. I told him I'd call him as soon as I could to let him know more about when and where we'd be getting married so he could meet us. Williams also scribbled his phone number for both of us, but he was going to go visit his cousin for a few days, so he wasn't sure he could make it back for the wedding. I told him not to worry about it, that I understood how much he missed his "cousin." Doc put him in a quick headlock and teased him about the possibility of him going even more blind this trip.

The clanging of the bell at Easton Avenue let me know it was time to hop off so I could catch the car running west out to the Ville. We quickly said our good-byes and shook hands. Williams came over and hugged me. Doc laughed and pulled him off me with a gruff, "Good grief! He's just getting married—not dying. Leave the poor man alone."

"You boneheads take care of yourselves," I said as I stepped down from the car. "I'll be seeing you soon."

Williams saluted me.

"No, you idiot!" I shouted. "You *don't* salute sergeants!"

"I know," he responded, grinning. "Just pulling your leg."

Doc jerked him back in his seat and started yelling at him again. I just shook my head as I watched the trolley roll away into the darkening night.

The Easton Avenue trolley, a brand-new one in what we called the Wellston Line, pulled up a few minutes later and I climbed aboard. "Where you headed, soldier?" the conductor asked.

"I wish I knew," I said. "I really wish I knew."

* * *

When the trolley stopped at Goode Street., I suddenly felt at home. I got off there and started walking, continuing west up Easton. I immediately started passing familiar sights. There was Baker's Hardware. Tillman's Billiards, where I had killed more than a few of my summer evenings playing eight-ball. Moore's Florist Shop. Garles Cage's Restaurant. Lorraine Irby's Beauty Shop, where Olivia had that sweet-smelling Sweet Georgia Brown Hair Dressing put on her hair to help keep it straight. Enterprise Cleaners, where many Sumner students worked after school and during the summer months. My mouth started watering as I passed Tobias's Delicatessen. Everyone thought Mr. Tobias was a genius. He had his exhaust fans routed out toward the front sidewalk so that over the noon hour the always delicious aroma of the "soup of the day" was carried through the breeze and advertised throughout the neighborhood. I had forgotten just how much I had missed his soups. I finally passed the building housing "Madam Wright, Spiritualist," and laughed. I remembered Olivia wanting us to go in there one time so Madam Wright could tell us how many children we were going to have. I suggested instead that we work on that ourselves.

When I got to Newstead, I headed north up to Cottage Avenue and doubled back east. I knew no one would be there this time of night, but I just had to see Sumner, even if it was only from the outside. As I headed that direction, I realized I was stalling. I should have turned south off Easton and headed down to West Belle Place, but I felt my knees shaking. I had proposed on the record I sent, but I hadn't heard a single word from her since the night of the phone message. I still wasn't entirely sure her "Yes" was in answer to my proposal. And even if it was, I was still going to have to propose again in person. And what if she had said "Yes" and had now changed her mind? Even on this cool night, sweat started forming on my forehead as that thought hit me.

When Sumner first came into view, it looked absolutely beautiful in the shadows of night. The columns to the sides of the main entrance stood as majestic as ever. The small panes of glass in the entrance doors sparkled with the reflections of the stars in the clear night sky. I stood there reminiscing about my days teaching science and math—and even laughed out loud as I recalled the close calls of driver's training. I could remember sitting at my desk and suddenly becoming aware of the odor of bread baking in the school kitchen. I could hear the clomping and shuffling of feet between classes. I remembered the thick cloud of cigarette smoke in the teachers' lounge and how it had stung my eyes as I tried to grade tests there. But more than anything, I remembered how proud I felt when I was invited for the first time to stand on the front steps of the school with the permanent staff so we could all have our pictures taken for the school yearbook, the *Maroon and White*. I was so excited that day I was positively giddy.

I looked at my watch. I wasn't sure how long I had been standing there, but it was already nearing 8:00 P.M. St. Louis time. I should walk to Olivia's before it gets any later.

I headed back south toward West Belle Place, my mind racing a mile a minute. When I finally got there, I paused at the sidewalk entrance of 4341. Part of me was telling me to keep moving, to just keep walking down the sidewalk, but I soon found myself pushing the buzzer, practicing the Morse code we had been taught in basic. I spelled out "SOS" over and over. I thought that appropriate.

From inside the apartment I could hear, "Hold your horses! I'm coming—I'm coming!"

When the door opened I knew I had made the right decision. Standing there, baking powder on her face and spatula in hand, stood the love of my life. She didn't say a word. She dropped the spatula, ran down the steps, and jumped into my arms. I lost my balance and we fell to the ground. We kissed so long and so deeply we finally both gasped for air, moving our lips away from each other at the same time, then instantly pressed them together again. Our arms wrapped around each other, hands searching up and down each other's backs, feeling each other as if to make sure this wasn't all just another dream.

I was still on my back when she moved over to straddle my waist, sitting on top of me. The whole time her lips never left mine. I moved my hands up to feel the smoothness of her face, finding the softness of the dimples at the side of her mouth, then moving back to circle the lobes of her ears. Her breathing was labored, coming in short gasps, as she moved her lips from mine, down my cheek to my neck, where her kisses made me shiver—gave me goose bumps—as she kissed the skin at the hollow of my shoulder. I took her face in my hands and raised her back up, looking deeply into her eyes. I kissed her again, this time, softly, gently, almost pecking at her lips with mine.

She unbuttoned the top three buttons of my uniform and pressed herself closer to me, never taking her lips from mine. It was now my turn, and I kissed slowly down her neck.

I reached up and put my arms back around her, rolling her over on her side, our lips still pressed together, when the porch light came on.

"What's going on out here! Liv? You OK?"

Then a few seconds later, "Oh, my God! Get off her, you son of a bitch!"

I looked up just in time to see a shoe coming right at me. I rolled back to the side a split second before my face would have been caved in. I reached up, grabbed the leg, and twisted it, causing another body to fall on top of us.

"It's OK! It's me! Bud, it's me!—Perc!"

Olivia's brother, Bud, now had his arms and legs mixed in pretty well with ours. He stopped squirming long enough to soak in what I was saying.

"Perc? That really you? Sweet Jesus—you scared me to death. I almost killed you. What the hell are you doing here?"

"I'm home on leave. I just got here."

Bud laughed and said, "Well, I don't think you *just* got here."

He stood up and towered over us, catching his breath. He then brushed the dirt from his pants and studied both of us before saying,

"I was just on my way to get a paper. I think I'll be gone a long time." He winked at me and saluted as he stepped over us and headed down the sidewalk. He stopped at the gate and repeated, "A *long* time."

At that moment I realized Olivia and I still hadn't said a single word to each other. I stood up, pulling her up with me. I drew her to me and kissed her one more time, this time trying to show her through my kiss how much I loved her.

I then backed away from her and asked, "So, how you doing these days?"

"Oh, it's you, Perc? It was so dark I wasn't sure who it was."

"Very funny," I said. "You do this with all bums and hoboes who come around looking for a handout?"

She smiled and said, "Well, we each contribute to the war in our own way."

"Come here, you," I said in my new sergeant voice. "That's an order!"

"No, *you* come here," she responded, motioning me to step forward.

I looked down and for the first time noticed I had lost a shoe in the melee with her brother. With the tip of the remaining shoe I made a line in the grass.

"How about if we meet in the middle?" I asked.

"How about if we go inside?" she responded.

I picked her up and carried her up the steps. When we were inside the living room she turned and said sternly, "How could you not let me know you were coming home? Look at me. I'm a mess."

"I am looking at you," I said. "I don't see a mess. I see the most beautiful woman in the entire world. And I'm in love with her."

She pressed a finger to my lips. "Shhhhhh!" she said. "Don't say anything. Just kiss me again."

I was home.

15

MARRIAGES

The next morning I was jolted awake by a heavy autumn sunlight creeping through the thin, flowered curtains covering the living room windows. I had not slept well. Olivia's couch had a sharp spring that seemed to follow my back every time I tried to get comfortable, so I never actually did fall into a sound sleep. While trying to rub the kinks out of my neck, I saw Olivia quietly tiptoeing toward me from her bed room.

"What do you want to do today, soldier?" Olivia asked as she knelt down next to me and kissed me softly.

"I think it should be a rule from now on that we start each day by kissing. Don't you?"

The way she then pulled me close and kissed me told me it was pretty plain she had the same notion.

* * *

Olivia fixed breakfast while I shaved and got dressed. After army food, I could have eaten wallpaper and been tickled. But Olivia was an incredible cook, one who took great store in presentation of the foods she prepared. The breakfast table looked like something out of a magazine. The table had a red-and-white checkered tablecloth and the dishes and silverware were arranged neatly. A small vase of dried flowers sat in the middle of the table. Napkins matching the tablecloth were folded into the shape of fans and were put into our glasses. It all looked so nice, so fancy, I hated to sit down and mess it up. Compared to our mess hall at Fort Bliss, this was pure heaven. "Yes," I thought. "I *am* the luckiest man in the world."

I was glad we had at least a little time to ourselves the night before because it soon started to look like we'd never be alone again. Bud came home right in the middle of breakfast and said, "That bacon I smell? And biscuits?"

That was all he said as he sat down at the table—right between us. He had been nice enough to leave us alone the night before, so I didn't growl too much as he devoured most of the food Olivia had prepared.

After breakfast I cleaned up the kitchen while Olivia got dressed. I had to take a turn at KP only twice since being in the service, but I still kept laughing at the thought of how clean the men had left their plates the nights I washed dishes. Each time I'd laugh, Bud would look over his paper and ask, "What's so funny." Each time I started to explain, he'd interrupt and yell either "OK!" or "Dammit!" as he scanned the scores and stories on the sports page.

Olivia finally finished dressing and came in to rescue me. I was wearing her apron so I wouldn't get anything on my uniform.

"Cute," she said, eyeing me as she came into the kitchen. "I can get you a job down at the lunch counter at Woolworth's if you'd like."

"Very funny," I responded. "I think I'll stick to the army a little longer. You meet a better class of people there," I teased while flinging soap suds on Bud's lap. Without looking up from the paper he said, "Damn. That wrestling has got to be fixed! My guy Moose lost again!"

"Let's go," Olivia said, rolling her eyes. "He'll be in his own little world until he's read every last word on his sports page. He won't even notice we're gone."

She patted him on the shoulder and said, "Bye, Bud. Perc and I are running off. See you in a couple of months."

"OK," Bud said. "See you later. Damn—he lost *again*! Would you look at that!"

She was right. Bud didn't even notice us leave.

* * *

Olivia thought I had lost my mind, but because the weather was unseasonably warm, the first thing I wanted to do was take a walk with her through the Ville to see familiar sights. It had become my home, and it seemed like I had been gone forever. I was aching to see if any changes had been made and to hear news of old friends and acquaintances. Olivia loved to tell stories about people in the neighborhood, so I knew she'd be the best guide and source of news I could have. Some people at school teased that she was the worst gossip in all of St. Louis, but the teasing was all done to her face. Even she laughed at that assessment. She may have "carried tales," as some put it, but there was never a mean side to the way she relayed the stories. I always thought of her as something of a "town crier," like towns used to have back in the old days. She never meant any harm to anyone; she just enjoyed passing along information about who was doing what and when. It was as simple as that.

The timing of my leave couldn't have been better. As luck would have it, Olivia had already made arrangements to have most of the day off from teaching to help organize the neighborhood scrap drive, so we were going to be able to spend just about the whole day together.

And then tomorrow, I figured, would be the big day. Knot-tying day. Hitchin' day. Ring day.

Ring day! I had forgotten completely about getting the rings! I was going to have to sneak away at some point in the day to get them, but, again, it would have to be on the sly. I'd have to get it done somehow without anyone else knowing about it. Secrecy was still the order of the day thanks to the Board of Education's rule about females and marriage not mixing, that is, if they intended to keep their jobs.

It suddenly dawned on me that for as much as I worried and stewed about whether she had said "Yes" in response to my Pepsi-Cola proposal, I hadn't even asked her about it yet. The night before had been so beautiful, so wonderful, I hadn't thought to bring it up. But I knew I should now.

There was a bench at the corner of Sarah Street and Finney. We were already holding hands, so I tightened my grip and led her over to it.

"Let's sit a minute," I said.

"My, my. Soldier boy already tired? I would have thought they'd have whipped you into shape by now."

I didn't laugh, so she could tell something was up. "What is it?" she asked. "You OK?"

"I'm not sure," I replied. "I think I'll know in a minute."

"What is it? Tell me."

"Listen to me a minute, OK?" I said, my voice cracking. "This is serious. I have been meaning to ask you something. Did you get that record I sent to you? You know, the Pepsi-Cola record?"

Olivia studied my face for a minute before responding. She cleared her throat and said, "Yes, I got it."

"Well?" I asked.

"Well what?"

"Did you hear what the record said?"

"It was awful scratchy. It sort of sounded like you were playing a banjo or something. But I did like the song—what I could hear of it. You know, it's a funny thing, though. It sounded near the very end like your friend Doc proposed to me. Why, I don't even know the man."

She pretended to clear her throat again. I could also see the faintest hint of a smile starting to creep up and knew I'd been had.

"Ha ha," I said. "You're a stitch. You should get a job with the carnival as the Laugh Lady."

Then I added, "I hope you and Doc will be very happy together. Be sure to name your first kid after me."

She could tell I had been tortured enough. She reached over and took my hand and said, "I guess that wasn't Doc, right?"

I nodded my head.

"Then I guess it was you, right?"

I nodded my head again.

"Then I'm also guessing you didn't get my message when I called the base. Heaven help me, but I said *Yes*."

I pulled her over and hugged her as tightly as I could. A little too loud I said, "The message Doc gave me was 'Yes,' but I didn't know for sure what question you were responding to. You don't know how miserable I have been thinking about this. For all I knew you could have been answering my question about whether I should go to OCS."

I pulled back from her and, lowering my voice, said, "Look, I know I'm not the best catch in the world. I'm flat broke, I'm in the army for goodness knows how long, so we won't even be together again for a long, long time. I can't offer you anything for the present except my love. But I offer all of it to you. Every ounce of it. Every speck of it. I'd give anything if I could look into a crystal ball to see the future, but I can't. All I can say is that for now, for right this minute, all I can give to you is me—all of me. That's all I have to give. If you were smart, you'd get up and run. As fast as you can."

She jumped up and pretended she was going to bolt off. I grabbed her and pulled her back down. She squinched up her eyes and said, "Well… I guess that will have to do for now. As you know, I come from a long line of gambling people. You may be a long shot, but I think I'll take a flyer on you. I just have this feeling, as Pop would say, that you'll go wire to wire. But you *are* right. I *should* get up and run."

"You do realize if we go through with this we can't tell anyone but our families and just a few other folks. If anyone finds out, you'll lose your job. I won't stand for that. Losing your job would kill you, and I know it."

"You really are slow, soldier. What do you think I have been doing since I got that record? I did some checking, and we can drive over to Illinois for a nice, quiet ceremony. If we marry in Illinois, the news won't appear in the St. Louis papers. No one will be the wiser. As a matter of fact, I already know a justice of the peace just outside East St. Louis who said he'd be glad to help. And more important, he said he'd keep his trap shut."

"You mean you had all this already figured out and didn't say anything to me? You let me go on and suffer?"

"Come here, you," I said, drawing her close again.

Her kiss told me everything else I needed to know.

* * *

We sat on the bench for the longest time kidding each other about what we imagined our children would look like once we actually could start a family. Olivia said they would take after her side of the family and the boys would be built as strong as Bluto and the girls would be slim and tall like singer Bea Roxie. She said if they looked like my side of the family the boys would look like Popeye and the girls like Olive

Oyl. I responded that I thought the boys would look smart like their father and the girls would be as pretty as my mother. I also added I hoped none would have Olivia's father's nose, which looked to me as big as a pear.

I also added, "Actually, as soon as we can, I think we should shoot for 'Irish twins'."

"Irish twins? What in the world is that?" Olivia asked.

"That's when you have two babies so close together that both are actually born in the same year. Can be done, you know. One of the guys in my outfit knows a guy who has kids that are just a little over ten months apart. Both born in the same year. Now *I* think that is a worthy goal to shoot for, don't you?"

"Are you out of your mind?" she shrieked. "Two babies in the same year? I don't think so! That's never going to happen unless you carry one of them!"

"Oh, I'll be glad to 'carry' them, one in each arm. You just have to have them first."

She playfully punched at me, and I grabbed her to kiss her again when, out of the corner of my eye, I saw Reverend Daniels, the minister of her church, and his wife coming straight toward us.

Reverend Daniels shouted, "Why, Inman Perkins! What in the world are you doing here? It's so good to see you, my son!"

He shook my hand, then pulled me to him and hugged me.

"Hi, Reverend. It's good to see you, too. I've really missed you. And you, too, Mrs. Daniels. I didn't know we were getting leave until right before we left, so I couldn't let anyone know my plans. I guess I just sort of showed up."

"And I suppose this young lady was happy to see you? Hello, Olivia. How are you?"

Then a quizzical look came over his face. Before Olivia could reply, he added, "What, no school today?"

"I couldn't be better," she responded. "I'm playing hooky. I hope the truant officer doesn't catch me."

We all laughed as she continued, "I'm the faculty sponsor for the new scrap drive. I'm going to meet some kids and their parents in the parking lot over at Waldman Auto Parts in a few minutes. And Inman has volunteered to help."

"Didn't they teach you not to volunteer for anything in the army?" he asked me.

"Seems like a good cause," I said. "I read that the city of St. Louis set some kind of record for donating scrap metal. Believe me, we can use it."

"You're right, of course. It's good you're going to lend a hand while you're back home. I know you must have a lot to do, a lot of people to see."

"Olivia and I were just taking a walk around the neighborhood. I miss this place so bad. I didn't live here all that long, but my heart is here now. This is where I belong."

I looked over at Olivia, who was making a face that said, "Let's get out of here! Time to go!"

"And we want you back here as soon as we can have you. The war won't last forever."

Suddenly his eyes lit up and he continued, "Why don't you come over and stay with us while you're here? We've got the extra bedroom. It'd be no trouble at all. We'd be glad to have you. What do you say?"

"Thanks, Reverend, but Bud already set up a place for me to stay at their place, so I'm all set. But thanks for asking. That's very kind of you."

Mrs. Daniels raised an eyebrow but didn't say anything. Before Reverend Daniels could respond, Olivia stood up and announced that we really did have to get going, that the kids helping with the scrap drive were waiting for us. We quickly said our good-byes and started walking toward Waldman's when Reverend Daniels shouted back at us, "I'll expect you in church. See you again soon!"

"Boy is he going to be surprised," Olivia whispered. "And mad, too, when he eventually finds out someone else married us."

"I know," I said. "But I think he'll understand. I think everyone who knows us will understand. Understand?"

"Not a word, soldier. But I'll take it on faith. And, by the way, what did you mean when you said to him you were 'all set'? I think I resent that," she said playfully.

I took her hand in mine and said, "You'll find out. Believe me, yes you will!"

We walked quietly for a while until I said, jokingly, "Think we'll go to hell for this?"

"Why, Inman Perkins—you getting cold feet?"

I frowned and said, "Hardly. I'm just sorry we have to sneak around so much. It just doesn't seem fair."

"It isn't fair," she said. "But I can live with it if you can. What do you say?"

"I say I'm the luckiest man in the world."

And I meant it.

* * *

We walked to Waldman's Auto Parts, where students and their parents were sorting donations for the scrap drive. Mr. Waldman deserved a medal for allowing this. His parking lot looked like a junkyard. Stacked everywhere were piles of tires and other rubber items, old pans and metal kitchen utensils and appliances, and old newspapers and magazines. To the right of the magazines was a makeshift storage bin for miscellaneous metal objects, like old car parts, timeworn store signs, and even a pile of broken toys. I even saw coffee cans filled with bottle tops and old keys. In the back corner of the lot someone had also constructed a huge pyramid from tin cans of varying sizes. One of the parents had a camera, and the students were taking turns getting their pictures taken in front of it.

"Holy Moses! Would you look at that!" I said as I looked over next to the building. There, neatly rolled together, was the largest ball of tinfoil I had ever seen. It was about three feet in diameter. Right behind it was an even larger ball of string.

Olivia said hi to a few parents and walked around thanking the students for their hard work. She then called for the attention of the group.

"I'm impressed. Really impressed. This is coming along beyond my wildest dreams. I'm so proud of all of you, and I know our soldiers defending our country would be proud of you, too."

She walked over to the giant ball of tinfoil, touched it, and said, "Do all of you really understand what you see here? This isn't tinfoil, and those aren't piles of cans and bottles and pans over there. What you're really looking at are tanks and jeeps and bullets and bandages and airplanes."

Olivia paused before adding, "It's even more than that. What you're looking at is our victory, our freedom. You'd never know it to look at that pile of old fruit cans over there, but those are going to help us all keep this great country of ours safe from our enemies. There's an old saying, 'One man's junk is another man's treasure.' Well, what some would call trash here is something we can all treasure. I'm proud of all of you."

The students and their parents applauded and cheered. She waved for them to stop and continued, "But don't take my word for it. Let's hear from one of our own fighting men, Master Sergeant Inman Perkins of the United States Army Air Corps!"

I hadn't expected this and said, "Thanks..." to Olivia as she shoved me forward toward the group. I looked out at the faces staring at me and felt proud. Proud of the students and their fathers and mothers. Proud of Olivia. Proud of the Ville.

"I didn't know I'd be saying anything," I began, staring over at Olivia again. "But I'm happy to do so. Miss Merriwether is right. Your efforts are helping us win the war. And make no mistake about it, we *will* win this war."

The students and their parents cheered again.

"We're going to win because people like you care—because of the work like all of you are doing right here. I've seen the planes, the jeeps, the munitions that grow from drives like this. Heck, from the looks of things, I think you've got at least a tank or two right here."

I walked over next to the ball of tinfoil and continued, "I never thought I'd be so thrilled to see so much junk, but I agree—these piles really are treasures. I want to thank all of you for helping with this drive. Keep up the good work. Bless you all."

The group applauded as I stepped back and let Olivia take over again.

"It's obvious you don't need me here anymore, so I'm going to be taking off in a minute," she said to the group. "You're all doing just fine. I'll walk around before I leave and take a few notes about all the different items we have so I can put it in my report. Then I'll make arrangements to get someone here early next week to pick up everything. Parents, you can really help today before you leave by making sure the new things that just came in get sorted and put into the right piles. That would be a big help. And don't forget—we'll meet here again at some point next week to see what the Boy Scouts are bringing over. I'll let you know when. I'd really appreciate it if some of you parents could come back then to lend a hand with the sorting."

Olivia paused before adding, playfully, "And you kids—get back to school now. Shoo! Go on now."

We walked around the various piles while Olivia made a few notes. "I really am proud of them. Look at this stuff. Can you believe how much they've scrounged and rounded up?"

"I'm proud of them, too," she said. "More than they will ever know."

* * *

When we finished there, Olivia wanted us to make a quick stop a few blocks up the street to visit with one of her girlfriends, but I begged off at the last minute, saying I just remembered I wanted to get a decent haircut while home. Henry Austin's barbershop, where I used to get my hair cut, was only a few blocks away and I asked if she minded if I ran over there. Before she could respond, I took off my hat and pointed to the bald spot near my right temple and said, "Do you really want to get married to a guy who looks like the Wild Man of Borneo?"

Olivia laughed and said, "OK, I get your point. But I also know men and barbershops. I don't want you staying there all day shooting the breeze with your loafer friends."

She looked at her watch, tapping it and then lifting it to her ear. "Great. Broken again. I don't know what time it is. Do you?"

"It's 1100," I said. "Don't worry. It won't take long for the haircut. Where should we meet up and when?"

"I don't know about 'eleven hundred'," she laughed, teasing me about the military time reference. "How about if we meet at the Steamboat Cafe around the corner for lunch right at noon?"

I smiled and responded, "How about Woolworth's lunch counter instead?"

"Want to show off that uniform, do we?" she teased.

"Very funny. Actually, yes. But besides that I've been craving one of their cherry Cokes ever since I left. That be OK with you?"

"I'll treat," she said. "Noon it is."

We headed our separate directions. I walked as quickly as I could to Evans Jewelry Store over on Taylor Avenue to see about buying our rings. The clerk there, a very tall and thin young girl who didn't look old enough to work in a store of this type, showed me several different styles of gold bands, some plain, others with etched designs on them. The plain ones were more in line with the price range I had, so I picked out one for me and then guessed at Olivia's ring size. The clerk said she could always have it sized later if it didn't fit. It suddenly dawned on me that I needed a cover story. I didn't know the clerk, but the grapevine at the Ville was very short and I didn't want anyone to know about the rings. Just to be on the safe side, I told the clerk the rings were actually for a buddy of mine in the service who was getting married back at Fort Bliss. I said I was just doing him a favor by picking them up for him while I was home on leave because the jewelry store in El Paso was incredibly expensive and gouged the soldiers. I went on and on to the point the story started getting out of hand.

"And besides," I added, "My buddy hurt his leg on the obstacle course and can't get out to the jewelry store there now anyway." I realized how dumb that sounded and added, hoping to make the story I was weaving a little more plausible, "And his fiancée was in a car wreck and is laid up, too." I was so deep into the story I figured I might as well add, "But they don't want to postpone their wedding just because they're a little banged up. They might both be in 'Roosevelts'—wheelchairs—but they'll both make it to the church."

The clerk gave me one of those "You've got to be kidding" looks and smiled at me, but to her credit she didn't say anything except, "I'll wrap these up now. Anything else I can help you with?"

While I waited for the rings to be put into boxes, out of the corner of my eye I noticed a watch very similar to the one Olivia had. I wanted her to have a special wedding present, so I bought it too. It was already on sale, and the clerk said she could take an extra 10 percent off because I was in the military. That was the new store policy, and I thought it a good one.

Just as I was getting ready to leave, the clerk said, "Oh, and by the way, please tell your 'buddy' I wish him good luck with his marriage—and that I hope he gets out of the wheelchair real soon. That's got to be uncomfortable."

I was so thrilled to find the watch for Olivia that the clerk's words didn't register right away. Then, too quickly, I responded, "Oh yeah. Thanks. I… I know he'll appreciate your kind words. I'll pass them along."

As soon as I was back out on the sidewalk I could hear the clerk howling with laughter. What a dope I was. I just hoped she would keep her mouth shut.

I was so excited about the rings and the watch I completely forgot about getting a haircut. I was about a block away from Woolworth's when I thought of it, but it was too late to run back. I had beaten Olivia to the lunch counter, so I decided to go ahead and order something to drink while I waited. The cherry Coke tasted just like I remembered. I had them put an extra couple of squirts of cherry juice into it, and that made it so sweet the back of my throat started tingling.

I just finished the last of it as Olivia walked in. We had a great lunch of hamburgers, french fries, and cherry Cokes. I stopped at two hamburgers, but I could have eaten three. I had three cherry Cokes. That lunch may sound pretty ordinary or dull or odd to some home on leave, but to me it was just what the doctor ordered. I was in heaven.

I also had some quick explaining to do. When I took off my cap, Olivia noticed right away that I hadn't gone to the barbershop. I told her I ran into some old friends and used up all my time visiting with them. I don't think she believed me, but the second hamburger came just in time for me to stuff my mouth so that I couldn't keep talking.

The rest of the day flew by. We walked down my old street, Easton Avenue, so I could visit with old neighbors and see how the local businesses were getting along. We stopped at Baker's Hardware and found out that his son, Tom, an old cardplaying buddy of mine, was stationed somewhere out in the Pacific. As a matter of fact, most of the sons and daughters of those on my street who were in the military seemed to have been sent to the Pacific theater to fight the Japanese.

I hadn't realized just how far we had walked, and Olivia's feet were killing her, so we hopped the next streetcar we could and headed back. Olivia complained again about her watch, and I just smiled. That is, I smiled until I realized how late it was getting. We made it back to Olivia's as quickly as we could so we'd have some time alone before Bud came home from work. However, when we got there, the floodgates opened. As soon as we sat on the couch, there was a knock on the door. Reverend Danielson stopped by to give me a special, smaller version of the Bible that he was sending to all those from the Ville serving in the armed forces. Of course, before he left he took the time to point out several verses that he said would be particularly appropriate for me to study.

It wasn't ten minutes after he left that our principal from Sumner, Mr. Brantley, stopped by to say hello and fill me in on his plans for me after the war. In addition to teaching science classes, he wanted me to continue teaching driver's training. I laughed and told him about my experiences teaching those in the outfit how to handle jeeps and trucks. I assured him I had learned much and wouldn't let my Sumner students get as out of control as the men had.

Next to knock on the door was Al Worthington, a friend of Bud's who was being trained at Wagner Electric to make brake parts for military vehicles. Al said he wouldn't bother us—that he'd wait out on the porch swing for Bud to get home. Olivia and I sat on the couch and turned on the radio. However, every time I got ready to put my arms around her, the porch swing would bang against the side of the house, causing us to jump. So much for our plan to steal a quiet moment together in the late afternoon.

Soon after that Bud came home, and Al followed him into the house. About five minutes later, two more of their friends came over to have a beer and talk sports, so Olivia and I moved out to the porch swing. Once in the swing we might as well have been waving flags because it seemed like every person who walked by had to stop to pass the time.

I finally suggested we move to the back porch to get a little privacy, but she responded, "Won't do a bit of good. Hear that clanking?

They're already out there pitchin' horseshoes, in the middle of winter! And besides, horseshoes and beer aren't the best combination to sit around, if you know what I mean."

I didn't admit it, but the attention we were getting as folks walked past was nice. It was also another way to find out how others in the Ville were getting along, so I didn't complain. I think Olivia was uncomfortable because she was now the focus of the conversations—instead of the person passing along the information. I teased her and said I thought that was good for her for a change.

She went into the house to get us some coffee while I sat back in the swing and gave it a big push. When she came back out she was rolling her eyes as she said, "It figures."

"What figures?" I asked.

"Well, guess who else is spending the night with us tonight? Bud's friend, Al. His landlord sprayed some kind of bug killer all over his flat and he isn't supposed to sleep there tonight. So, good old Bud told him he could stay here. You know what that means, don't you? Al gets the couch tonight, and you get to sleep with Bud, the human buzz saw. Lucky you."

"Not to worry," I said. "I'll get my rest. I've got a big day tomorrow, and I'll be ready for it. You forget I have been sleeping in a barracks full of snorers and sleepwalkers of all types. They snore even worse than you."

"I don't snore!" she protested in mock disgust. "Thanks a lot!"

"Like the dickens, you don't! Last night I thought the Missouri-Pacific was coming right through the house. Shoot—I almost jumped off the couch and grabbed for my luggage! I almost yelled for a porter!"

With her index finger Olivia motioned me to bend down so she could whisper something in my ear. Instead of whispering, she playfully bit my ear and said, "If you notice any snoring tomorrow night, it will mean you're doing something wrong."

I pulled her close to me. "Heaven help me, I do love you. Snoring and all."

I started to kiss her again when I noticed Reverend Danielson running up the sidewalk toward us. "One more thing," he said, out of breath. "Inman—I forgot to ask if you'd be willing to say a few words tonight at the church supper. I know it's short notice, but can you two make it?"

Olivia and I looked at each other, and at the same time said, "What the heck. Might as well!" We both laughed.

Reverend Danielson smiled curiously at both of us and said, "Good. See you both at six. Don't be late!" With that, he headed back down the sidewalk, pretending to cover his eyes with his hands so he wouldn't see any more of our kisses as he departed.

"So much for spending a quiet evening together," I said.

Olivia put her arm around me and said, "Don't worry. We'll make up for it tomorrow."

"Darned if I don't believe you," I said pulling her close again. "Darned if I don't."

I could tell from the way she smiled back at me that there'd never be a dull moment in our marriage.

Yes, I really did feel like the luckiest man in the world.

16

PROMISES

Charles Dickens hit the nail right on the head at the beginning of *A Tale of Two Cities* when he said, roughly: It was a good day. It was a bad day. It was the best of times. It was the worst of times.

Our wedding day seemed to start out exactly the same way.

And it certainly was a morning of contrasts.

I woke up so much in love I wanted to shout it to the whole neighborhood from the roof of Sumner High School. Actually, it was Bud snoring beside me that woke me, but after I brushed the cobwebs from my eyes and got my bearings, I lit a cigarette, propped myself up in bed, and lost myself in my dreams for the future. Unfortunately, that peace and tranquility didn't last long. I suddenly felt like I was back at the barracks. Bud's friend Al came wandering in, apparently looking for something—or possibly sleepwalking—and left as quickly as he had entered the room. I crawled out of bed and looked into the living room to make sure he was OK and saw that all the other horseshoe players had decided to spend the night and were sleeping all over the place. The living room looked like a flophouse, bodies tangled up like a pile of twisted rope. I stepped on someone's hand as I gingerly made my way to the bathroom, and the poor soul let out a sleepy howl.

I decided as long as I was up I might as well go ahead and get cleaned up and dressed for the day. Once in the bathroom, I drifted back into thoughts of what the future would hold. Mixing shaving and daydreaming turned out not to be such a good idea. Just a few strokes into attacking my whiskers, I cut my throat as badly as I had since I first started shaving. It had to happen on my wedding day. Blood continued to ooze down my neck and onto my chest as I continued my shave. I tried sticking toilet paper on the wound to see if I could stem the flow, but even that didn't work. "You look like you work in a slaughterhouse," I said to myself as I stared into the mirror and shook my head.

On most mornings, my shaving time was my "thinking time," time I used to ponder everything from the upcoming day's events to longer-term issues and dreams. While I continued to shave, I realized there were still many contrasts that I hadn't yet sorted through in my own mind. I had become used to giving orders and being in control. By contrast, for my own marriage ceremony, my future wife had made all the arrangements. All of them. With Olivia, I knew life would be a partnership. I *hoped* we'd always share in making decisions, but as bullheaded as we both were, I knew that was going to take some work. As I started wiping the rest of the soap from my chin I realized that while I was a free man now and master of my own fate, I would be married in just a few hours—and immediately take on the responsibilities of being a husband, even if I would be thousands of miles away. Related to this was the biggest contrast of all. I was home, happier than I had been in a long, long time. I was getting married to the love of my life. Then in a few more days I'd be headed back to Fort Bliss. How ironic: Fort "Bliss." For all the bliss I was feeling on this morning, another "Bliss" was going to take much of that away from me all too soon. What bothered me most was the almost certain knowledge that the battalion wouldn't even be staying there much longer. Scuttlebutt, which had been right more than wrong of late, was saying we were shipping overseas within the month. It would be bad enough being apart, but an ocean between us, too? This was some way to begin the responsibilities of being a husband.

Other contrasts drifted through my head as I continued shaving the same spot on my left cheek over and over. I was so happy, I wanted everyone to know we were tying the knot. The school board rule made that impossible. I wanted to start a family right away. However, that couldn't be done because, again, no one could know we were married or Olivia would lose her job. My thoughts bounced from Olivia's job to thinking about my own future employment. Mr. Brantley had plans for me at Sumner that sounded pretty darn good. I didn't even want to think about what would happen when I got back from the service. If the marriage rule didn't get rescinded, how could we hide our marriage then? On the other side of the coin, Colonel Ellis seemed to think that I was a sure bet to be sent to Officer Candidate School. A career as an officer in the army would open so many new doors. There were too many contrasts, too many choices ahead.

The more I stood there thinking and trying to get my neck to stop bleeding, the more I realized the scales really did seem to be tipped heavily toward the good side of the ledger. Yes, it was true that I didn't have much to offer Olivia but a very uncertain future at best. But even in that uncertainty, I was positive that our love would get us through whatever obstacles and potholes showed up in the road along the way. Was I being fair to her? Was it right to get married when we'd be spending the first part of our marriage apart? There were so many questions I didn't have resolved yet in my own mind. Our journey certainly wouldn't be easy, but I felt as long as we were together, there wouldn't be much we couldn't overcome. Was all of this cold feet? I didn't think so. It was just plain common sense creeping in. When two people are in love, common sense doesn't always rule the day. On this day, our hearts would rule. We'd just have to trust fate. It would be interesting to see which way the scales tipped after a few areas immediately out of our control got sorted out. Time is both an enemy and an ally.

I was jolted back to the present when another of Bud's friends sleepily threw open the bathroom door, which hit my arm, which caused another gash on my cheek the size of the Grand Canyon.

I was going to look plenty handsome for Olivia this day.

* * *

The night before I had called Doc to let him know the tentative schedule for the day and to ask if there was any way he could drive us over to East St. Louis. He said he'd be glad to and that he'd have no problem getting a car from his uncle's garage. He asked if he could bring Judy along, and I said that would be just fine, that I was looking forward to meeting her. I also asked him if he wanted to make it a double ceremony, and he stuttered and stammered so much I suggested that just maybe he wasn't ready to make such a big leap.

"It isn't the jump I'm worried about," he responded. "It's the landing that has me spooked."

We both laughed, but it was clear he felt that he and Judy had a few matters to discuss before they'd be ready to exchange vows.

Doc also told me that he had been in contact with Williams. He wasn't going to be able to join us because he was visiting his "cousin." Doc cleared his throat and said, "It's more than kissin' those cousins are doin'. Hell, if she's as pretty as he says, he may just go AWOL and we'll never see him again. Wouldn't that be something?"

"I'm not worried about Williams," I said. "He can take care of himself. I'm sorry he can't make it, but I'm sure he'll keep himself entertained today. I can certainly understand that."

"Entertained? Is that what they are calling it now?"

"Now, let's not tease him about this too much when we get back to the base. OK? If you do, I'll have to tell Judy about a certain incident with a wolf spider one night in your bunk...."

He cut me off, "OK, OK. My lips are sealed. At least until he gets on my nerves again."

Doc asked me what time we needed to head over to East St. Louis. We decided he and Judy should come over to pick us up about 9:00 A.M. Olivia had said the justice of the peace had told her to be there by 10:00, so I figured we'd make it in plenty of time if we left about an hour before that. It was just going to be the four of us going together. Bud had been told the day before he was going to be moved to another shift at work, so he wouldn't be able to make it. We decided against taking Olivia's parents with us, whom she had already taken into her confidence about all this, to avoid suspicion if others from the Ville saw us all heading down the road. I hated all this sneaking around, but under the circumstances, there wasn't much else that could be done.

After shaving and putting on my uniform, I made my way through the pile of bodies in the living room, stepping on a foot this time, to the kitchen to see what I could scare up for breakfast. I had just sat down to a bowl of Wheaties when the kitchen door opened and Olivia walked in. I dropped my spoon back in the bowl and said, "Wow! Would you look at you! You look incredible."

She was wearing a light blue skirt and a white blouse. She also had on white gloves that ran all the way up to her elbows. I had seen these gloves in magazines, but this was the first time I had seen them in the flesh. She was wearing white shoes, and had a matching white purse over her arm. In her left hand she carried a white hat with a cloth band matching the color of the dress. I whistled again, "Would you look at you!"

I motioned for her to come sit on my lap.

She shook her head and said, "Put your tongue back in your mouth, soldier. No tasting the fruit until the tree's planted in your yard."

I pulled her down on my lap, but before I could kiss her, four sleepy and hungry ex–horseshoe players started circling the kitchen as they foraged for food. They completely ignored us, finally pulling chairs right up next to us at the table.

"Are we ever going to get some time alone?" I asked to no one in particular.

"It will be a miracle if we do," Olivia responded. "A complete miracle."

* * *

Doc and Judy knocked on the front door about ten minutes to nine. I was glad they were early because I wanted us to have a little time for introductions and for visiting before we hit the road. Doc had been right. Judy was a knockout. She was a tall woman, built like actress and singer Lena Horne. She had a great sense of humor, which became obvious the minute we met. As she extended her hand to shake mine, she said, "I'm so pleased to meet you. You don't look nearly as mean and ugly as Doc said you were."

"Just wait until you get to know him," Olivia chimed in, stepping over to shake Judy's hand.

Judy and Olivia hit it off right away. I have absolutely no idea how it came up so quickly in conversation, but almost immediately it was determined they both had the same size feet. Before Doc and I could get a word in edgewise, they were both off into Olivia's bedroom to look for different pairs of shoes to go with their outfits.

"What about my shoes?" Doc asked, mimicking their voices.

"Think I should put on my combat boots to match my eyes?"

"We better get used to this," I replied. "I have the feeling we're going to be spending half our lives waiting for them to do something. It'll be just like the army: 'Hurry up and wait!' But they're going to be worth it. And by the way, you didn't half describe how pretty Judy is. She's knockdown gorgeous."

"And Olivia. Wow! Pardner, you know you don't deserve her, don't you?"

"Don't I know it," I responded. "But she hasn't figured it out yet, so keep quiet."

Before too long, and both sporting new shoes, Olivia and Judy rejoined us. "So, what should we do today?" Olivia asked. "You boys have any plans to speak of?"

"Very funny," I said. "No, actually I don't have any special plans. You, Doc? If you don't, I think we can catch the ponies in the first race over at Fairmount Park. Want to go?"

"Now who's being funny?" Olivia asked. "Get your big rump out in the car and let's get over to East St. Louis before I change my mind. Get going," she said as she made a shooing motion toward the door.

"Yes ma'am," I said. I bowed and continued, "Anything you say."

I felt a playful kick against my rump and bolted for the door. Doc said, "I don't need to be kicked. I'm going! I'm going!"

I was the first one out the door and the first one to see it. Doc had said he'd be able to drive us to East St. Louis. What he didn't say was what kind of vehicle we'd be in.

"You've got to be kidding," I said, stopping short at the edge of the porch.

"Oh, no!" Olivia shouted right behind me.

There, parked next to the curb right in front of us, was a hearse. A Johnson and Harms hearse. Very black. Very long. Very loud.

So much for sneaking around.

A crowd had already assembled on the sidewalk, spilling into Olivia's front yard. As soon as Olivia came out onto the porch I heard someone say, "Well, it isn't her."

Reverend Danielson, clutching his Bible, came barging his way through the crowd. Out of breath, hands resting on his knees, he gasped, "Olivia, is it your brother?"

The crowd let out a collective gasp as they waited for her reply.

"No, Reverend. We're fine. I'm fine. Bud's fine. We're all fine. Really."

"Then what's this hearse doing here?" he said, panting and gesturing back toward the curb.

Olivia looked at me and said, "Why don't you tell him, Perc. What is that hearse doing here?"

We were caught red-handed, but at least no one knew what we were guilty of. At least not yet. I didn't want to lie to a minister, so I pointed over to Doc and said, "This is Doc, my best friend. We're stationed together at Fort Bliss. He's from Kinloch. And this is his girl, Judy. She's from Kinloch, too."

Reverend Danielson just stood there, staring at me, still gasping for breath. The look on his face said, "So?"

So I continued. "Doc's a mechanic. His uncle has a garage. We're taking our girls out this afternoon, and he was able to borrow this… this…this hearse to drive. Right, Doc?"

Before he could say anything, a police car, siren blaring, came roaring down the street, inching its way through the crowd until it was parked right in front of the hearse. Two officers ran through the crowd yelling, "Let us through! Make way!" They stopped when they saw Reverend Danielson and asked, "What's going on here? We got word someone was shot."

The crowd gasped again.

"Not yet, they're not," Olivia said, smirking, first looking at me and then at Doc.

In the assembled crowd I could hear people asking "Who died?" and "Who got shot?"

"We're all OK, really," I said to the officers. "This is my friend, Doc. He's a mechanic. He just borrowed this…. Well, he borrowed it so we can take our girls out today. That's all, really."

The officers eyed Doc. In his uniform, he looked anything but a mechanic. "That true?" the older of the officers asked. "Where'd you get this hearse?"

Doc explained the situation to the officer and Reverend Danielson, repeating what I had just said. While he had their attention, Olivia kicked me in the shin like a mule kicking a fence post. I grabbed my left leg and hopped up and down, nearly falling off the porch. A few nearest the porch laughed. Word was starting to spread toward the back of the crowd that no one had died, so my hopping was now the center of attention.

"What's the matter with you, Perkins?" Reverend Danielson asked.

Olivia responded for me, "Oh, he hasn't seen anything yet."

Raising her voice so that everyone could hear it, she continued, "Can you believe it? He comes to take me on a date in a hearse! Can you believe it!"

There was a collective groan from the women in the crowd and laughter from the men.

Finally Reverend Danielson told the officers he'd vouch for us, so they headed back through the crowd toward their car. The younger officer turned and said, "Wouldn't catch me riding around in that."

Someone nearby shouted, "Hell, I wouldn't be caught dead in that!" much to the approval of the crowd, a crowd now buzzing with nervous laughter.

Just as the police car pulled away, Bud and his horseshoe buddies came staggering out to the porch. Al had on Olivia's robe and was smoking a cigar. "Damn, who died?" he asked.

"It'll be all of you if you don't get back in that house right this instant," Olivia shouted.

Practically clawing each other, they shrank back into the living room. From the crowd I could hear new voices saying:

"Wouldn't catch me in that thing."

"Bad luck to ride in a hearse."

"Don't look right at it or you'll be the next to die."

"We're sorry, sir," I said to Reverend Danielson. "We really are. We're home on leave for just a couple of days, and this is the only way we could get around today. Isn't that right, Doc?" I asked while giving him my best glare.

"That's right. We were just thinking about our girls. We're here for only a short time, and we were dying to see some of the city."

I cringed the minute he said it. Olivia did, too, and then kicked me in the shin again. Then she kicked Doc.

Reverend Danielson, not one known to have the best sense of humor, dryly said, "Well, you better get going before the entire neighborhood shows up. Look at that crowd," he said, motioning to the swelling number of curious onlookers. "I didn't have that many for my last sermon."

We laughed, but it was a nervous laugh. A grateful laugh. At least he had broken the tension somewhat.

"OK, back away!" Reverend Danielson ordered the crowd. "Make way. They're leaving."

Like Moses parting the Red Sea, Reverend Danielson got the crowd to move back enough for us to make it to the curb. When I reached for the door handle, a chill ran up and down my back.

"I don't think I'm getting in. I think I just thought of something I have to do."

From behind me, Olivia whispered, "If you don't get in that car under your own power, you'll be getting in it another way!"

So I got in the hearse. In the mix-up, Judy followed, sitting right next to me. It was too late for her to get back out, so Olivia went around to the other side and climbed into the front seat next to Doc. Once in the vehicle, she turned and, squinting, gave me that look she was so good at giving. The one that this time said, "This may not be the last time today you ride in this!"

To add insult to injury, the motor would turn over, but it wouldn't start. Doc cranked it half a dozen times before the motor roared to life.

"For goodness sakes!" I shouted. "Let's get the hell out of here."

Doc pulled the hearse away from the curb, inching slowly so as not to run over those packed close to it and those who were still running down the street to see what was going on.

The last thing I heard as we picked up speed and left the crowd behind was an older gentleman who must have been ninety who shouted after us, "Ha ha! Missed me again!"

No one said a word for blocks, until Judy broke the silence. "I told you this was a bad idea," she said to Doc.

Olivia hit Doc on the back of the neck with her purse. She then looked at Judy, and they both burst into laughter.

"These two are peas in a pod," Olivia said. "You're not going to marry that guy, are you?" she asked, hitting Doc playfully again with her purse.

"Not unless he promises to pick me up in a hearse on our wedding day," Judy replied.

"OK, I get your point. Maybe this wasn't the smartest thing I could have done. But the only other thing running this morning was a dump truck, and you two would have had to ride in the back of it with the garbage. All the other cars weren't fixed yet. I thought I was doing something nice. This thing is great, isn't it? What a vehicle!"

To this point I had kept my mouth shut. "I told you this was all to be on the hush-hush. Why didn't you just get a fire truck and come with the sirens blaring? That wouldn't have brought as big a crowd out."

Olivia started laughing again and said, "Oh heck. Leave him alone. He had good intentions. He must be a pretty good friend to take it as good as he's taking it now. What the hell. This will certainly be a day we'll never forget."

Just then we pulled up to a busy intersection where a policeman was directing traffic. When he saw us he gave a sharp blow on his whistle and stopped the cross traffic immediately and flagged us through.

Once through the intersection, we all burst into laughter.

Yes, this would be a day we'd never forget.

* * *

After that, the marriage ceremony itself was a cakewalk, but even that had its moments. The justice of the peace had lost his glasses earlier in the morning and was half blind without them. At one point he had Olivia and Doc standing together, holding hands.

"Hey, wait a minute!" Judy and I shouted at the same time.

Once we were all in our proper places, the ceremony took about three minutes. Three minutes to get married—forever and ever. In sickness and in health. In wealth and in poverty. For better and for worse. Until death do us part. His words all seemed to run together as I stood there, looking at the most beautiful woman I had ever known. Beautiful both inside and out. Doc was right. I *didn't* deserve her, but I was going to enjoy every minute I could fool her into thinking I was right for her. She was in my first thoughts upon waking in the morning and my last thoughts before going to sleep at night. She was grace and beauty rolled into one. She was, now and forever, my sun, my moon, and my stars. I was the luckiest man in the world, and I knew it.

The next thing I knew Doc was hitting me on the back and saying, "Well, go ahead. Kiss her—before I do."

Olivia and I took each other by the hands, squeezing them tightly. She moved slowly toward me and gently brushed her lips against mine. Then, she kicked off her shoes and jumped up, wrapping her legs around my waist, and kissed me so hard it staggered me. Doc's sturdy arms were the only things that kept me from falling completely to the ground. Then he let go, and we did crash to the floor, Olivia still wrapped around me. Judy was laughing so hard I looked up to see tears streaming down her cheeks. Tears of joy. Tears of laughter. We all had some of each.

Doc reached down and pulled Olivia off me, saying, "It's customary for the best man to kiss the bride, and I don't plan on getting cheated."

Olivia nearly shocked the socks off him when she kissed him hard right on the mouth. Doc staggered worse than I had, almost falling down. She then loosened herself and came over to help me off the floor.

"Good grief!" Doc shouted. "Perc—if you don't want her, I do!"

"Not as long as I'm around, mister," Judy said, standing on tiptoes and planting a deep kiss on him, too.

"Doc, I think it's time we get back in that meat wagon and get the hell out of here before these two cause another crowd to gather."

"I'm with you, Perc. Lock and load—let's get going!"

Bowing slowly toward the girls, we gentlemanly motioned them to walk ahead of us. As soon as they passed us, we kicked them playfully on the rumps. They both screamed in mock horror.

"OK," Olivia said. "Truce?"

"Truce," I said.

* * *

I didn't have enough money saved for us to spend the night in a hotel, especially after buying the rings and the watch, so we were going to spend our first night as husband and wife at her house. That meant we needed to stall and give Bud and his friends time to clear out before going back there. I had enough money left for the four of us to grab a bite to eat, so I suggested we stop for a late lunch at one of Olivia's favorite restaurants in East St. Louis, McCrorie's. Eating at restaurants was expensive, but I wanted this day to be perfect for Olivia. McCrorie's was something of a combination barbecue and seafood place, a combination that I would never have put together in a restaurant. But it was the perfect place for us because ribs were my favorite food, and she always raved about their shrimp. Doc and Judy said they'd be glad to join us, so we headed to the restaurant.

No sooner had we been seated when the owner, Mr. McCrorie, came to our table. "How nice," I thought to myself. "He can tell this is a special day and wants to make sure we are going to get great service." Instead, he barked to Doc, "That your hearse outside?"

"Yes, sir, it is," he replied.

"Bad for business," he said, shaking his head. "Please pull that thing around back where no one can see it before people think someone died in here."

Doc started to get up. "Wait a minute," Olivia said. "What'll you give us if we move it?" she added, smiling up at Mr. McCrorie.

Mr. McCrorie smiled back at her and said, "OK—drinks all around—but move it now!"

"Sold!" Olivia replied. "OK, Doc. You can move it now."

Mr. McCrorie threw his hands in the air and said, "Women!"

"I agree," I said. "Women!"

The lunch was perfect. Doc and I each got a rack of ribs, and Olivia and Judy ate a mound of shrimp. Mr. McCrorie kept bringing us beer and the girls some kind of mixed drink. He came back to our table right before we were getting ready to leave and asked me quietly, "Today is a special day for you two, isn't it? I can tell these things."

"Well, I…we…" I stuttered. "You see…"

"I *do* see," he said, laughing. "You two have no idea how much trouble you've just gotten yourselves into. But I want to give you a good start."

With that, he tore up the check right in front of us. "Now I want you to do two things for me. First, you need to name your first kid after me—Max. It's a good name. It can be for a boy—Max, or a girl—Maxine. See? Second, when you drive that hearse out of here, take it down the road behind the building so no one sees you. OK?"

Doc and I stood up and shook hands with Mr. McCrorie. "Max it will be," I said. I pointed to Judy and said, "I bet she comes up with a Maxine before too long, too."

"Good luck to all of you," he said. He turned and headed back to the bar area, whispering over his shoulder, "Down the back road—OK?"

* * *

Olivia figured we still had some time to kill to make sure everyone would be gone from her place, so she suggested we head to Forest Park to take our wedding pictures. She was the sponsor of the photography club at Sumner and had borrowed a camera for us to use to capture our first day together.

"Forest Park?" Doc asked.

I could tell from the tone of his voice that he was thinking about more invisible fences. "You think that's a good idea?"

"I go all the time now," Olivia responded. "Besides, we're in a hearse. I don't think anyone will bother us, do you?"

We laughed, but it was more out of nervousness than anything else. In the short time I had lived in St. Louis I discovered there was an unwritten rule that Negroes weren't especially welcome in Forest Park unless it involved some type of school or church outing. I had never heard of anyone actually being given a hard time for being in the park, but from Doc's reaction I could tell he had heard of this before, too.

I thought about it for a minute and then said, "Olivia's right. We're in a hearse. Who's going to bother us? Besides, this is our wedding day. I want my picture taken on the top of Art Hill overlooking the lagoon below. That's my favorite place in St. Louis, and I want my wedding picture taken there."

"OK," Doc said with more than a tinge of doubt in his voice.

"You're the sergeant."

I pulled Olivia toward me and kissed her. "He's right, you know. I *am* the sergeant."

"And I'm your general from now on, and don't you forget that," she said, hugging me tightly.

* * *

When we reached Art Hill, Doc pulled the hearse into a parking spot directly between the Art Museum, a remnant of the 1904 World's Fair, and the statue of Saint Louis riding his horse, which was across the street and overlooking the lagoon below. From the spot directly behind the statue, one could see for miles. The skyline of the city, to the right, was majestic against the midday sky. The lagoon below reflected the sunlight, making it appear mirror smooth. Off to the left, the dense trees of Forest Park cast tall shadows that bent toward us and swished and swayed with the gentle breeze that always seemed to be atop Art Hill.

"Without a doubt, this is my favorite place in all of St. Louis," I said as we all sat on the soft grass behind the statue. "This is also where I want to be buried someday—so I can overlook the lagoon and the city."

"What a morbid thing to say," Olivia said. "Especially with that hearse parked over there."

"Not morbid at all," I replied. "Isn't this the most beautiful view you've ever seen in all your life?"

"I've never been up here before," Doc said, still visibly uncomfortable at being in the park.

"It's beautiful," Judy said. "This would be a great place for someone to propose. It would be so... so memorable."

"OK. Let's get married—and let's get out of here," Doc teased.

"Relax, my friend," I said, reaching over to rub his shoulder. "This is our time, too."

I could tell by the way Olivia looked at me she also knew Doc was feeling pretty unsettled. She suddenly jumped up and said, "Hey, I've got a great idea. Let's walk down to the Bird Cage. I haven't seen it in years, and I hear it is now loaded with flamingos."

"Why not?" I said. "I've only been there once, but it was really fun.

Doc? Judy? How 'bout it? Let's go."

"I think we'll stay here," Doc replied, not raising his eyes to look at us. He was pulling weeds out of the grass growing in front of him and flinging them down the hill.

"It'll be OK," I said. "We can go down there."

"It's not that," he said. "Judy and I need to talk about something. We'll just stay right here."

"What?" Judy asked. "What'd I do? You mad at me?"

"Just wait," Doc said. "We'll talk in a minute."

Olivia said, "I guess we know when we aren't wanted. I certainly don't have to be hit over the head with a board. Let's go, Perc. I don't want to be around when the feathers start flying."

"It's nothing like that...." Doc protested as we started walking down the long hill toward the Bird Cage, but we didn't stop to hear the rest of his words. I took Olivia's hand in mine and started rocking our hands back and forth as we walked, like a couple of schoolkids.

The Bird Cage at the St. Louis Zoo was a famous St. Louis landmark. It was one of the favorite attractions at the zoo and a popular location for weddings of those high up in society in St. Louis. I had been to the Cage once before when Sumner sponsored a trip for the Boy Scout troop from the Ville and I had gone along as a chaperon.

The Bird Cage was basically a huge, oblong wire dome that allowed the birds to fly freely inside it. What made it so special was a covered tunnel, also made of wire, that ran its entire length so that visitors to the zoo could get right in with the birds and observe them while they were resting and in flight. Birds would fly constantly overhead while visitors shielded their heads from anything that might drop from the sky. However, it was also local legend it was great luck to be hit by bird droppings while walking through the tunnel. One of the boys on our field trip, Tommy Johnson, got splatted on his shoulder, and within a week he was named "paperboy of the week" by the *St. Louis Post-Dispatch*. Coincidence? Not according to the rest of the scout troop. Never mind that Tommy had sold more papers than any paperboy in St. Louis the week before. All were convinced that his good fortune was tied in with the Bird Cage. Thus are legends born.

The St. Louis Zoo was free to all. However, there was a belief by most back in the Ville that the only admission one needed was the color of one's skin—and it wasn't black. Negroes did go to the zoo, but, again, it was usually in conjunction with a trip set up by a school or church. Olivia didn't appear uncomfortable in the least as we made it to the bottom of the hill and the Bird Cage, at the north edge of the zoo, came into view. I couldn't say the same thing for me, but I didn't want to show it.

There were only three families in the tunnel when we entered it, and none of them seemed to pay any attention to us. Rather, all eyes were pointed up, watching the antics of some giant macaws in the tree overhead. Below the tunnel, a group of about two dozen pink flamingos suddenly ran for cover behind a row of small trees near the outer wall of the cage. Two birds that looked like starlings swooped down and harassed the flamingos, causing them to take off running again.

"Let's sit here and watch a minute," Olivia said, pointing to a bench about halfway through the tunnel.

"OK, but I'd feel a lot better if we had an umbrella. Look at this!" I pointed to bird droppings covering the ground around us.

"Oh, don't be such a scaredy-cat," she said. "Besides, we've got hats on. Relax."

We sat quietly, holding hands, watching the flamingos run back and forth below us as the starlings continued to swoop down at them.

Olivia squeezed my hand and said, "Perc, thank you."

"Thanks for what?" I asked.

"Thanks for marrying me."

"*You* are thanking me for marrying you?" I replied. "I'm the one who feels darn lucky right now."

"It's a difficult thing for a woman to explain," she continued. "Ever since I was a little girl I dreamed of this day—of the day when my knight in shining armor would come sweep me away. Well, you aren't exactly wearing armor, but your uniform will do," she said, smiling. "And I'd guess I'd have to say you did sweep me off my feet."

She paused, moving closer to me and putting her arm around me, and then continued, "You don't have any idea how much I love you, do you?"

"Frankly, I don't see how you couldn't love me," I joked. "Look at me. I'm broke. I look like my hair's been cut with a saw blade. I'm stuck in the army for goodness knows how long. I cry at movies, especially westerns. And I'm crabby in the morning. But other than that… go ahead. Ask anybody—I'm some 'catch-of-the-day.' Do you have any idea what you did today by marrying me?"

"I think so. I married an incredible romantic, who won't admit it. I married a man who is kind and gentle. I married a man who is good and true and honest. I married someone who will always make my heart smile. You even have one of the most—how should we say it?—most *amazing* haircuts I've ever seen. Now what other man can top all that? My question to you is, why me? Why in the world did you want to marry me?"

I scooted back from her and studied her, from feet to face, while rubbing my chin and saying "Hmmmmmmmm…"

She playfully slapped at me. I grabbed her hand again and continued, "I married you because you are the love of my life, and I know it. I tried explaining this to Doc one night back at the barracks…"

"Explained it to Doc?" she shrieked, this time whacking me on the leg with her purse.

I put my finger up to my lips and said, "If you want to hear this, let me talk. Like I was saying before, I know you are the love of my life. You make me laugh. And you're smart. Not as smart as me, of course, but you ain't bad."

I quickly added, laughing, "Now don't hit me again. I'm just telling the truth. And besides being smart, you are absolutely gorgeous. When we kiss I feel it throughout my whole body. Like I was telling Doc, you make me feel like a man. I'm a chemist, so I know—there is a chemistry between us that I've never felt around anyone before in my whole life. You see the world as beautiful. I don't always see it that way, and I like—no I *love* the way you see something good in everything. I need that in my life, and you'll give it to me. Those are the reasons I love you, but there is one more thing. I don't think, as long as I live, I'll ever be able to tell from one minute to the next what you'll do. You're just like those flamingos over there. You never roost in one place for too long."

I avoided her eyes and continued, more seriously this time. "There are more question marks ahead of us than Carter has pills, and I don't have very many answers right now. Who knows what the future's going to bring? I certainly don't know about the future, but I do know about the present. For now, I'm just going to love you with all my heart. For now, that is all I can promise you. Whatever else comes, will come. But now—our time begins now."

I started bending down to kiss her. She had already closed her eyes and was waiting for my kiss when it suddenly dawned on me I had forgotten to give her her wedding present.

When I didn't kiss her, Olivia opened her eyes and said, "What in the world are you doing?"

I reached in my pocket and pulled out the small package.

"Our time really does start now," I said, handing her the package.

When she opened the box she said, "Oh, Inman, this is beautiful. It's like my old watch, but this one has stones where the numbers would go. It's so beautiful! Thank you so much. I love it—and I love you. Hold the box while I wind it up."

Holding her arm out so we could both look at the watch, she added, "Now I know what you meant by our time starts now. You're really something, you know that?"

"And by the way," she added. "I got a little something for you, too." She reached in her purse and pulled out a small box.

I opened it, and inside was a silver cigarette lighter. My initials were on one side. On the back were etched the following words, "With all my love...now and forever."

"It's perfect," I said. "And so are you. Lean over here and kiss me, Mrs. Perkins."

"Not so loud," she whispered. "That has to be our little secret, remember?"

I sat my lighter down on the bench, put my arms around her, and kissed her gently. "Now and forever," I said. "And so it shall be."

I reached back to grab my lighter and immediately dropped it back on the bench. A bird had hit it dead-center, and its silver case was now milky white, with a little purple thrown in for good measure.

"Would you look at this!" I said, picking it up and wiping it off with my handkerchief. "I'll be damned. Do you suppose it's the same good luck if my lighter gets hit instead of me?"

Olivia laughed out loud, so much so that everyone else in the Bird Cage looked over to see what was going on.

"It's OK," she said to the others. Pointing up to the sky she said, "He got hit!"

"That's good luck," a large man in a green suit coat yelled over. He then added, "Hey, buddy. Make a wish and it'll come true. Everybody who gets bombed gets one wish."

I waved to him and said only, "Thanks." I then turned to Olivia and said, "One wish? I know exactly what I'll wish for."

I closed my eyes tightly and made my wish but I didn't tell her, for fear of jinxing it. I wished our love would always be as strong as it was on this day, at this moment.

"Let's go," I said, standing up. "I made my wish. I know it'll come true. I know it will."

"Are you going to tell me?"

"Nope. I'll show you, every day of our lives."

I took her hand, and with one last look at the birds flying overhead, we headed out of the Cage and back up the hill.

* * *

When we got back to the statue of Saint Louis, Judy was crying.

"You poor thing," Olivia said, kneeling down to put her arm around her. "You big lummox," she yelled up at Doc. "What did you do to her?"

Doc, pacing back and forth behind the statue, responded, "I just asked her to marry me—that's all."

"Well, obviously, that was enough," Olivia shot back.

I laughed. Doc reached over and knocked my hat off. "Quiet, or the next time your head goes with it."

"Congratulations!" I said, slowly dragging the word out and reaching over to shake Doc's hand.

Doc stopped his pacing and stood in front of me, a blank expression on his face.

Judy wailed even louder. "There, there," Olivia comforted her, patting her on the back.

"All I did was ask her to marry me," Doc said, his voice full of confusion.

At the same time, Olivia and I said to Doc, "That was enough!"

"What do I do now?" Doc said.

"Let's take a walk while the girls have a talk."

"But all I did was ask her to marry me!" he kept muttering over and over.

"Just leave us alone for a couple of minutes. She just needs some time, that's all."

We headed down Art Hill toward the lagoon. "No fair jumping in," I said to Doc. "You're an engaged man now. You've got responsibilities. Oh, brother, do you now have responsibilities."

Doc looked up at me, blinking rapidly in the sunlight, fumbling in his shirt pocket for a cigarette. I had never seen him at such a loss for words before, and it tickled me. I pulled out my new lighter and lit his cigarette, handing my handkerchief, bird droppings and all, to him. "Here's a blindfold to go with that last cigarette."

"I think I'm going to be sick," he said.

I looked up the hill and saw Olivia and Judy walking slowly down toward us.

"You'll get over it," I said. "You're not sick. Brother, you're in love. There isn't much difference, is there?"

I paused and added, "I know because I've been there. I *am* there."

I was there all right. As I watched Olivia coming toward me, I felt it in every fiber of my body and wasn't ashamed to admit it.

I was in love with the most wonderful woman in the world, now and forever.

17

GAMES

Our leaves were over all too quickly. The men streamed steadily back to the base, for the most part relaxed—but also very tired. They were still so happy they had been able to see their families for a few days they didn't even seem to mind the medical going-over, and the shots they all got, the minute they stepped back on the base. I was given three shots, all in the right arm, and within the hour was so sore I could barely lift a fork to eat.

"SOP—standard operating procedure," Sergeant Ingram told me. "The Army always does this just in case we were exposed to something horrible while back home."

By 1600, the ordered reporting time, all but one of us had returned. Clark had caught the measles from his little brother while home. He had been ordered not to report back until a doctor could certify he was no longer contagious. But other than Clark, we all fell back pretty quickly into our army routines.

That is, all except most of the men of Barracks N-1. By the time we returned to the base, they were gone, shipped out, we were told, to another base for special training in flight support. They were being reassigned to another battalion at their new destination, so they wouldn't be joining up with us again down the road. I was upset I hadn't been told of this in advance, but Sergeant Ingram also reminded me that I wasn't in the "need to know" circle on this—that movement of troops was one of the most carefully guarded secrets of all. Still, I had formed friendships with several of the men in N-1, and I was going to miss them.

While the rest of the men seemed pretty happy and loose, I was brooding. I missed Olivia worse than I ever imagined I could. The last days of my leave, our "honeymoon," had flown by. We did a lot of talking about the future, mixed in with visits to relatives and friends. We also took Bud's car one evening, thanks to the last of the gas ration stamps for the month, and drove back to Art Hill, where we sat behind the statue of Saint Louis and watched the small boats floating by in the lagoon below. Sitting there on the grass, holding her hand, I felt closer to her than I had ever felt before. I wanted to capture that feeling forever. We sat there for almost an hour without saying a word to each other. No words needed to be said. None at all.

And then, as quickly as it seemed to start, the honeymoon was over. When she dropped me off at Union Station, I asked her not to come inside. I didn't want to put her through standing on the platform and watching the train pull out, and I didn't want my last sight of her to be with tears in her eyes. We said our good-byes in the car.

Doc got back to the base right before the deadline. He took the train after mine because he and Judy lost track of the time while they were, as he said, "getting to know each other better." I knew what he was talking about and didn't tease him one bit. Williams came back on the train with him, but Doc said he slept nearly the whole way. Evidently, he got to know his "cousin" really well this trip.

I missed Olivia horribly, but in an odd sort of way I was also happy to be back. While it was expected that all of us should crab about being in the army—and I crabbed with the best of them—deep down I found the army fascinating. I had no idea what the future would hold, but as much as I wanted to go back to Sumner, I wasn't about to rule out the possibility of staying in the army, especially if OCS was really in the cards. So, I went along and complained like everyone else, at the proper times, but I wasn't closing any doors behind me, either.

Meanwhile, rumors were flying everywhere that we'd soon be shipping overseas, either to Italy or North Africa. But even in the face of these rumors, I had never seen the men so relaxed. Time with loved ones and friends had fortified them emotionally. They were also so physically exhausted from trying to cram so much into their short visits home they were all limp as dishrags. Along with this, something had also changed that was difficult to put a finger on. As all fell into their normal routines and the tempo of the days quickened, there was a new atmosphere in the battalion, one of cautious optimism tempered by the uncertainty of the future. A pride was also building, but that climb was still a slow one.

Now that basic training was over, the men were assigned to squads to learn their specialized training. Some were being trained to serve as ground support for our bombers. Others were learning general construction skills so they could tear down and rebuild camps as our troops advanced in combat. Still others were learning how to work with the Army Corps of Engineers to build and repair airstrips so our planes could move with the rest of the army. Most of the men, even those also getting other specialized training, were rotated in and out of special classes where they were learning to string and maintain lines for communications. If our battalion was going to be known for one skill in particular, it suddenly seemed that was going to be it. Even our truck and jeep drivers attended the communications classes when they weren't pulling special duty with the convoys constantly bringing fuel to the base. Those poor men were kept so busy we seldom saw them anymore.

The men were all required to have at least one special skill, but I had to run, literally, each afternoon from one training session to the other because all sergeants were expected to have a good, working knowledge of all areas. Then, after classes each day, we all worked on and cleaned our gear, got the barracks ready for inspection, dug in at chow, and came back to the barracks for a couple of hours before lights-out.

This schedule left precious little time for leisure activities, but that didn't mean the men weren't up to a little fun and couldn't find diversions in the evening. It just meant they had to be more creative in using what little free time they did have.

These men loved games. All types of games. Gambling wasn't allowed in the barracks, but Sergeant Ingram and I usually looked the other way as long as the men didn't fight over bets. The most popular games were pool, Ping-Pong, and cards. Tournaments were held almost nightly in all three areas. It came as a huge surprise to everyone, but Williams and Tyler were incredible bridge players. They were challenged by every team in the barracks, including me and Jamieson, who was a pretty fair player himself, but no one could beat them. Jamieson and I didn't even come close. Williams and Tyler didn't just beat all comers—they destroyed the competition. It beat anything I ever saw.

Less popular, but one could still find a game going most of the time, were checkers, dominoes, dice games of all types, and chess. There were also games and activities of less traditional types. It only lasted for a week or so, but Williams gathered up a stable of cockroaches and held races on a makeshift racecourse he made in the shower area. This was pretty overt gambling and shouldn't have been allowed in the barracks, but I looked the other way because I wanted to see just how he could pull this off. The cockroaches in El Paso were proportionally in size with the giant spiders that seemed to be everywhere, so they were truly something to behold. Some were as much as five inches long and had shells so hard they were almost impossible to kill. They were found often in our boots, which sent men screaming and jumping all across the barracks. Between the spiders and cockroaches it felt like living in the middle of a minefield.

Williams painted the backs of his cockroaches different colors to make it easier to follow the races. He posted daily odds for each of them and set up what would have been pretty big payoffs for things like trifectas and exactas, but no one ever won those. According to the men, the races were all "rigged." Just how one could rig cockroach races escaped me until I caught Williams pulling the back leg off one of the favorites before a race. He saw me watching him and said only, "He was in pain." It wasn't only that poor cockroach that was in pain. Williams wanted the races to, in racing parlance, "make him well" financially. And they did. He made so much money over the course of that week, accepting everything from cash to cigarettes as acceptable betting currency, he had the entire barracks cleaned out. He was doing fine until Albertson lost three dollars on a roach called Speedball and became so angry he decimated the field with his GI boots. He jumped up and down in the middle of the racecourse shouting, "Sons of bitches! Sons of bitches!" Williams watched in horror as most of his stable was wiped from the bottom of Albertson's boots. So much for the roach races.

When the weather cooperated, the men went outside the barracks after evening chow for other types of games. Horseshoe tournaments were held every night possible. However, there was also constant bickering involving the makeup of the teams. Because of men being rotated to guard duty, mess duty, and everything else that could come up, the teams changed so often it was hard to tell who had beat whom—and by how much. I finally had to step in and order that written records be kept of team performance to keep them from killing each other with the horseshoes.

Still others played a very similar game called "washers," a game tremendously popular back in St. Louis, where there seemed to be "washer pits" in every city park. Washers was played exactly like horseshoes. As the name implied, the participants threw large, metal washers, about three inches in diameter, instead of horseshoes. The object of the game was to toss the washers into a two-foot square box, made out of two-by-fours. The ground served as its bottom. A hole was dug in the ground in the middle of the box. A washer landing in the hole was worth three points. A washer landing in the box was worth one point. The first team to get to eleven points was declared the winner. Washers was a faster game than horseshoes and didn't produce as many fights. Washers were either inside the box or were in the hole—or they weren't. There wasn't much to debate. The games were fast and fun to watch.

And the men were still baseball crazy. It was usually too dark and too cold to play over at the field at night after finishing their evening duties, so the men stuck close to the barracks and played elaborate games of catch, with as many as ten men throwing the ball back and forth in some type of geometric pattern that I never really did get the hang of. It looked like a wild game of pepper, only without the bat. It was dangerous to come up the walk outside the barracks while games of catch were in progress. The men were known to throw at those walking by if they weren't paying attention. More than one man slumped to the ground after getting beaned. The men roared with laughter when this happened, all yelling at the poor, unfortunate victim, "You never hear the one that gets you!"

The games were ways for the men to relax, to forget the duties and responsibilities of the day. And no one kidded themselves—we all understood these games were also a way to move our thoughts, at least temporarily, away from those we missed back home. The men played games, all kinds of games, and they played to win when they played—but the real challenges were more within themselves at this point.

* * *

As far as the games were concerned, the most anticipated night of the week was Thursday night. Thursday night was our one and only night to use the base Service Club. We had our own recreation area in the barracks and had converted part of the motor pool into our own version of a Service Club, but it wasn't even close to being in the same league as the base club. For the men, the base club was like entering the gates of Shangri-La.

Colonel Ellis had stuttered and stammered that first week we came to camp when he explained to me that our battalion would be allowed use of the club only on Thursday evenings. I asked if all the other groups on the base had special nights as well. His response was, "Well, others use the club the rest of the time."

I was sorting files at the time and pretended not to hear him. Without looking up, I said, "I'm sorry, Sir. I was looking for something and missed what you were saying. So, other groups on the base have their own special nights, too?"

"Sort of. They all…that is…it's used by…" he said, struggling for words and chopping sentences in two. Finally he just blurted out, "Well, it's restrict…."—and the minute he said it I saw out of the corner of my eye his eyes widen as he realized what he had started to say. He quickly shouted out, louder than he probably meant to, "I mean it's *reserved* the rest of the week!"

He paused a minute, taking his glasses off to wipe them with his handkerchief, and added, softly, "Our battalion gets to use it Thursday nights. OK?"

"If you say so, Sir," was all I could think of to say. I understood perfectly what he meant. Perfectly.

The Service Club was popular with the men because it had brand-new pool tables with smooth felt, Ping-Pong tables that were level, shuffleboard tables of regulation size, and card tables and chairs that didn't collapse when leaned on or sat in. The Club also had a jukebox stuffed with the latest Glenn Miller and Benny Goodman records and a large dance floor right next to it. Opposite the dance floor was the bar. Only beer was served, and low percentage alcohol beer at that, but the bar still gave one the feeling of being in a "real" bar. The rest of the club had new, overstuffed chairs and couches where men could lounge, sip their beer, and soak up the music and games around them. There were also large oak tables spread throughout the room. These tables were well lighted, something our barracks and our motor pool weren't. The Red Cross kept the drawers in the tables stocked with stationery and pencils and the men took advantage of this, and the lighting, by sitting at the tables and writing letters back home since postage was still free for military personnel.

In addition to being their sergeant, I had also taken on another role: their dictionary. Men were constantly yelling over the music and buzz of the room, "Hey, Sarge. How you spell this word?" If I had a nickel for every word I spelled for them… Oh well, at least they were making the time to write to those who worried about them back home. Lifelines.

* * *

At first it seemed like so much sound and fury signifying nothing. Shortly after breakfast on Thursday morning, Albertson ran up to me on the parade ground and said he heard a rumor floating around that we were being bumped from our night at the Service Club—and asked me to check to see if there was any truth to it. I hadn't heard anything about it, so I said I'd do some investigating. At first I didn't give it much thought because, normally, it wouldn't have been a problem at all to shift nights or have the men just come instead to the motor pool for a movie in our makeshift theater. I had forgotten this week was different. Very different. The men had gone to great lengths to convince, and then to make the proper arrangements for, a group of girls from a Methodist church in El Paso to come to the base for a combination dance and "game night," and they didn't want to have to cancel it at the last minute.

Albertson also said he had somehow been assigned the role of social chairman for the event, and he needed to make one last phone call before evening chow to make sure the girls had been able to find suitable transportation to the base and to confirm their arrival time. He continued to pester me about it so much I finally headed over to battalion headquarters, not just to get some information, but to get away from him, too.

When I arrived at headquarters, I was stunned to see Colonel Ellis sitting alone in the outer office and cleaning a rifle.

"Expecting Indians, Sir?" I joked.

"Very funny, Perkins. You better watch it or I'll have you standing guard for those Indians tonight."

I couldn't say that Colonel Ellis and I had become good friends, but my respect for him had grown because I felt he was sincerely trying to do well in a situation I knew he did not want to be in. He had requested transfer half a dozen times to a new Signal Corps training outfit being put together in Washington, D.C., but for whatever reasons, he was still with us.

Over time, our working relationship had become a pretty good one, in large part because he wasn't a "by-the-book" officer like most I had come to know. He also wasn't one to mince words or beat around the bush when it came to the daily operation of the headquarters. If he wanted something done, he said so, plainly and bluntly. If the job was done well, he was happy and quick with a compliment. If it wasn't done well, he was very "colorful" in his use of language to express his displeasure. Still, while he often had an outward commanding presence in headquarters, more than a few times I saw him standing next to a window, staring forlornly off into the distance, no doubt dreaming of better places for him to be. In many ways, I saw him as a man divided between his duty and his dreams, areas that were clearly oceans apart.

He had that same forlorn look on his face as he cleaned his rifle.

"Sir, if I'm not bothering you too much, I'd like to ask you something," I said, realizing that I was interrupting his thoughts.

He motioned for me to sit down. "What's on your mind?" he asked.

"I just heard something and wanted to check it out with you. Word has it that we aren't going to be able to use the Service Club tonight. Have you heard anything about that, Sir?"

Colonel Ellis had now started cleaning the outside of the rifle, working on the barrel first. Without looking at me he said, "I just got a call a few minutes ago. I was going to send for you as soon as I finished up here. I know the men will hate it, and so do I, but it looks like we are being given the heave-ho tonight."

"But, Sir..." I started to interrupt as he cut me off with a wave of his hand, and continued.

"I know, Perc. This isn't fair. I know the men have spent a hell of a lot of time getting their little get-together arranged. I understand they even had girls lined up. You got to give them credit. They're nothing if not creative—or maybe the better word would be persistent. No, I take that back. They seem like a bunch of con artists to me. I'll still never understand how they actually convinced a group of women to come to a base full of wolves. I'm actually kind of proud of them."

"This isn't a 'little get-together,'" I said, repeating his words. "The men worked their tails off getting everything ready for this night. It wouldn't be right to yank it all away from them now, especially after all they've done."

He shrugged and continued, "I agree with you, but I don't think there's really anything we can do about it at this point. Did you also manage to hear through the grapevine who's coming to the base? The mayor of El Paso. Can you imagine that? The damn mayor himself. He's supposed to be bringing some rich folks with him, too, the upper crust and cream of the town, those with more diamonds than brains. Ladies with big hair and men with tuxedos they haven't been able to fit into since Coolidge was president. I'm not completely sure, but I think this is all supposed to be part of some fund-raiser the mayor started last month. From what I can gather, the mayor wanted to have it here on the base because the fund-raiser is tied in somehow with that drive the Red Cross has been having. My opinion? It's all just going to be a political show for the mayor. That's the way these things usually end up."

I had done my best to keep my mouth shut while he tried to explain the situation. But when he paused to click open the bolt and turn the rifle around so he could check the barrel, I jumped in.

"I understand, Sir. But that still doesn't make it right or fair. The men get to use the club just once a week. This is their night. If this gets pulled out from under them—especially this week—they're really going to be hurt. Can't the mayor and his group go to another part of the base? Surely there's someplace else they can go, right?"

Colonel Ellis got up and put his rifle in the rack on the wall by the entrance to his office. "It's already been decided, Perc. Tell your men they'll have to wait for another night. I'm sorry, but that's just the way it is."

"I'm sorry, Sir, but this really stinks. How am I going to explain this to them? They've gone to so much trouble and this is so important to them."

"I tell you what I'll do," he said. "I'll dig up some passes for tonight. Why not take them back to Mexico? I hear they had one whale of a time down there the last time they went. Think they'd like that?"

"I think they'd like to have their party here more," I said. "If we can't do anything about tonight, how about seeing if we can switch nights and let them use the club tomorrow night or Saturday night? They wouldn't be happy about it, but that would sure help."

Colonel Ellis walked over to the window and stared off into the distance. "I'm sorry, but I don't think that is going to happen. There'll be other weeks."

"You could ask, Sir," I suggested.

"I know what the answer would be," he said, his voice firm, final. He then continued, "Mexico might not be a bad idea. See what they think about that. Tell them I'm sorry. But also tell them my hands are tied. Mexico is the best I can do under the circumstances."

"Sometimes our best isn't enough, Sir," I said sarcastically, getting his complete attention. The tension between us at that point choked the air.

He finally looked me in the eye and said slowly, "That will be all, Sergeant Perkins. I'll have the passes for the men on my desk by 1600. You can pick them up then. That *will* be all."

He turned to leave and I snapped to attention and saluted him, crisply. A little too crisply. He saluted back, turned again, and walked into his office, closing the door behind him.

I stood alone in the outer office, staring at the closed door. What

I had just seen wasn't his "best." I knew what it was, and I knew the men would, too. As I stood there, I kept thinking about one of my grandfather's favorite sayings when he felt someone was being less than completely honest with him. Grandfather would say, "Don't piss down my back and tell me it's raining."

It wasn't raining.

* * *

I did my best to explain everything to the men, but I don't think I did a very good job. I couldn't. I didn't really understand it all myself. I explained how the mayor and the cream of El Paso were coming for a fund-raising event of some type, but that didn't seem to justify taking away their one night of the week in the club, especially not after they had poured their hearts into getting their own get-together ready. And now they looked as if those hearts were being stomped on. They stood in silence in front of me, staring at the floor, occasionally shifting their weight.

I think as much as anything, it was the principle of the act that rankled them most. Their "game night" could be held another week. That wasn't the point. And the girls could always be invited back. The point was, the base seemed to be getting smaller and smaller for them ever since I had "the talk" with them about where they were, and were not, welcome on the base. Yes, the fences were still there, and none of us wanted them to be drawn in any closer. But now it seemed they were.

I told the men that Colonel Ellis was issuing passes for the evening, and those who wanted to could head down to Mexico. I was just finishing news about the passes when the back door to the barracks was kicked open. Davis had kicked it open. Under one huge arm was Tyler. Under the other, Williams.

They had been beaten—and badly.

The sound of the door being kicked open drew the attention of all.

"Oh, God, no…." I shouted, running to the back of the barracks. The men followed closely behind me, circling in around Davis, who gently lowered Tyler and Williams to the floor. Tyler was unconscious. His shirt had been ripped nearly off his body. His face looked like someone had used it as a punching bag, and his eyes were nearly swollen shut. A thin line of blood trickled down from the corner of his mouth.

Williams didn't look any better. He was conscious, but barely. It was obvious his nose was broken, and blood had pooled up above his upper lip. His left eye was bloodshot, and there was a deep gash on his cheek under it. I got down on the floor and cradled his head in my lap. I felt the lump, about the size of an egg, on the back of his head.

They both needed help—and quick.

"Somebody run for a truck. Now!" I screamed.

Jamieson ran out the door while I instructed others to get water and some towels.

I had just started blotting blood away from Williams' mouth when he suddenly swung his right arm up, catching me high on the cheek with his fist.

"It's OK! It's OK!" I said, holding him back down. "It's me—Perc. You're going to be OK. Just take it easy and try to rest. We're going to get you to the infirmary. You'll be OK."

When he had calmed down, I leaned over and asked Davis if there was any change in Tyler. He was still holding him in his arms, rocking him gently.

"He's bad," Davis said softly. "He needs a doctor right away."

"Soon as the truck gets here we'll move them," I said. Then, looking around me, I said, "You four men here—and you four men over there. Pull two of the mattresses off bunks. We'll use them as stretchers. Each of you take a corner to make sure we don't drop them."

Williams moaned and moved his head from side to side. "Perc— there were too many of them. We tried to run, but…"

"Shhhhh," I said, wiping his forehead with my sleeve. "You can tell me about it later."

Davis spoke softly, "I found them in the bushes behind the Service Club. I had gone over to see if they needed any help with the decorations and couldn't find them. I checked out back to see if they were throwing away trash—and there they were. Before Tyler passed out he said some goons told them to beat it or they'd get beaten good. I guess Williams said a few choice words, and the next thing they knew they got jumped. There were four or five of them."

Davis then added, "I got scared, Sarge. I'm sorry. I didn't know what else to do, so I brought them back here. I probably should have taken them…"

"You did just fine, soldier. We'll get them help as soon as the truck gets here. You did just fine."

"Funny thing," he continued. "Now that I think about it, there were a bunch of guys over by the club who saw me carrying them, but no one offered to help."

Williams coughed deeply, spitting up blood. I wiped his mouth and yelled, "Somebody go see where the hell the truck is!"

"It's here, Sarge," Albertson said. "Just pulled up."

"OK, let's do this the right way," I said. "Put the mattresses on the floor right next to them. Then we'll lift them slowly onto them and carry them out. Try to keep the mattresses level. Got that?"

Tyler was still unconscious and as limp as a sack of rags. Williams was becoming more alert, but it was more and more obvious he had some broken ribs. No matter how tightly the men held the mattress as they carried him outside, each time they took a step he cried out in pain.

"Albertson, I'm putting you in charge. You drive. Davis, you get in and go with him. You men carrying the mattresses—climb in the back of the truck and hold your corners tight so they don't roll around. Now get to the infirmary as quick as you can. I'm going to go see what the hell happened and then be right over. The rest of you stay here around the barracks."

As the truck pulled away, I turned to the rest of the men and added, "I'll take care of this. Don't do anything while I'm gone. You hear me? I mean it. I'll take care of this."

When I got to headquarters, the door to Colonel Ellis's office was still closed. I could hear the radio playing softly inside. I knocked and opened the door before I was instructed to.

Colonel Ellis was startled and shouted, "What in the hell is going on?"

"Excuse me, Sir. That's what I'm here to find out. We've got a problem. Two of my men—they're near dead."

"What? What do you mean 'near dead'?" he asked, standing up behind his desk.

"They were beaten. Over at the Service Club. I've got some men taking them to the infirmary right now."

I then added, moving toward his desk, "Please help, Sir. They're in bad shape."

He grabbed his hat and without another word brushed past me and out the door. I followed.

A doctor was already working on Tyler, who was still unconscious, when we arrived at the infirmary. Colonel Ellis looked at Tyler's swollen face, looked back at me, and said, "What in hell's name is going on here?"

The doctor motioned for us to step back. "Please keep your voices down," he said.

"How is he, Doctor?" Colonel Ellis asked.

"I'm going to do some more tests, but I'd say this one has a pretty nasty concussion. I've seen better." He continued to wrap Tyler's head and added, "The other one's not in the best shape, either. Pretty banged up. What happened?"

"I don't know, but I'm going to get to the bottom of this if it's the last thing I ever do," Colonel Ellis said, a little too loud. The doctor asked him again to keep his voice down.

"Nurse—I want you to finish wrapping here while I look at him again," he said, pointing to Williams.

"You two get out of here," he ordered. "I'll send word when I know something more."

"Can I stay and help?" I asked, motioning toward Williams.

"No. I'm going to put a few stitches in that cheek and then give him something to make him sleep. There's really nothing you can do right now." He then added, "I think they'll be OK. I'll take good care of them."

"Let's go," Colonel Ellis said, slapping me on the arm. "We've got some work to do."

Outside the infirmary, the men who had brought them were still standing beside the truck, waiting for news.

"You did fine, men," Colonel Ellis said to them.

"How they doing, Sir?" Davis asked.

"The doctor is still working on them. I think they'll be fine. You men get back to the barracks—and stay there. We'll keep you posted."

The men didn't move. They looked at me, waiting for me to say something. "Colonel Ellis is right," I said finally. "They'll be all right. I'll meet you back at the barracks in a little while. Now go ahead. Get going."

As the truck pulled away, Colonel Ellis said to me, "I want you to go back to headquarters and wait. I don't want to argue with you about this, Perc. This is something I need to take care of. You stay out of this. The lieutenant is still not back from leave, so I'm putting you in charge of HQ until I get back. OK?"

I wanted to go with him, to find out what had happened, to find those responsible for beating Tyler and Williams. But I also knew he was right. This *was* something that he, as the commanding officer of our battalion, should take care of. He must have read my mind because I was going to argue with him, but I didn't.

"OK," I said. "But please, Sir, let me know as soon as you find out anything."

"It may be a while before I get back," he said. "I'm counting on you to run things while I'm gone."

"Yes, Sir," I said. "Will do."

"I know you can," he said, putting his hand on my shoulder. With that, he turned and headed toward the front of the base. I walked quickly to headquarters, where Doc was pacing back and forth in front of the door.

"I just heard," he said, running over to greet me. "How's Williams doing? He going to be ok?"

"He got knocked around pretty bad," I said. "He's pretty busted up. Broken nose and some ribs, too, I think. I'm guessing it will take a while, but I think he's going to be OK. The doc said he'll send word as soon as he knows something more. Tyler's about the same."

I was about to say it could have been much worse, but I wasn't so sure that was true. I kept seeing the blood trickling from Williams' mouth.

Doc looked right at me, not blinking, and asked, "Who did it? Do we know yet?"

"Davis said Williams kept saying one of them was called 'Martin'—or something like that. I don't know. Colonel Ellis is going to find out right now. He said he'll take care of it."

"And so will I," Doc said, pounding his right fist into his left palm.

"This isn't the time," I said. "We've got to let the colonel take care of this, and you know it."

"I can wait," Doc said slowly and deliberately. "But you can bet one thing, this 'Martin' or whoever it was is going to be one sorry son of a bitch."

"Let's wait and see what happens first," I said.

Doc wasn't really paying much attention to me at that point. The look in his eyes said it all. He wanted revenge and I had the feeling before this was over he was going to get it.

18

RETRIBUTIONS

When Colonel Ellis came back to battalion headquarters, he entered the building slowly, almost shuffling past me as he went into his office. He didn't say anything. He didn't need to. His body said it all.

I followed him in and asked, "What did you find out, Sir?"

He sat down in his desk chair and put his face in his hands, wiping his forehead with the tips of his fingers.

"I talked to that son of a bitch Rogers," he said. "I don't think there's any doubt it was his men who did this, but he didn't seem all that interested in finding them. I demanded they be brought in for questioning, and he laughed and said, 'You demand? How dare you! You demand?' After that, it was all downhill from there. He said he'd conduct an 'investigation,' and if any wrongdoing was found on the part of his men, he'd take appropriate action. I bet."

He continued rubbing his forehead. "I'm not finished yet, though. Far from it. I went to see the base commander, but he's in Washington. Won't be back for a couple of days. I told them I wanted to see him the minute he gets back. For now, we have to wait."

"Wait? That's going to be hard to explain to the men," I said. "Waiting isn't exactly what they'll have on their minds. Isn't there anything else we can do right now? We've got two men in the infirmary who are in bad shape. *Something* needs to be done."

"Just what in the hell do you want me to do, Perkins? Go out and form a lynch mob?" he practically screamed at me.

He looked up and said, gently, "I'm sorry. I didn't mean to yell at you. I feel so damn helpless. So damn frustrated."

He paused before adding, "Something *is* being done. We're waiting. And you tell the men this: We aren't going to get mad—we're going to get even. One way or the other. Oh, those men who did this will pay. I can promise you that. It may take some time, but they'll get theirs. That much I do know."

"I'll tell them exactly that, Sir."

He stood up and said, "No you won't. *I'll* tell them. You follow me."

* * *

It had been weeks since Colonel Ellis had actually set foot in the barracks. The men sitting on the ground outside who were waiting for some news were shocked when they saw him and froze.

"Ten-hut!" I shouted as we made our way up the walk and into the barracks. The men immediately got up and snapped to attention. I motioned for them to follow us inside.

Colonel Ellis walked quickly to our recreation area, turned around to face everyone, and said firmly, "At ease, men. Gather 'round. I want to talk to you a minute."

Every man in the barracks dropped what he was doing and moved into the semicircle forming around Colonel Ellis.

"First of all," he said, "I just came from the infirmary. Williams and Tyler are going to be fine. Doc says they'll both be down for a week or so, but they'll be good as new."

A collective sigh of relief swept through the men as he continued, "I still don't know exactly what happened. No one knows for sure right now. But I wanted you to know this—I'm not going to let this go. If the fight wasn't their fault, there'll be hell to pay for the men who did this."

A low rumble also suddenly made its way through the group. When Colonel Ellis said "If the fight wasn't their fault…"—it was the first time anyone in the barracks, and especially me, even considered the possibility that they might have been the instigators. A horrible thought came to me right at that moment. I knew Williams well, and I knew that he could be a real pain in the ass. What if it *was* his fault?

Colonel Ellis half answered my question when he added, "Regardless of who started the fight, we can't have any more of this. And that's an order. I know some of you would like to find the others right now and take care of this yourselves, but I'm ordering you not to. I'll take care of this. I'm scheduled to see the base commander when he gets back. We'll get to the bottom of everything. In the meantime, go about business as usual. Tyler and Williams are going to be OK. That's the most important thing right now. I'll take care of the rest. Everyone understand?"

Heads nodded all around the room.

"Sir, can we go to the infirmary to see them?" Albertson asked.

"We don't want a mob over there," Colonel Ellis responded. "The doctor said you can go two at a time. And that's all. But don't go tonight because they're supposed to get all the sleep they can right now. You can see them tomorrow."

He added, "Any more questions?"

I spoke up. "On behalf of the men, I want to thank you, Sir. Thank you for everything you've done."

The men joined me as Colonel Ellis walked toward the back of the barracks. When he got to the door, he turned and said again, "Wait until tomorrow to go see them. OK?"

After he had gone, the men asked me if I had any other details. I probably shouldn't have said anything—I probably just should have kept my mouth shut—but I kept thinking of how Tyler and Williams had looked lying there on the floor of the barracks. I told them it was likely men from Colonel Rogers' battalion who had been involved. I also told them Colonel Rogers had said an "investigation" would be done.

"Yeah, right," Davis said sarcastically. "We know how those investigations go, don't we?"

"That was my first reaction, too," I said. "I don't like it any more than you do, but I think Colonel Ellis is right. We are just going to have to wait and see what happens. Colonel Ellis was right about something else. Tyler and Williams are going to be OK. That's what's most important right now. So, we wait."

I checked my watch. "I know it's late, but none of us have had anything to eat. You men wait here while I run over to the mess. I'll get them to put something together. Give me about half an hour and then come on over. If we are going to have to wait, there's no sense waiting on an empty stomach. Right?"

The men were in total agreement.

* * *

While the men finished a late meal, I went over to the infirmary to check on Williams and Tyler, to see if there was anything they needed or if there was anything the doctor wanted us to do. They were both sleeping when I arrived. The doctor wasn't around, but an older nurse, one who looked like she had probably made the army her career, met me at the door and told me there had been no change, that they were both resting as comfortably as could be expected under the circumstances.

"The one in the far bed," she said, pointing to Williams. "He must be some little scrapper."

"Why do you say that?" I asked.

"His right hand is swollen about the size of a small melon. I've seen that a hundred times before. I'd say he got in a few good licks of his own. He also has four broken ribs, as far as we can tell. When he landed a punch, those ribs must have hurt like hell. I'd say he's a tough little so-and-so, but you'd never know it to look at him. Take a good look at him right now. He looks like a little kid, doesn't he?"

"That little kid has turned into one heck of a man," I said.

I then added, "When I first met him, he was so shy I'm not sure he spoke even to his own mother."

The nurse laughed and said, "You two must be pretty close. Am I right?"

"I don't think I knew just how close until right now. But don't tell him I said that. He's also a little character, and I'm going to have to keep chewing his behind or I have the feeling this won't be the last time I'll be standing over him."

"What about Tyler?" I then asked. "How's he doing?"

The nurse didn't respond. She kept looking at me while she put down a stack of clean sheets she had been carrying. Coming closer to me, she reached up and rubbed my left eyebrow.

"Ouch! What are you doing?" I yelped as I drew back from her.

"I thought so," she said. "Here, you sit down a minute. I want to take a look at that."

"Take a look at what?" I asked, rubbing my eye.

She started laughing again, quietly at first, then so loudly she had to cover her mouth.

"I'm sorry," she said. "I shouldn't be laughing."

She then laughed so hard she picked the sheets back up and hid her face in them.

"What's so funny?" I asked. "What is it?"

I walked over to a mirror hanging on the wall by the door and studied my face as she tried to control her laughter. My eye was puffy, almost swollen shut. I hadn't even realized it. Suddenly it came to me. I remembered that while I was cradling Williams in my lap over in the barracks he came to just long enough to swing his arms out, cuffing me right in the eye. I hadn't thought anything about it at the time.

The nurse, finally controlling her laughter, motioned for me to come back and sit down.

"Let me take a good look at that," she said, prying open my eyelid and examining my eye. This time her touch was soft, gentle. After she finished she said, "I think you'll be OK. I don't see any damage to the eye, and the soft tissue should heal in a few days."

I was relieved. I could just see the letter back home to Olivia: "Sorry, dear, but I lost an eye today when Williams slugged me...."

I thanked the nurse for taking a look at me and then asked, "Say, what was so funny? Mind telling me?"

"I'm really sorry," she said again. "That was *very* unprofessional of me. I shouldn't have...."—and here she paused and looked away from me, biting her lip to keep from laughing again.

"I want to know," I said. "What is it?"

She paused a minute, appearing unsure if she should say anything, but finally spoke up, "It's just that you...well...you've got a black eye! First one I've ever seen!" And with that she put her face back into the sheets to muffle her laughter again.

At first I didn't get it. What could be so funny about a black...?

Then it hit me, like a fist.

On any other day but this one I might have laughed right along with her. But not today. Looking over at the limp bodies of Williams and Tyler, I felt my temples start to throb. I drew back from her, removing her hand from my forehead. Today there wasn't anything I could find funny about the color of a man's skin, even if it wasn't said with malice.

The nurse wasn't being mean, and she wasn't teasing me. But this wasn't the time. And after today, I didn't know if there'd ever be a time when I'd find comments like hers the least bit funny again.

I finally said to her, "If you look closely, I have two black eyes. One of them is bruised, like them," I said, pointing to Williams and Tyler.

I studied her face. All trace of laughter had evaporated. She stared at me, unblinking.

"This bruise will heal," I said, rubbing my eye. Then, pointing again to Williams and Tyler, I said, "Think theirs will?"

"I'm sorry," she said, apology filling her voice. "I didn't mean anything. I didn't."

"I know you didn't," I said. "No one ever does."

I walked over and pulled the covers up around Williams' neck. Then I turned and walked out of the infirmary.

* * *

Doc was running up to greet me as I left the infirmary.

"They're OK. They're going to be fine," I said, anticipating his questions.

"You better come with me—and hurry," he said, a panicked look on his face.

"What's going on?" I asked as he grabbed my shirtsleeve and practically dragged me down the street.

He was out of breath, his sentences coming in short bursts. "A couple of jerkheads from Rogers' battalion. Came by in a jeep right after we got back from chow. They stopped outside the barracks and threw all the decorations we had over in the Service Club out on the walk. Right in front of us. Most of it was ripped to shreds."

He paused to catch his breath, tugging on my arm to get me to stop walking. "That would have been bad enough, but as they drove off one of them said, 'That'll teach you to stay on your own side of the street!'"

"That did it, Perc. I'm telling you—the men snapped. Right then they decided that 'waiting' stuff was for the birds."

"What did they do?" I asked, afraid of what was coming next.

"You'll have to see for yourself," he said. "I saw it, and I still don't believe it. I think it was Albertson who got them to do it."

"Don't tease me, Doc. What did they do?"

"It isn't what they *did*—it's what they're still doing *now*. You better take a look for yourself."

As we rounded the corner the Service Club came into view. There they were, lined up in a perfect row, standing in the soft rain that had started falling.

In full uniform, standing at attention, in complete silence, they were facing the Service Club.

Colonel Rogers came out of the club, screaming at them as he came toward them, ordering them to leave.

"If you don't get the hell out of here—and I mean right this minute—you're all going to spend the rest of this war in the stockade. I'm going to have you arrested, and don't you think I won't. Now you get your asses out of here before the MPs come."

He was screaming at the top of his lungs. Even in the darkness, I could see his face was beet red.

His guests in the Service Club were pressing their faces against the windows, straining to see what was happening outside. A window flew up, and a soldier inside called out, "Colonel, want us to come out and help?"

He didn't answer him. Just as he got right up in Davis's face and started screaming again, a six-by pulled up and MPs jumped out, rifles clutched to their chests.

At almost that same instant, Colonel Ellis came roaring up in his jeep, skidding to a halt between the MPs and the men. He jumped out and shouted to the MPs, "Hold it! Don't any of you dare move!"

Colonel Rogers ran over to him, his arms flailing, still screaming back at the men.

"This is it, Ellis," he then shouted. "I've had enough of this shit. They're all going to the stockade—and you'll be going too if you don't get the hell out of the way."

Colonel Ellis looked like he wanted to take a poke at him, but instead he put his hands in his pockets and smiled. "And what are you going to arrest them for?" he asked. "For protecting your guests?" He pointed to the Service Club.

"Protecting my guests?" Colonel Rogers shrieked. "Protecting my guests? What the hell are you talking about?"

The men finally moved, but just barely. At Colonel Ellis's last words, almost in unison they moved their heads to look at him, also curious what he was talking about.

"Didn't you hear?" Colonel Ellis continued. "It looks like someone—not one of ours—got on the base and is beating up military personnel, and the *investigation* hasn't come up with anything yet. Hell, that fiend might just attack your guests tonight. And I hear the mayor is in there, too. How would it look if the mayor got attacked while here as your guest?"

Colonel Rogers was dumbfounded and started stammering, "What are you... What are you..."

Colonel Ellis didn't give him a chance to get his thoughts together and jumped right in again. "I ordered these men to protect your guests. They're here under my direct orders," he said, pointing to the men, some of whom were now smiling.

"Not only that," he continued, "I ordered them to use all available means of force, if need be, to protect the mayor and his party. *That's* what they are doing here."

He paused one more time, for emphasis, and continued, "This afternoon it looked like you didn't have time to do anything to increase security around here, so I stepped in and took care of it myself. You don't have to thank me now—I know you appreciate it."

Before Colonel Rogers could respond, another jeep pulled up. The acting base commander, General Mann, stepped quickly from the jeep and asked, looking back and forth from Colonel Ellis to Colonel Rogers, "What's going on here? Explain!"

Colonel Ellis beat Colonel Rogers to the punch and said, "Everything's under control, Sir. I ordered this 'security detail' to form here to protect the mayor and his party."

He pointed again to the Service Club and added, "You were out this afternoon when I came to HQ, Sir. All indications are that someone snuck on the base and attacked some of our men."

Colonel Ellis was on a roll, his words coming so fast no one could get a word in edgewise.

"I was concerned, as I knew you would be, about the safety of the mayor and our other guests. That's why I ordered this. Better safe than sorry. Right, Sir?"

General Mann looked at the faces pressed against the windows of the Service Club and then at the men, who were still standing at attention.

Then he looked at Colonel Rogers, "That right?" he asked.

"Well, Sir... I guess..."

It was obvious from the look on his face. He knew he'd been had. What could he say? It would have been one thing if Colonel Ellis had said "soldiers" had been involved in the beatings, but he had been smart enough to hint that it was someone from outside the base, some fiend, who had been the perpetrator. If there was one thing that was true about the army it was that it protected its own—to all lengths possible. Colonel Ellis had played upon this so much that there wasn't anything that Colonel Rogers could say back to General Mann except, "That's right, Sir."

He said it like he had a fishbone caught in his throat.

A broad smile came across my face. Colonel Ellis had been so convincing, I almost started wondering myself who the "outside" fiends were who had beaten up Williams and Tyler.

"Well, then, OK," General Mann said. He then turned back to Colonel Ellis and said, "For godsakes, Ellis, you didn't need to turn out half the damn base to do this. Get some of them the hell out of here. Leave about a dozen men here and the MPs, too. That'll be more than enough for security."

He then said to Colonel Rogers, "Under the circumstances, I think you better consider escorting your guests back to town. Ellis is right. If the mayor would get hurt, we'd all be digging outhouses the rest of our lives."

With a sweep of his arms, he ordered, "OK, break this up. Ellis— have a dozen fall out and get the rest out of here. You MPs—take charge of this. Let's get everybody safely escorted home."

With that, he shook his head, climbed back in his jeep, and said to his driver loud enough for all of us to hear, "Get me the hell out of this loony bin."

As soon as he pulled away, Colonel Ellis quickly ordered, "From this end—count off to twelve. The rest of you men, head back to the barracks."

And then, louder, for the benefit of Colonel Rogers and all the noses pressed to the windows, he said, "Good job, men. Good job."

Other than the twelve who were now on "fiend patrol," the men started heading back to the barracks. I quickly walked over to Colonel Ellis as he started getting back into his jeep and stuck out my hand, reached over and took his, and shook it firmly.

"I don't know what to say, Sir. That was magnificent."

"Keep your voice down," he said. "Look at that bastard Rogers staring at us. He's probably already trying to figure out a way to get even."

"He probably is, Sir," I said. "But for the time being, I'd say this round was ours, wouldn't you?"

"You really think so?" he replied.

"Just look at the men," I said.

They were now walking slowly back to the barracks, many with their arms around the shoulders of the man next to him.

"Just what the hell did they think they were doing anyway?" he asked with a hint of a smile across his lips. "Just what the hell were they trying to prove here?"

"Sir, you'll have to ask them, but I'm pretty sure I can guess. I don't think there's any doubt part of it was what happened to Williams and Tyler. And I'd guess part of it was losing the Club tonight—and then having to look at those faces in the windows. And probably part of it was just, well, being plain mad."

Colonel Ellis sat back down in his jeep. "You're probably right," he said, shaking his head. "But what a way to show it. I've never seen anything like that in my life, have you?"

I hadn't.

"I'm going to have to talk to them about this, you know," he said.

"Please don't come down too hard on them, Sir. This had to be done, and I think, deep down, you know that, too."

"I know," he said, looking down at the ground. "I know."

He pulled a cigarette from his pocket and lit it. Looking over at me, he pulled out another and offered it to me. I took it, and he handed me his cigarette so I could light mine off the end of his.

We smoked together in silence.

As we watched the mayor and his guests being escorted from the Service Club by our men and the MPs, we looked at each other and I knew we were both thinking the same thing.

This battle had been won.

And those involved would never forget it.

19

BOMBERS

I didn't want anyone to know it, but I was worried.

Very worried.

Even though Colonel Ellis had quickly and shrewdly diffused the explosive situation at the Service Club, I was starting to worry that repercussions from that night would be fast and furious. Colonel Rogers didn't seem to me to be the kind of man who could just walk away from a showing-up like he had been given. He had been fit to be tied when Colonel Ellis jumped in and suddenly turned attention from what our men were doing there to the need to find the "fiends" who had beaten up Williams and Tyler—and who might have still been lurking in the shadows, posing a threat to the visitors to the base. Colonel Ellis had, plain and simple, made Colonel Rogers look bad in front of everyone, and in my gut I had the feeling we hadn't heard the last from him.

Almost immediately, the full story of what was now jokingly being referred to in the battalion as "Albertson's Last Stand" came out. Albertson had been the one who first took a stand, literally, in full view of the mayor and the rest of his party that night outside the Service Club.

For Albertson, already angry about what had happened to Williams and Tyler, the last straw had been Colonel Rogers' men shredding and then dumping our Club decorations out in front of the barracks that same evening. As soon as Colonel Rogers' men had driven off, Albertson, without saying a word, walked inside the barracks, got dressed in full uniform, and then headed back outside. A few curious onlookers asked what he was doing as he then started marching down the road. In response, he said only, "I've had it."

With a few men trailing behind, he continued marching down the road until he was outside the Service Club. Once there, he stood next to the sidewalk where those coming into and leaving the Club couldn't help but see him.

The sight of him standing at attention in the rain was like a call to arms to the other men. Within minutes word spread, and a line soon started forming next to him that grew until almost every man in the battalion not pulling special duty had joined in.

They stood their ground and made their point that night, and they had done it together, but they still woke up the next morning to the same everyday realities that had surrounded them before. Only now they had the aftertaste of the previous evening's events lingering in their mouths.

The mood in the battalion changed again and might best be described as "defensive." The men became very protective of each other, and the almost constant teasing and ribbing that had been a daily part of their lives in the barracks slowed almost to a halt. It was pretty clear to me they were circling the wagons—both physically and emotionally.

One thing that helped lift their spirits in the days that followed "Albertson's Last Stand" was how quickly Williams and Tyler started to recover. Both were kept under close observation in the infirmary until one afternoon when Williams, sneaking a smoke while the nurse was out, accidentally set a trash basket full of bandages on fire, resulting in enough smoke pouring out of the building that the base fire trucks were summoned. Williams protested his innocence when questioned, and no one could prove otherwise, but the doctor decided if he was well enough to jump out of bed and run for help, he was well enough to rejoin the battalion. He was released the next day.

When he got back to the barracks, his arm was in a sling. Several of us were just heading out for a quick game of catch but stopped to welcome him home. The men gathered around as he told them about his wounds.

I stood off to the side where he couldn't see me. This was Williams at his conniving best, and I didn't want to break the spell he was weaving. He told the men he wouldn't be able to do any type of work for several more weeks. He even went so far as to say he had been given permission to assign his regular duties to other men in the barracks—and would especially need help doing things like making his bunk and cleaning his rifle. He might, he said, even need help eating.

He was really getting wound up when I coughed and got his attention. Upon seeing me, he said, "Well, I *should* get some extra help. Shouldn't I?"

I had been to the infirmary earlier in the day, and the doctor told me that other than having some sore ribs, Williams was recovering nicely. The sling he was now wearing was *his* idea. His arm was fine.

When I casually mentioned this to the others, they circled in around him and pretended to beat the stuffing out of him.

It was good to have him back.

Tyler was another story. His concussion wasn't a "million-dollar wound," as the men described wounds and injuries that were serious enough to send men back home. But it was cause for enough concern that the doctor wanted him to be put on light duty for several more weeks just to be on the safe side. For as small as he was, he turned out to be one pretty tough little bird.

Having Williams and Tyler back was a definite shot in the arm, but I was still hoping and praying for some sort of diversion to break the tension and take our minds off what had happened that night at the Club. None of us would ever forget it, but it was also time to stop looking back. It was time to look forward again. It was time to recapture the laughter and pride that formed the foundation of the battalion.

At the same time, a diversion wasn't needed just by our men. It was needed by everyone on the base to put that horrible night in the distance. It was time to come together, to put differences behind us and a unified effort up front above everything else.

And the time for all of this was now.

* * *

About a week after Williams and Tyler returned to the battalion, my prayers were answered. A better diversion could not have been designed than the one that suddenly appeared to be falling right into our laps. It seemed for all the world like a miracle.

Word came that Joe Louis, the heavyweight boxing champion of the world, the "Brown Bomber" himself, was coming to Fort Bliss.

And not only that, he was coming because he specifically wanted to visit our battalion.

He had made a big splash the previous year when he joined the army, putting his boxing career on hold to join in the war effort. From what I could gather from the newspapers, he was now touring the country as something of an ambassador for the army, helping with recruiting efforts wherever they sent him. Along the way, he held boxing exhibitions for the troops, and that was what he was scheduled to do during his stop at Fort Bliss. Diversion? Definitely—but I soon started to think "blessing" was actually more like it.

As soon as word leaked to the men, they whooped and hollered as if they had been granted two weeks leave. Brown was so excited he jumped up and darn near scalped himself when he caught his head on the edge of the door frame. Ten stitches.

Joe Louis wasn't just a boxer to them. He was a symbol. Actually, he was many symbols rolled into the most powerful right hand in the land. He was, first and foremost, a symbol of America's power and strength. Back in '38 when he had resoundingly defeated Max Schmeling, Hitler's fair-haired symbol of Aryan supremacy, the country had rejoiced. Outside the ring, that fight was considered a victory of democracy over fascism—of "right" over "might." In that rematch, Louis had moved in quickly and knocked Schmeling out in the first round, leaving no doubt whatsoever as to whom was the better fighter.

Radios all across the land were tuned to that fight, and when the referee stopped the fight and declared Louis the winner, all America cheered—and let out a collective sigh of relief as well. Germany's continued march across Europe was plastered all over the newspaper headlines every day. Countries were falling like dominoes. Louis's victory stopped those headlines for a day and even seemed, and not just in a symbolic way, to halt the German advance, at least temporarily, at a time when the dark clouds over Europe were growing even larger.

Joe Louis was also a symbol of a different sort to the men. He

wasn't just a man who had excelled in athletics. He represented someone who had made it over the fences that seemed to form boundaries
all across society, boundaries to keep some Americans, at the same
time both in and out of the current. Just how far he had been able to
travel on the other side of the fence was often hotly debated, but all
had to admit he had at least made it over. Many others still had not.

Immediately the men started putting their newly learned construction skills to work, building a boxing ring right next to our baseball field. Williams, now fully recovered, scrounged not only posts for
the corners of the ring, but ropes as well. None of us knew where he
got the material. None of us wanted to know.

He also "found" several parachutes that he hoped could somehow
be pieced together and stretched into a passable floor for the ring,
replacing the canvas that was normally used. However, no matter how
tightly it was stretched, the parachute material gathered when walked
on, which caused dangerous footing. Albertson and Brown climbed
inside one day to try it out, and both kept tripping and falling to the
ground. The parachute material idea was scratched. There was no way
we were going to subject Joe Louis to possible injury if we could help
it. We finally decided that the ground would be a suitable floor for the
ring if all rocks and pebbles were removed and the area was smoothed
down. Those who had received special training in helping build "on-
the-fly" runways were put in charge of leveling the ground. They did
just fine.

While the ring was being built, others started work on two sets of
bleacher seats, one for the north side and the other for the south side
of the ring. These were impressive structures, each ten rows high, and,
as Jamieson described them, "fifteen butts long." They were not built
as permanent structures. Rather, they were built in interlocking units,
a skill several had just learned. These units could later be moved to our
baseball field. Jamieson had thought of that one.

During the initial stages of construction it looked like gallows
were being built. Several joked to Williams that they had been ordered
to build them in case he got caught stealing anything else around the
base. He had laughed and then nervously lit up a smoke, burning his
fingers in the process.

"Last cigarette?" I teased as I watched him dance around in pain. He didn't find it funny. My teasing also didn't deter him in the least.

I did find out where the wood for the bleachers came from and wondered if he wouldn't have been marched up real gallows if someone like Colonel Rogers ever found out. It seemed that construction materials intended for use in building new latrines on the other side of the base had suddenly up and disappeared one night. Those on guard duty that night could remember seeing a small convoy of trucks driving around the base about 2200 hours. The guards had even helped change a tire on one of the trucks, but neither of them had seen anyone go near the supply depot.

Williams again.

From the minute he got out of the infirmary, Williams was a man possessed, a man on a mission. Anything not nailed down was fair game for his sticky fingers. His funniest and best piece of "borrowing" came to light one night when I opened the door to the supply closet in the barracks. There, stacked from floor to ceiling, were dozens of rolls of the new, softer, GI toilet paper.

Confronted by me about this, he replied matter-of-factly, "Well, I figured as long as they weren't going to be able to build those new latrines, they wouldn't be needing this stuff, either."

I was beginning to like his logic.

* * *

As the time for Mr. Louis's visit to the base drew near, I was also wrestling with a very difficult decision I had to make. I was fully aware that whichever way my decision went, I'd end up making plenty of the men mad at me, and my stomach was starting to burn every time I thought about the subject.

Mr. Louis was bringing with him his regular sparring partner for the main exhibition bouts, but he also sent word ahead that he'd like a couple of the men from the battalion to step into the ring with him. This wasn't to be for any serious kind of boxing. Rather, it was going to be more for show than anything else. He just wanted to make the event more interesting for the men, to boost morale, to give them something more to talk about after he left.

And it was my responsibility to choose the men who would step into the ring with him.

This was a once-in-a-lifetime opportunity, and the men were well aware of that. After the men found out I was the one who would make this decision, they tried to bribe me with every manner and form of flattery and gifts. Brown, who was now being called "Ten-Stitch" because of the gash in his head, stole a whole cherry pie from the mess and left it on my bunk with a note that read, "For the best sergeant in the army!" Not too subtle. I came into the barracks one afternoon to find Sanders sitting on my footlocker and shining my other pair of shoes. When I asked why he was shining my shoes, he replied, "Well, I know you want to look your best when Mr. Louis gets here." He then looked up at me with the most pitiful look on his face I had ever seen. Even Williams pled his case, saying that he had it set up so that pictures would be taken when he was in the ring with Mr. Louis, and a fortune could be made selling those pictures later on—a fortune he was willing to split with me. Why someone would want to buy pictures of Williams in the ring with Mr. Louis was a mystery to me, but I knew if Williams was involved, money would definitely be changing hands.

The bribery got so out of control and so ridiculous that Clark even offered me a date with his girlfriend—and said the date would be one I'd never forget. Doc, who had seen Clark's girlfriend, described her as having the face of a Missouri mule and legs to match, so I was guessing it really would have been a date to remember. When his girlfriend actually called me at the base one night and invited me to her house, that was the last straw. I finally couldn't take the attention, the "overwhelming adoration," anymore and announced my decision so the men would stop bothering me.

In addition to stepping into the ring with his sparring partner, Mr. Louis would also be dancing around the ring with Doc, Davis, and Tyler.

To me, Doc was a logical choice because he was in the best physical shape of anyone in the battalion. Doc "looked" like a fighter. I knew I'd be mobbed with charges of favoritism for choosing him, and there might have been more than a little truth to that, but I also knew the rest of the base would also be watching and wanted someone in the ring who could put up a good show for the battalion. I was hoping the men would understand that.

I chose Davis because he actually had some boxing experience back in his hometown of Atlanta. He had three professional bouts under the name of "Dynamite Davis." He was knocked out in the first round in all three bouts, but he knew his way around the ring. Sort of...

Then I chose Tyler. He was more and more becoming a symbol for the battalion. He was a scrawny little runt, but he was the kind of guy none of us could get mad at for long, no matter what he did. He just had this incredible bad luck of being in the wrong place at the wrong time. One day on the parade ground a bird flying overhead dropped a bomb right on top of his head. The men laughed so hard they quit their calisthenics and fell laughing to the ground. Another day he got his shirtsleeve caught on the side of a jeep just as Williams started driving away, and the whole sleeve, all the way up to the shoulder, just ripped right off his uniform. Brown laughed so hard at the sight of that, he pulled a stomach muscle and had to be helped to the infirmary to get checked out. Still another night, Tyler was sitting next to the projector in the motor pool as we watched a Hopalong Cassidy movie. While the rest of us watched the movie, he stuck a pencil in the take-up reel, causing it to jam, which led to the film snaking and flying all over the room before we knew what had happened. The film was ruined, and we lost movie privileges for two weeks over that incident. He later just said his curiosity got the best of him. But how could we be mad at him? There wasn't a malicious bone in his body. He was just unlucky—which made us feel all the more lucky by comparison.

It would be a good show to see Tyler climb into the ring. David versus Goliath wouldn't even begin to describe the contrast between Tyler and Mr. Louis. The men would howl, and right now they needed a good laugh. And so did I.

I wanted Tyler to get into the ring so that everyone on the base— everyone—could see he had recovered. He had taken a beating, and a bad one, but he had also gotten up before the count reached ten. It was important for all to see this with their own eyes. Mr. Louis may have been a symbol of strength and might for the entire country but, closer to home, Tyler was our own symbol of quiet strength and perseverance. If Tyler could succeed, we all reasoned, then there was hope for all of us.

* * *

The morning Joe Louis arrived, Fort Bliss looked like it was receiving royalty, which, in a way, it was. Welcome banners hung from every building on the base. They said things like:

"Axis vs. Louis—No Contest!"

"Watch Out, Krauts—The Brown Bomber's Going To Knock Your Block Off!"

"B-17s and Joe Louis—What a One-Two Punch!"

"Beat the Tar Out of Tojo, Joe!"

I didn't want to know where Williams found it, but he had the men string red, white, and blue bunting all along the road leading to our new boxing ring and bleachers.

The camp band turned out to play a rousing version of Sousa's "Stars and Stripes Forever" as he entered the base.

Colonel Rogers had left instructions for Mr. Louis's jeep to stop in front of his own battalion headquarters so he could personally welcome him to the base. However, the jeep didn't even slow down as it rounded the corner, throwing up a cloud of dust that swirled around a coughing and sneezing Colonel Rogers.

When Mr. Louis had found out about the 449th being on the base, he had his representatives contact Colonel Ellis so that he could specifically have time with our men. Colonel Ellis put me in charge of the official welcome. I thought about giving some type of speech when he arrived, but I didn't want to burn up the time he was going to be spending with us with a lot of my words.

When his jeep finally pulled up to the ring, I walked forward, saluted smartly, and then reached out to shake his hand.

"Mr. Louis," I said, heart pounding. "Welcome to Fort Bliss. Thank you for coming—we really appreciate this."

I then turned and said as loudly as I could, "Men, I'd like you to meet Mr. Joe Louis, the heavyweight boxing champion of the world!"

The roar that followed could have been heard all the way in

downtown El Paso.

The men stormed past me to shake his hand and ask for auto-graphs. I had to fight my way back through the crowd to referee the situation before it got completely out of control.

"That's enough!" I shouted. "Get back and give the man some air for goodness sakes!"

Then, as the men slowly backed up, the questions were thrown out, like a flurry of punches:

"Mr. Louis, when you fightin' again?"

"Who's the toughest man you ever fought?"

"You're not duckin' that bum Conn, right? When's the rematch?"

After this last question, the rambunctious crowd suddenly grew absolutely silent. Louis looked up from signing an autograph and sternly scanned the crowd to see who had asked it. The question was in poor taste, and those standing around Clark, who had asked it, let him know it by pounding on him.

Back in '41, during just one of those things that happens on the spur of the moment, about a hundred of us from the Ville gathered around a radio in the gymnasium at Sumner to listen to Mr. Louis fight Billy Conn. When word got out around the neighborhood that folks were starting to gather there to hear the fight, others came streaming in like ants. It was a rough fight for Mr. Louis, who didn't appear to be anywhere near his best that night. In the later rounds, the announcers hinted that Conn already had the fight won, and a gloom settled over the gymnasium. However, Conn made a costly mistake and tried to move in for a knockout, leaving himself open for a right-hand "bomb" that staggered him. Mr. Louis then moved in and hammered him, finally knocking him out. When the referee's count reached ten, those assembled let out the loudest cheer I had ever heard inside a school—and it was sweet music to all of our ears.

Billy Conn was a dangerous fighter, and some suspected Mr. Louis was now ducking him on purpose. Clark had just put into words what many were already thinking—but he shouldn't have done it in front of Mr. Louis.

To his credit, Mr. Louis didn't pretend like he hadn't heard the question. Instead, he smiled and said, "Men, I'm in the army for the duration. Sure, I'd like to fight Conn again—and I'll whip him again—but there's another fight that needs to be taken care of first. We need to pulverize Hitler and Tojo—and by God we're going to do it!"

Those who weren't standing jumped up and joined those who were and let out a cheer that sent chills down my back. Men from "both" sides of the base pounded each other on the backs, punched fists into the air, and screamed over and over, "Damn right! Damn right!"

While the roar grew louder, Joe Louis just stood there, smiling and shaking hands. I had seen pictures of him in newspapers and magazines, but nothing I had seen had prepared me for just how physically powerful he looked in the flesh. He was built like the proverbial "brick outhouse." His arms were so muscular they looked like twisted wire cable. Even through his uniform shirt I could see the muscles of his chest rippled when he moved. At first it surprised me that his legs seemed so short. Then I realized they just "appeared" to be short because his upper torso was so massive.

When the crowd started settling back down, someone else yelled out, "Hey, Mr. Louis, how much money you make last year?"

That last question got a lot of laughs. It also provided a perfect pause for me to jump in and get back at least a semblance of control.

"Mr. Louis doesn't have much time today," I shouted out. "So, let's get on with the exhibition. I'm sure there will be time for you to ask more questions later."

I turned to Mr. Louis and said while pointing to the ring, "It isn't much, but we did the best we could."

"Looks just fine," he responded. "Shoot, about a month ago I got in a ring that had chicken wire strung around it instead of ropes. I've still got scars on my back from that day. Compared to that, this'll be perfect."

When we got to the ring, Mr. Louis started undressing right then and there. He had worn his boxing trunks under his uniform so he wouldn't have to waste time finding a place to change. As his uniform shirt came off, a collective gasp could be heard. Mr. Louis's chest looked like it had been chiseled from rock.

He turned to me and said, "I usually start the exhibition with one of my own guys. That OK with you?"

Here was the heavyweight champion of the world asking me for permission to do something. All I could do was stutter, "S-Sure. That sounds good."

The bleachers were overflowing. Jamieson may have designed each row to be "fifteen butts long," but there were now a good twenty in each. I started praying they wouldn't collapse from the extra weight.

Seats in the first row of both bleachers had been reserved for officers. As a gesture of goodwill, a spot had been saved in the middle of the first row of the north bleachers for Colonel Rogers, who was still brushing dust from his uniform as he sat down. I was shocked to see Colonel Ellis walk over and sit down right next to him. The thought was he did so in order to keep an eye on him and head off any ugly situations that might pop up. Colonel Rogers didn't look all that happy about the seating arrangements, but he was trapped. It would have caused another scene if he had gotten up to move.

I wondered how the men would seat themselves in the bleachers. Even though Mr. Louis specifically wanted to visit with our battalion, everyone on the base had been invited to come see the exhibition. Doc and I talked about this the night before. He was sure all the Negroes would sit in one set of bleachers, and those from the other side of the base would fill up the other. I wasn't so sure.

As it turned out, Mr. Louis was almost an hour late getting to the base, and a rumor started making its way around that he wasn't coming at all because he had been delayed at his last stop. As the rumor spread, about half the men who had gathered dejectedly started heading back to their barracks. Then, when word came that his jeep was at the main gate, they turned around and ran as fast as they could back to the ring. In the midst of all this confusion, the men practically ran over the top of each other as they bolted for seats in the bleachers, and there wasn't time for any sorting. Judging by the looks on some of their faces as twenty butts were crammed into rows designed to hold fifteen, there were a lot of surprised soldiers of both colors as they realized the rows were being shared. But no one got up to move. No one was going to lose the chance to have one of the best seats in the house. The men weren't exactly chummy to each other, but they didn't say anything to each other either.

I looked up and down each row of the bleachers and held my breath.

Mr. Louis walked over to me and said, "My man Gans is going to get in first. OK to start now?"

"If we don't, the men are going to be all over us again in a minute," I joked. "I've got someone to ring a bell to take care of the timing. I was told you wanted to keep the rounds three minutes. That still right?"

"Three is fine. I'll do a round with Gans first. Then get your first man in the ring as quickly as you can after that."

He smiled and added, "And tell him to go easy on me."

"I don't think you have anything to worry about," I replied, smiling back.

I motioned for Williams to bring his hammer down on an old fire truck bell that he just happened to come across the other day. The banging of hammer on bell produced an odd clanging sound, almost like the sound of a streetcar bell, but it was good enough to get the attention of all.

I stepped into the ring and waved my arms, motioning for the men to quiet down.

"Men, may I have your attention please," I shouted. "The exhibition will now begin. Mr. Louis will first show us his boxing skill by going one round with one of his own sparring partners. After that, we have a couple of surprises for you. But first, I give you Mr. Joe Louis, the heavyweight boxing champion of the world!"

Applause erupted as Mr. Louis moved forward and immediately exchanged punches with his sparring partner, Gans, knocking him back against the ropes. When Gans regained his footing, they traded soft left jabs for a few seconds before Mr. Louis went into his trademark footwork, quickly moving in and out, head bobbing and weaving, throwing punches while moving in, and ducking side to side as he backed out of reach of his opponent. Gans continued to alternate left jabs with crossing rights that Mr. Louis easily blocked. After Gans had thrown one wild right, Mr. Louis moved in and with a sharp uppercut nailed Gans on the chin, staggering him. Mr. Louis followed the uppercut with a left that caught Gans completely off guard. He dropped to one knee, shook his head as if trying to get rid of cobwebs, and attempted to get back up, falling forward so that Mr. Louis had to catch him.

Mr. Louis turned to the north bleachers and said, obviously enjoying playing to the crowd, "What do you think? Think he's had enough?"

The applause indicated they agreed.

As Gans climbed out through the ropes, I quickly motioned for Davis to enter the ring. Even Williams couldn't find anything resembling boxing shorts, so we ended up making him some by cutting the legs off an old uniform. That was all he was wearing as he entered the ring. Gans, still visibly woozy, helped him into his boxing gloves and tied them. Mr. Louis came forward and introduced himself to Davis. Davis was so awestruck he was speechless. He just nodded toward Mr. Louis and looked like he was going to faint.

When Davis's gloves were secured, Williams hammered his bell again and the two boxers moved toward each other. The crowd, and especially those from our battalion, cheered wildly.

It was obvious, in spite of the early knockouts he suffered in his own professional fights, Davis knew his way around a boxing ring. Mr. Louis was going easy on him, but the two traded punches equally, both moving in and out of range of the other's punches with ease. To be honest, Davis didn't look all that interested in getting in close enough for Mr. Louis to tag him with a strong punch. Each time he moved in, he quickly moved back out of range. The two finally moved around the ring in little circular patterns, each man catching the other with light, easy blows.

The three minutes seemed to come so quickly. The clang from Williams' bell startled me, and I nearly tripped and fell as I climbed into the ring to shake the hands of both boxers.

"Good job, Davis," I said, patting him on the back.

He was so winded he couldn't reply. He just nodded his head and gasped for breath as Gans ran over to remove his gloves. Mr. Louis also stepped back over and said, "You're not bad. You've fought before, haven't you?"

One of the biggest smiles I had ever seen spread across Davis's face. When he had sucked in enough air to talk again, he responded,

"A few fights. I'm not very good. Thank you, Mr. Louis. I'll never forget this."

"Keep at it, son," Mr. Louis said. "Your footwork is OK!"

Davis, upon hearing this, looked like he could have died right at that moment and been perfectly happy.

As Davis climbed through the ropes and out of the ring, Doc was already stepping in. Gans quickly put the gloves on him as whistles and shouts of "Wow!" started spreading through the crowd. Doc, while not in the same league physically as Mr. Louis, was still an imposing figure. He had what many called a "washboard" chest, rippled and appearing hard as steel. His arms were huge compared to anyone else's in the battalion, including Davis's. His legs were so muscular the tendons seemed to pop up and down as he walked.

When his gloves were secured, I motioned for both men to step to the center of the ring. I joked, "OK, let's keep it clean—no low blows."

Mr. Louis smiled as he eyed Doc. "Where'd you find these guys," he asked, shaking his head. "These two look better than the 'bums' I've been fighting."

Mr. Louis was making reference to a comment made by a sportswriter a year or so back that had, unfortunately, stuck to him like flypaper. The writer had said something like, "When is Joe Louis going to fight a real opponent—instead of these bums and has-beens that keep parading out of the woodwork? 'Bum of the Month' club—that's what his competition has been…."

Personally, I didn't think it was his fault the competition wasn't that strong. Mr. Louis had beaten every major contender. Who was left? Maybe it was true that some of his fights right before he entered the army had been against less than stellar opponents, but that certainly didn't seem his fault.

I didn't know how Doc would hold up in the ring, but he sure didn't look like any bum. When Williams hit the bell to start the round, Mr. Louis and Doc met in the middle of the ring and tapped gloves, the boxing version of shaking hands. Then they started circling each other, throwing out soft, exploratory left jabs. Doc had never boxed before, but it quickly became obvious he knew how to take care of himself.

His reach was long, and he kept his left out almost constantly to help deflect Mr. Louis's jabs. He appeared to be cocking his right hand, waiting for an opening. Mr. Louis saw that and kept moving to the right, away from Doc's power. He wasn't the heavyweight champion for nothing.

While Mr. Louis was moving to his right, lulling Doc into the rhythm of the soft jabs, he suddenly changed course, catching Doc completely off guard. Doc, inexperienced as a boxer, had been standing flat-footed and couldn't keep up with Mr. Louis's swift movement. Before Doc could reset himself, Mr. Louis landed a sharp left, left, right combination, the last punch harder than the rest and catching Doc under the left eye. His knees buckled. His balance gone, the only place for his body to go was down. His back hit the ground first, followed by his head.

He got up quickly, smiling, motioning Mr. Louis to come back to the center of the ring for more. Mr. Louis laughed loudly and said, "OK, son, but don't say I didn't warn you."

Doc moved in quickly, jabbing with his left and keeping Mr. Louis honest with his right. Suddenly both men threw a flurry of punches, both landing some good ones. Doc tagged him with one good right that bent Mr. Louis's head back. Mr. Louis countered with a right hook to Doc's left ear. Out of the corner of my eyes I could see men in both bleachers wince after that blow. Mr. Louis was playing with Doc, but the two of them were putting on quite a show. For an instant, it really did look like two professional fighters going at each other.

The clanging of Williams' bell signaled the end of the round, but Doc and Mr. Louis kept slugging it out. I jumped into the ring and stepped between them, not the smartest thing I had ever done. One of them—or maybe both of them—clubbed me on the forehead, snapping my head back. They stopped boxing when Doc reached down to catch me just as I was about to hit the dirt. I was fine, but my temples immediately started to throb.

The men applauded wildly for Mr. Louis and Doc. Then some joker yelled out, "Way to take a punch, Sarge!" The men clapped for me, and I gave an exaggerated bow, my knees buckling again in the process.

Doc used his teeth to undo the knots on his right glove and

removed it. He extended his hand to shake Mr. Louis's glove and said, "Mr. Louis, I don't know what to say. I'll never forget this as long as I live. Thank you—and God bless you."

"You've got a mean right," Mr. Louis said in response, smiling again. He came over and hugged Doc and patted him on the back. "You're OK, son. You take care of yourself, OK?"

"And you, too, Mr. Louis. Please take care of yourself. You don't have any idea what you mean to us, and I don't think you'll ever really know. It's hard to put into words, but we're so proud of you. So damn proud."

"Thanks," Mr. Louis said, reaching over and tapping Doc on the shoulder again with his glove. Then he nodded his head and added, "Let's all keep fightin'."

I hated to break up their conversation, but I knew time was growing short. While the crowd continued to buzz about their round, I quickly made my way to the side of the south set of bleachers. I yelled in to Brown and Jamieson, "It's time. Bring him out."

I had put Brown and Jamieson in charge of keeping Tyler out of sight under the bleachers until it was his turn to step into the ring. And what a sight he was. He, too, was wearing cutoff uniform pants, but his were made from a pair of Brown's, which meant they were so large on Tyler he looked like he was standing in a barrel. There was no way those shorts were going to stay up by themselves, so suspenders had been made from rope. The shorts were synched up so high they came up practically to his armpits. He also had his own homemade boxing gloves, which were about twice the size of normal ones. They were so big they looked like hams. To top it off, he was wearing a crown Albertson had made from tinfoil.

Once out from under the bleachers, Brown and Jamieson lifted Tyler on their shoulders, and with a fanfare provided by Clark and his trumpet, they brought Tyler to the ring. The crowd, and Mr. Louis, took one look at Tyler and started laughing so hard I thought the bleachers were going to collapse. Unfazed, Tyler jumped down from their shoulders and climbed under the ropes and into the ring, bouncing up and down and pounding those huge gloves together to show he meant business.

I was still a little worried about Tyler taking part in this. When I had talked on the phone with Mr. Louis's manager to set up the rest of the details of his visit, I had mentioned wanting to put Tyler in the ring. I had also told him about Tyler's recent concussion and asked that he relay this information to Mr. Louis. The manager told me not to worry about it, but that was easy for him to say. He hadn't seen Tyler unconscious in the infirmary.

I jumped back in the ring and yelled for the crowd to pipe down so I could announce the last fighter of the day. At the same time I motioned for Williams to hammer his bell to help get their attention. Williams continued banging so long and so loudly I ended up having to go over and take his hammer away from him. He looked up so sadly I gave it right back to him, scolding, "Enough! Don't you touch this until I tell you to!" The men thought it was funny, but I didn't. Time was wasting.

"Gentlemen! Gentlemen—may I have your attention please!" I shouted from the center of the ring. "It's time for the main event."

When the crowd quieted, I continued, waving my arm toward Tyler, "In this corner, weighing 107 pounds soaking wet, wearing… well, the highest trunks I've ever seen, the terror of Tennessee, the 'Memphis Mauler' himself, Johnny Tyler!"

The men went wild. A chorus of "Memphis Mauler! Memphis Mauler!" rang out as the men stomped their feet on the bleachers.

"And in this corner," I continued, shouting above the buzz of the crowd, "Weighing in at about, oh, I'd say about as much as a tank and built like one, too, wearing black trunks, the heavyweight champion of the world, the Brown Bomber himself, Mr. Jooooooeeeee Louis!"

Shouts of "Brown Bomber! Brown Bomber!" immediately filled the air. The men again stomped their feet up and down on the bleachers, only this time in unison. "Brown Bomber! Brown Bomber!" they continued to shout as Mr. Louis raised his arms and waved to them.

Mr. Louis then stepped to the middle of the ring and bowed, first to the north, and then to the south set of bleachers. As the men continued to stomp, a loud crack suddenly pierced the air. The bottom row on the north bleachers snapped right in the middle, causing the men on both sides of the break to slide together toward the center.

When we saw that no one was hurt in the pileup that resulted, some muffled laughter and a few giggles could be heard, but no one dared laugh out loud. That first row had been reserved for officers, and the men knew better than to laugh at them. Still, I could see more than a few men biting their shirtsleeves and covering their mouths to keep from howling. The officers quickly climbed off each other and brushed themselves off. At the bottom of the pile, the last man to get up, face covered with dirt, was Colonel Rogers.

A more beautiful sight I had not seen since entering the army.

Those in the second row quickly moved down from their seats and sat on the ground so the officers could move up and take their places. When all had quieted down again, I motioned Mr. Louis and Tyler to come back toward the center of the ring.

"Now, no low blows," I sternly admonished Mr. Louis, pointing to Tyler's hiked up shorts.

"Then where in the hell am I going to hit him?" he replied, laughing.

"You'll just have to do the best you can," I said, motioning for both men to step forward and tap gloves.

I pointed to Williams, who hit the bell, signaling the start of the round.

Tyler immediately started swinging his arms around and around like windmill blades as he cautiously inched forward toward Mr. Louis. Mr. Louis stood, hands on hips, laughing at Tyler's exaggerated swings. He turned to the south bleachers and threw up his hands, as if to say, "What in the world should I do?"

Just at that moment, Tyler jumped up, arms still swinging around, and his huge right glove came down right on the side of Mr. Louis's face. Mr. Louis staggered back all the way across the ring until his back was against the ropes, shook his head from side to side, and fell forward to the canvas. He lay motionless.

Instantly, everyone in the crowd became absolutely silent. Tyler pulled off his gloves and bent down, shouting in his high-pitched and now panic-stricken voice, "Mr. Louis—you OK? You OK? I didn't mean it!"

Mr. Louis rolled over on his back, moaning loudly, "Oooooohhh!

Oooooouucchhh!" I ran over and knelt down next to him. When he saw me, he winked—then groaned again louder than before.

I started to smile but bit my lip before anyone could see me. The men in the bleachers were all now standing, craning their necks to see what was going on. The men who had been seated on the ground had moved forward and were all now hanging over the ropes.

I pushed Tyler back and ordered, "Get back to your corner!"

"I didn't mean it!" he continued to shout. "I didn't mean it!"

Then to the collective horror and disbelief of the crowd, I started the count—"One, two, three…"

The men looked at me like I had lost my mind. When I got to the count of "five," Mr. Louis reached out, grabbed the rope, and slowly pulled himself up. He was upright completely by the time I reached "nine."

"Why you little…" he shouted over toward a still stunned Tyler. Then he started chasing Tyler wildly around the ring. The men roared again once they figured out what Mr. Louis had done.

I waved to get Williams' attention and made a hammering motion with my hand. He hit the bell repeatedly as Mr. Louis continued chasing Tyler.

I finally grabbed both of them and brought them back to the center of the ring. I held up their right arms and shouted over the laughter, "Gentlemen—your attention please. In a judges' decision, the fight has been declared a draw!"

"Quick count! That was a quick count!" Tyler shrieked, his voice cracking.

The men howled again.

"You were robbed," Mr. Louis responded. Then shrugging his shoulders and turning to the crowd he said, "That's boxing."

I motioned for Williams to hit the bell again so I could get the attention of the men one last time.

"Please, hold it down just for a minute. There's one more thing I want to say."

When I saw I had the attention of most, I continued, "I just want to say thank you to Mr. Joe Louis for taking the time from his busy schedule to stop by to visit with us today—and to show us what we already knew—that he's not just one of the greatest boxers in history, but one of the greatest men in history, too. Mr. Louis—on behalf of every man here I want to thank you. Thank you—and God bless you!"

The men applauded and cheered, "Hip, hip, hooorrraaaayyy. Hip, hip, hooorrraaaayyy!"

Mr. Louis bowed repeatedly to the crowd and then motioned for everyone to quiet down.

"Men," he said, "I'm not going to give a speech. I'm not good with words. I usually let my fists do my talking for me."

He smiled again before continuing, "But there's one thing I want to say before I go. I've been saying this every place I've been all across this country. Every time I step into the ring I give it everything I've got. Everything. I leave nothing in the corner when that bell rings. I expect that same kind of effort from all of you, whether you're diggin' ditches or flying planes. We're going to win this war, and we're going to win it because *none* of us is going to leave anything in the corner. Thank you for having me—and a special thanks to the men of the 449th. Good luck and Godspeed to you all."

Wild applause broke out as men poured into the ring to shake his hand. I knew he was on a tight schedule and would have to rush to catch his train, but I didn't move forward right away, like I should have, to help him out of the ring. Rather, I stood there, watching the men—"all" the men on the base, crowding around him.

He may have been a symbol of many things, but as he stood there in the ring, signing autographs and posing for pictures with the men, he was now, more than anything, a symbol of "unity."

Unity of men—and unity of purpose.

We desperately needed both.

* * *

For the rest of the afternoon the men could talk about nothing but Mr. Louis's visit. Every once in a while they would also square off, mimicking Mr. Louis's footwork as they pawed at each other. His visit had been just the boost in morale we had all needed.

This was also our night for the Service Club, our first time there since the week before "Albertson's Last Stand." Not long after we got there, I could see Mr. Louis's final words to the men had also been taken to heart. I watched the men closely, and the level of competition was definitely a few rungs higher than usual. On this night, during their games, the men left nothing "in the corner."

The Ping-Pong matches, in particular, were spectacular, with volleys often going for minutes at a time before someone mis-hit the ball. Even the checker games took twice as long as usual. The men studied each move like they were getting ready to move battalions of men to the front lines. When Clark beat Davis in a game that had drawn several onlookers, he stood up and shouted, "And the winner, by a knockout!" The others offered hearty congratulations, shaking his hand and patting him on the back.

Tyler and Williams also picked up the pace in their bridge game, wiping out Albertson and Jamieson so quickly they barely had time to get their chairs warm.

Just as Davis won his checkers rematch with Clark, Sergeant Ingram, wide-eyed and out of breath, ran into the club. "Perc, let's go!" he shouted, motioning me outside. "Now!"

Once outside, he took me by the arm and pulled me down the walk.

"What is it?" I asked. "What's up?"

"Get in and I'll tell you," he said, still out of breath.

We climbed into his jeep. He lit up a smoke and held out his pack, motioning me to take one.

"No thanks," I said.

"Take it," he said. "You'll need it."

"OK," I said, studying his face as I flicked my lighter. "Now tell me what's going on."

He looked around to make sure no one could hear us then whispered, excitedly, "I just got the word. We're out of here tomorrow. We've got to get these men back to the barracks so they can pack. And then…"

"Whoa! Slow down," I interrupted. "What do you mean we're leaving tomorrow? Leaving for where?"

"I don't know. Well, I do—and I don't. We're going to the Dyersburg Army Air Base in Tennessee first, but don't tell any of the men until we're already on the move. We don't want it showing up in any letters written tonight. I only got a quick look at the travel orders, but that's definitely our first stop. What really matters is, we're going east. You know what that means. Everybody who goes east, ships east—to Europe. I'd have bet money we'd end up in the Pacific. Doesn't look like it now."

"We leave tomorrow?" I practically shouted.

"Keep it down," Sergeant Ingram whispered. "We've got to get 'em back to the barracks right now. Colonel Ellis wants to say a few words to them before we take over and get them packed and ready to move out. We don't have much time."

He flicked his cigarette to the ground. "Perc, this is what we've been waiting for. Now we'll see what the men are made of."

"I'm not worried about them one bit," I said.

"You think they're ready?" he asked.

"I *know* they're ready," I said.

Without another word, Sergeant Ingram hopped from the jeep and ran back into the Service Club to round up the men.

I decided not to wait for them. I stepped out of the jeep and started walking alone toward the barracks. The evening air was cool, almost chilly. As I walked around the base, a flood of memories of our time spent there washed over me.

The men had come a long way.

They still had a long way to go.

But no matter what or where the final destination, the men of the 449th Signal Construction Battalion were going to make the journey together.

And I was proud to be going with them.

As proud as I could be.

20

CROSSINGS

Not a single one of us had ever been aboard a ship before, a fact that was easy to tell by the smell.

Within hours of leaving port, there wasn't a man in the battalion who wasn't at some stage of seasickness.

It also wasn't long before "Bombs away!" took on a whole new meaning. Whenever that was shouted, the men scrambled to give wide berth to the green-stomached man ready to let go of his payload. For the first two days at sea, this happened to someone at least once an hour, and typically quite a bit more often than that. The men on deck had been ordered to rush for the railing if they felt the urge coming on, but it was the rare man who actually made it there on time.

Then, like circling vultures, the cleanup crews would swoop down to try to clear the deck before the smell got to others who were on the verge of dropping their bombs, too. Cleanup detail, called "swab detail" aboard ship, became one of the dirtiest phrases we knew, and the men tried every trick in the book to get out of taking their turns at this. And I didn't blame them.

We had been assigned transport on the SS *Livermore,* a former liberty ship now used solely for troop transport across the Atlantic. We boarded at Hampton Roads, Virginia, after what seemed to most of us like an incredibly long journey. On the way to Hampton Roads, we had spent two weeks at Dyersburg Army Air Base in Halls, Tennessee. We didn't know it until we got there, but Dyersburg was one of the major training facilities for B-17 flight training, maintenance, and ground support. It was also one of the major supply depots along the route east, and we were to be completely outfitted there for our voyage across the Atlantic.

While at Dyersburg, our men who had already been given some training in air-ground support back at Biggs Field received the rest of their specialty training, especially in the areas of runway construction and maintenance. The rest of us spent most of our time on supply detail. Our stay there was unremarkable, except for being able to watch the daily formation training given to the B-17 pilots. The sight of those planes, in perfect formation, flying over the base each morning was a sight that none of us would ever forget. The first morning we were there, as we watched the planes thundering overhead, Doc was the first one to say it: "Men, we're going to win this war—and soon." Those majestic and powerful B-17s had that effect on all of us.

We were quite excited the day the cities of Little Rock, Arkansas, and Nashville, Tennessee, were "bombed." The B-17 pilots and crews were on base to receive a last tune-up before heading overseas, so simulated bombing runs were drawn up and carried out to give them more practice. On that particular morning, the two runs were carried out simultaneously. Both squadrons involved later reported that key targets in Little Rock and Nashville were "reduced to ashes." When word filtered down to the men, and especially to the squads that helped get everything ready for the attacks, they stood and applauded the pilots as they passed from the debriefing area back to their barracks. It was quite a sight to see.

But other than receiving more specialty training, getting supplied, and an occasional simulated "bombing run," the stay at Dyersburg was remarkably quiet. We received no liberty. We never got off the base.

From there we boarded another train east. This time our destination was Camp Patrick Henry at Hampton Roads, Virginia. We were there only three days, just long enough for our ship to be loaded and readied for sail and just long enough for most of the men to get themselves into a peck of trouble.

Only two in the battalion had ever seen the ocean before, and what seemed like something akin to group hypnosis set in as the men were drawn to the sound of the waves. When they weren't helping load the ship or given other duties, they were free to wander down to the nearby beach to a section designated for military personnel. Fascinated by the waves, they stripped down to their shorts and jumped right in, playing in the surf for hours at a time. Those who weren't crazy about the water walked the beach looking for seashells, something few had seen before. When one found a particularly pretty shell, sand dollar, or starfish, the resulting shouts of joy could be heard all the way down the beach.

However, their days at the beach came at a cost. Something else few knew about was the sunburn that would result from those carefree hours in the water and strolling along the sand. By the third night, about half the battalion became so blistered they could barely move in their tiny bunks aboard ship without screaming in agony. It didn't help that the medicated cream given to the men to put on their blisters seemed to burn the skin twice as bad as the sunburn itself.

For those who chose to skip the beach and didn't get too burned by the sun, there were other diversions. Each evening we were allowed to head into the nearby town, where more than a few of the men got a quick introduction to women who, for a few dollars, provided companionship. Women were everywhere. Lots of women. All types and sizes of women. Women inside bars. Women outside the bars. In the evening there were women sitting on windowsills of motel rooms beckoning men to come inside. There were all types of women, but they had one thing in common: They were very good at selling their wares. The women charged through the soldiers' money like Sherman marching to the sea. Several men regretted this "companionship" later when they discovered they had been given something else new to them, a little going-away present called venereal disease. Sadly, the films we saw in basic hadn't deterred them.

Doc and I visited the beach quickly the first day we were there, staying only long enough to stick our toes in the surf so in our letters back home we could honestly say we had been in the ocean. The next two evenings we went to a small restaurant on the edge of town run by a man who was the spitting image of Sergeant Ingram. He took an immediate liking to us, so both nights we were served what he called sampler platters of the different types of fish they prepared so we could try a little of each item. After rejecting most of the samples as too fishy, we stuffed ourselves with fried crab cakes and sea bass. We ended up joking that we ate so much fish we could have swum ourselves across the Atlantic.

We also saw plenty of women as we walked up and down the sidewalks across town, but neither of us felt tempted. A nearly naked woman sitting on a bench outside a bar at the north edge of town winked at us and said, "Ready for a good time, boys?"

Doc turned to me and said, "Judy would kill me dead."

I replied, "Olivia would put my head on a pole right next to the statue of Saint Louis."

We both nodded to each other. That particular form of temptation wasn't going to be a problem for us.

It was with great relief for me that the men were ordered to board ship for good at 1100 the fourth day. I had been given the responsibility of checking off their names as they came aboard ship, and I asked Doc to help with this. To put it bluntly, it was a motley looking group that reported that morning. It was hard to believe these were the same men who had arrived at Hampton Roads just three days before. As we checked their names off the list, I began to understand the meaning of a new word I had heard several times since our arrival: ship-bum. We now had what looked like a whole battalion of them.

As soon as we were out of the harbor and the tugboats escorting us turned and headed back to shore, the men, who had all stayed on deck to watch us leave, became absolutely silent. We weren't just leaving port. We were headed for adventures and destinations unknown, and we were all anxious about this. We were leaving behind family and friends for a duration known to none. Not even scuttlebutt was venturing a guess. We knew it was probable that some of us would not be returning, and that thought sobered even those who had closed down the bars in town the night before. As we stood there along the rail and watched the buildings on shore shrink and eventually evaporate into the distance, the uncertainty of the future suddenly became just that much larger.

Many of us, myself probably more than anyone in the battalion, were also sad to be saying good-bye to someone who had become a good friend, Colonel Ellis. He didn't receive word until the day before we were to set sail, but he had been granted his wish and had been assigned to duty in Washington in the new Army Signal Corps Training Division being formed there.

There were times we worked together at Fort Bliss when I felt he was too much of a fence-sitter, especially when it came to making the tough decisions, but his heart was good. At the same time, in so many ways I saw him as an "explainer" rather than a "doer," a quality I figured would likely hold him in good stead in a training division. I couldn't be too hard on him for being like that, though, because there were times when, as much as I hated to admit it, I felt that characterization also fit me. I was a teacher, so I really was an "explainer" most of the time. I just hoped over time I would also learn to be more of a "doer," especially when it came to working with the men. I often thought if I could change one thing about myself, that's what it would be. It wasn't that I felt there was anything particularly wrong with being an explainer. I was just starting to understand that the best teachers were those who also practiced what they preached, especially here in the army.

I would also never forget how Colonel Ellis had stepped in during "Albertson's Last Stand" to diffuse that situation. There was some debate later among the men about his motivation that night, whether he was acting for the men or whether he was just trying to get the goat of his rival, Colonel Rogers. It may have been a little of both, but the end result, no matter his thinking that night, was an esprit de corps appearing in the battalion that wasn't there before. I was sorry to see him leaving us, but happy for him that his new orders had come before we got out to sea. In the army, timing can be everything.

I was going to miss him.

As soon as Colonel Ellis said his good-byes, I started stewing and worrying myself half sick that we'd end up with someone like Colonel Rogers to lead the battalion. However, my fears evaporated when the new colonel introduced himself to me later that same afternoon. Colonel Phillips wasn't much older than me, and like me, he had been jumped in rank just about as soon as he entered the army. He had graduated from the University of Missouri with a degree in engineering and explained he had sailed through the ranks so quickly because of a shortage of officer material Stateside, especially in the area of leadership for construction groups. His degree made him a natural choice for this job, but the higher-ups needed to jump him in rank quickly in order to put him in charge of a battalion, even a small one like ours. In short, he was now a member of a group known as "paper colonels" throughout the service. Paper colonels didn't earn the rank by past accomplishment. They were given the rank because of circumstance.

And now we had one of our own.

Colonel Phillips was also, and immediately, the most seasick of all those aboard ship. Before we even got out of the harbor, he became as green as new tomatoes. His last order before he took to his bunk was for me and Sergeant Ingram to take complete charge of the men until further notice because, for some reason never explained to us, no other officers had been assigned to go with us. Then it was nothing but "Bombs away!" for Colonel Phillips for the first two days of the voyage. Each morning a handwritten note of orders and instructions would come from him, but he never left his cabin.

The morning after we sailed, Sergeant Ingram and I assembled the men and assigned them their specific shipboard duties. This wasn't going to be a free ride—they were going to work their way across the Atlantic. First on the list was the rotation for swab detail. Out of sheer necessity, all were going to have to take a turn. Still, I had never heard such groans as I did when that schedule was posted. Because Colonel Phillips was dropping his bombs so frequently, we also had to form a special squad to do nothing but keep his cabin clean. I thought those men were going to threaten mutiny. Because of the heat and stuffiness belowdecks, Colonel Phillips's cabin soon became so rancid the men in the cleanup squad said their nose hairs were being burned out. I went to take some paperwork to Colonel Phillips one afternoon and discovered there wasn't much exaggeration in what they said.

If anything good could be said about all the vomiting that was taking place and swab detail, it was that the men didn't seem to mind any of the other duties they were assigned. The most popular assignment was KP duty, especially garbage detail, something the men had tried to avoid like the smallpox back at Fort Bliss. The reason they enjoyed this duty so much was they soon discovered sharks would often cruise in to pick through the food scraps they dumped overboard. This was fascinating to watch. For others, it produced an immediate "Bombs away!" just at the thought of those sharks being down there.

We assigned the rest to duties that ranged from general cabin and deck cleaning to supply inventory. Sergeant Ingram and I figured out almost immediately that we needed to keep the men busy and, if necessary, to invent duties to keep them occupied, especially during the daylight hours. Once the men finished their work, they started lounging on deck even though the late January air was brisk during the day and downright cold at night. They didn't want to go below because of the combination of the heat and the smell, and we couldn't blame them. However, while lounging on deck, their attention soon turned to the ocean and the waves and the rocking motion of the boat. "Bombs away!" would typically soon follow.

As the same time, we noticed that as long as the men were kept busy and their eyes were focused on something other than the waves, the bombing became much less frequent. Poor Brown seemed more miserable than anyone aboard ship other than Colonel Phillips. I felt sorry for him and knew something had to be done. To keep him busy after his regular duties were finished, and to keep his eyes away from the ocean, I came up with a special duty for him: inventory superintendent. As far as I knew, no such duty or job title existed in the army, but it sounded important, and the importance was what I wanted to impress upon him. It was my responsibility to keep track of the inventory of the supplies we were taking with us, but I didn't see why I couldn't add an assistant, or two, or three.

I sent word for Brown to report to me after his regular duties were finished. When he arrived, I said to him as seriously as I could, "Brown, I've got a job for you, an *important* one, and I want you to start on it right now. I know you can do this. I'm going to make you "inventory superintendent," and your first job is going to be to count all the nails in the kegs we're taking with us. These nails are like gold. Think about it. How can we build anything wherever we're going without them?"

Brown was staring blankly at me, like a man in a hypnotic trance. It soon became obvious, by how he kept swallowing and clearing his throat, that he was really staring past me, watching the waves slide up and down. I quickly grabbed his shoulders and turned him sideways so all he could see was the wall behind me.

When I had his attention again, I continued, "You may not understand how important this is right now, but get below and count out those nails into piles of two hundred nails each. That's about how many it will take for each of the small supply huts we're probably going to have to build. Then I want you to wrap each group of two hundred in paper and stack them back in the kegs. This will simplify our nail problem once we get to building things. Each crew can just grab a bundle and get to work. It will also help with security because we'll be able to tell if anyone steals one of the bundles. After you get all the nails bundled, it will be your job to count them, inventory them, every night. Got that? I'm counting on you."

Brown nodded his head. He looked like he wanted to say something, but it also looked like he was so queasy he was afraid to open his mouth. His silence was just fine with me.

"Now get below and get started." I guided him toward the steps and added, "Take a couple assistants with you. Sanders and Clark. They'll do, I think."

Sanders and Clark were running a close second and third to Brown in the "dash for the rail" steeplechase.

When the men weren't working, to pass the time they bundled up and played games out on deck. Dice games were the most popular, but checkers and cards were also constantly being played. The games weren't taken all that seriously, especially cards and checkers, because the sea breeze kept blowing cards over the rail and tipping over the checkerboards. The men finally got creative and solved this problem by weighting down everything that could become airborne.

At night, after chow, the men went back out on deck to relax in the cool evening air and to look at the stars. Out in the middle of the Atlantic the only light that could be seen was that produced by the heavens. Sprinkled across the thick darkness of the night, the stars were so bright they seemed like miniature spotlights one could reach out and grab. One night I was asked by Jamieson to point out the Big Dipper. I did, and this led to more questions from others until I finally ended up going from one corner of the sky to the other, pointing out the different constellations and the stories behind what they represented. The men seemed to enjoy this and started making up their own stories about a few of the more well-known constellations. However, their versions, more often than not, were on the bawdy side.

Their stories may have been a little crude, but at least while they were making them up they weren't throwing up. That was a welcome, and ironic, relief. It took a sick story to keep the men from getting sick themselves.

None of us minded one bit.

* * *

It was the second night out that Doc approached me about it.

I was sitting under a suspended lifeboat, the only place I could find on deck where the constant breeze could be blocked from hitting me in the face. This was especially important while smoking. Several of the men had red eyes as a result of ash from their smokes blowing back into their faces. The breeze also made the cigarettes burn down twice as fast, an important fact because cigarettes were becoming a valuable commodity. Somehow in all the rush to get supplied, cigarettes were left off the list. The men were going to have to start rationing what they had or it was going to be a long trip for some of them.

As Doc came up to me he held out his hand and asked, "How 'bout a smoke, Perc?"

And, like two kids playing a game, I responded as I always did, "No thanks. I already have one."

"Ha ha. Very funny," he replied, a frown on his face.

I pulled out my Luckys and let him pull one from the pack. He sat down next to me and lit it, after five or six attempts to keep his lighter going long enough in the stiff breeze. Inhaling deeply, then exhaling with a sigh, he said, "You notice anything funny about this ship?"

"Funny?" I replied. "How do you mean?"

"Well, does it strike you that something is missing? Look around us? Haven't you noticed it?"

I looked around at the men, most of whom were sprawled out on the deck, either playing cards or looking up at the stars. The stiff sea breeze also muffled sound on deck, but it was still remarkably quiet for how many men were lounging around.

"You mean how quiet it is?" I replied.

Doc didn't say anything. He stared straight ahead as he inhaled deeply again.

I knew what he was talking about, but I hadn't said anything to anyone else. I wasn't foolish enough to think if we didn't talk about it no one would notice. I just hadn't seen the importance of mentioning it so soon into the voyage.

I pulled a Lucky from my pocket and lit it on the first attempt. I sat back against the outer wall of the ship and closed my eyes, listening to the sound of the breeze as it whistled past.

"I've noticed," I said, quietly. "I noticed it yesterday afternoon. Other than what looks like a skeleton crew running this ship, I think we're the only ones aboard."

I took another drag on my cigarette and continued, "Last night I took a quick look below, went on a little scouting trip of my own. I saw enough empty rooms for us to be hauling at least one more battalion, maybe two. If we wanted to, we could split up the men and damn near give every one of them his own room. Yeah, we *could* be hauling more men, but it looks like we're it."

I stubbed out my cigarette on the bottom of my shoe, deciding to save the rest of it for later, and continued, "We really must be precious cargo."

I laughed. Doc didn't.

He flicked his cigarette over the side, something we were strictly ordered not to do for fire safety reasons because the breeze could blow lit cigarettes back on board. He then turned to me and said softly, "Perc, look around us. It looks to me like we're watching the mail again."

"I'm not sure," I replied. "Could be. I thought of that, too. Then again, it could be something else. I've been thinking about this a lot and have my own theory this time. Maybe this time, in an odd sort of way, *we* are the mail."

"We're the mail?"

"Yeah, in a way, I think so. And plenty of people are going to be watching us to see what kind of mail we turn out to be. You know how mail can be good news or bad news. Well, we both know that some are going to see us as bad news no matter what. I know it's a long shot, but we just might get a chance to show we're something else."

"Do you really believe that?" he asked.

"I *have* to believe that. You have to believe it, too. And the men have to believe it or we might as well just around and head back. I don't know where the hell we're going, but we both know where we've been. I'll take my chances with what's up ahead—for good, bad, or worse."

"Are you going to say anything to the men?" he asked.

I paused a minute before replying, "Some things are best left unsaid."

"And some things are not," he said, standing up. He looked at me sadly, turned, and walked away.

I leaned back again against the cold steel of the outer wall. I closed my eyes and tried to lose myself in the rhythm of the ship slicing through the gentle waves. The night air was also growing colder, and I shivered time and again.

I might have been shivering for us all.

* * *

The rest of the crossing was uneventful, with one night of exception. The night after we passed the Rock of Gibraltar the warning horn blared, sending the crew scrambling for their emergency posts. Even though we had been instructed to stay below in case of an alert, the men immediately headed up to the main deck.

And so did I.

A German submarine was reported to be in the area by one of the ships ahead of us. As we had practiced at least a dozen times in our lifeboat drills, the men lined up in an orderly manner and put on their life jackets. I went down the row checking them as they counted off. However, at the end of the count, I didn't know what else to tell them to do. There wasn't anything we could do. The SS *Livermore* had two guns, one mounted forward and one aft. They were each manned by three members of the crew. Other than that, the ship had no weapons aboard other than the rifles we were bringing with us, and it seemed silly for me to tell the men to run below and get them. What could they shoot at?

After completing the count, I told the men to stand at ease. From the scared looks on their faces I knew I needed to find something to keep them occupied, to put their minds at work. I thought for a minute, and it suddenly came to me.

I mustered up the best sergeant voice I could under the circumstances and barked, "OK, listen up. The best thing we can do is keep watch. Watch for light reflecting on the surface of the water. If we can help spot an enemy ship or sub, our destroyers can jump right in and take 'em out. So, stand at ease, but keep your eyes peeled. Keep as quiet as you can so we can hear if someone sees something and sings out. And no smoking. Your cigarette tips can be seen for miles on a night like this. Remember—sing out if you see anything—anything at all."

I was a sergeant and I was also becoming a pretty good situational liar. And I was beginning to understand the two often, out of necessity, went hand in hand. I was proud of how effortlessly I could now combine the two.

Giving the men a job had the immediate effect I had hoped for. They whispered among themselves, with someone occasionally pointing out into the ocean and asking, "What's that?" Others would gather around and take a look, following the sight line of the man's outstretched arm. They didn't spot any enemy ships, but it wasn't for lack of trying. They stood their ground in the face of danger.

As the men continued their watch, a member of the ship's crew walked by, stopped for a second to look at us, and then continued forward, shaking his head and smiling. The men ignored him.

About an hour after the first alarm had gone off, the all-clear sounded. If there had been an enemy sub, it had retreated before our destroyer escort could find it, which was fine with us.

When the blare of the siren ceased, I called out, "Pass the word down the line. Fall out and try to get some rest. This could be a long night. Now you can light 'em if you got 'em."

A few did, nervously flicking their lighters or striking matches in the strong evening breeze. Others, still shaken by the sub warning, ran to the rail as their pals, without any sympathy in their voices at all now, shouted, "Bombs away!"

The combined smell of cigarette smoke and vomit was something none of us would forget.

* * *

That was the only time, at least that we knew of, that we encountered the enemy on the whole journey across. The rest of the time the men kept busy with their regular duties during the day and their game tournaments at night. Days started to roll one on top of the other like the passing waves.

A few days after the submarine alert, Colonel Phillips finally emerged from his cabin. He asked Sergeant Ingram and me to meet him in the galley so we could give him a report on the status of the battalion. When I saw him, I was shocked. He was pale as a ghost and looked considerably thinner than I had remembered him at Hampton Roads. As we sat down at the table with him, I noticed his hands were shaking so badly he had to hold his coffee cup with both hands.

"I want to thank you men for taking care of things while I was under the weather." He frowned and continued, "'Under the weather' just doesn't do it justice, does it? I was sick. Sick as a damn dog. At first I was afraid I was going to die, and then I felt so lousy I was afraid I wasn't going to die. Anyway, my thanks to both of you. I hear you've done one hell of a job."

"Thank you, Sir," we both replied.

"We've got a few things to talk over," he continued. "I just talked to the ship's captain. We aren't that far away from our destination, so it's time I told you where we're going and what we'll be doing."

"Interested?" he asked.

Sergeant Ingram and I looked at each other. This is what we had been waiting for.

"I hope you understand that I was under orders to keep a lid on it. I was told not to say anything before now. 'Loose Lips Sinks Ships.'"

We nodded, leaning forward. "Let's have it, Colonel," I said. "Don't keep us in suspense. We've been dying to know ever since we got aboard ship."

He took several gulps of his coffee, still cradling the cup with both hands. He then sat the cup down and lit up a cigarette, at the same time offering one to each of us. I was glad to have it because I was down to my last pack and was already rationing myself to four cigarettes a day. Sergeant Ingram took one and put it in his pocket. I resisted the urge to laugh at that and lit mine up right away. Colonel Phillips took a short puff of his cigarette and blew one perfect smoke ring. As I watched it drift to the left, he looked around to make sure no one could hear us.

"What I'm going to say stays right with the three of us. That's an order, and let's have that straight right up front."

Sergeant Ingram and I nodded that we understood.

He then continued, "I'll let you know how much to tell the men and when to tell them. OK? I don't want a peep to get out until I give the word."

We nodded again.

He leaned closer to us and spoke softly, "We're headed for Naples. We've been assigned to the 12th Air Force, and we'll catch up with them there."

I let out an "All right!" and pounded my fists on the table, causing Colonel Phillips's coffee to spill. Fortunately, it missed him as it sloshed over the edge of the table.

"Sorry, Sir," I said. "That's great news. The 12th is a great outfit."

"Well, before you get too excited you better hear the rest of this. As soon as we get to Naples we're to report to a staging area at Bagnoli. There the battalion is going to be split into two companies. Supposedly, we've got airstrips all over the place over there. You know—the idea is if one gets bombed, the others will still be ready for action. I've heard we even got one in Pompeii, if you can imagine that."

"How come we're being split up?" I asked. My heart sank the minute I heard him say this, and my mind started racing a mile a minute.

"The orders are that one group will do nothing but communications work for the 12th. It's no secret that if we can someday break through to Rome, Italy will fall. There's an old saying that an army moves on its stomach, but there's something a hell of a lot more important than that. Without good lines of communication, an army can't move at all, no matter how stuffed the men are. And that's where we come in—at least part of us. Those men will need to maintain the lines we've already got while the army keeps moving ahead. Imagine what would happen if the guys on the ground got out of touch with our boys in the air. I don't even want to think about what could happen."

He paused and shook his head. He put out his cigarette and immediately lit up another. Leaning back this time, he continued, "Anyway, you're going with them," he said, reaching out and slapping Sergeant Ingram on the arm. "Your company will follow the troops and put up poles and string the lines, hopefully all the way to Rome. I assume the men have had the training to do this."

"They have. And they're good at it," I jumped in and said proudly.

Colonel Phillips smiled. "They'll need to be. That's going to be a hell of a hike."

"What about the other company?" I asked, my curiosity boiling over again.

"The rest of the men will stick close to Naples and have it as home plate. I'm staying with that group. And so are you. You're sticking with me. We'll still be moving around a lot from strip to strip as we're needed, but it looks like Naples will be our main home. Our job will be to help the engineers maintain the strips we've already got and maybe build a new one or two when we advance. At least I *hope* we get to do that. That's what I've been trained for. They need us more than anything, at least right away, to help take care of the ones we've already got. It seems the Luftwaffe has other ideas about us being in Italy, and they've been dropping little presents on the strips. I guess they're like a dog trying to swat flies off its back. And right now, we're the flies. They haven't been able to shake us off yet, but they're doing one hell of a job swattin' at us. And I hear tell the strips show it. We'll keep busy enough with that for a while, but we're also going to be in charge of keeping communication lines functional in the immediate area. The men are going to jump in and help with whatever construction needs to be done. We even have a few who can help get our planes ready to go. I suppose they're good at that, too, right?"

"They can handle it, Sir," I replied. "They were trained at Biggs Field and at Dyersburg on the way here."

"Then make sure they get kept in our company and don't get sent off with the others. I have the feeling we'll need them before this is all said and done."

He downed the rest of his coffee in one gulp. "Any questions so far?"

I looked at Sergeant Ingram, who was smiling. It was a smile of pride, a smile that said, "Let's get going. We're ready!" I felt the same way and let a smile slip, too. Colonel Phillips just said, "Good. Now I wasn't kidding when I said to keep a lid on this. I don't want to hear the men singing Italian songs tonight, if you get my meaning."

"Don't worry, Colonel," I said. "They're too sick to be singing anyway."

Colonel Phillips laughed, but immediately grabbed his stomach and groaned. "I wish you hadn't reminded me. If I don't get off this ship, and soon, I'm going to die. I know it."

"You'll make it, Sir," I said. "You aren't near as bad off as some of the men."

"Thanks. That's a comfort," he said sarcastically. "OK, that's all. You two get out of here and leave me alone to die."

As we started to leave, he motioned for me to sit back down. "You go ahead, Ingram. I just remembered I've got one more thing for Perkins."

Sergeant Ingram crossed the room and headed up the steps to the main deck. There was now a hop in his step. When he reached the steps, I sat back down and said, "What's up, Colonel?"

"They call you Perc, don't they?"

"Yes, Sir," I replied. "I don't know what they call me behind my back, but I'm called that a lot to my face anyway."

"Well, you're a sergeant. If you're any good at what you do, I'm guessing they have words they've invented for you."

We laughed. The ice was breaking. "Perc, this is the first chance we've had to talk. I got to meet with Colonel Ellis before he shoved off, and he said you were good people, said the men looked up to you and respected you. That's why I'm keeping you with me."

He paused a minute before continuing, "I haven't been doing this long, and I'm not exactly what anyone would call 'military' by any means. I'm an engineer, and I don't even know how good I'm going to be at that. I'm not exactly crawling with experience. I guess what I'm trying to say is I know I need your help. When it comes to helping repair or build airstrips or buildings, I'll be right out front giving the orders. But I want you to take over the day-to-day operations, especially when it comes to our communications work. If you can handle that, I think we'll make one hell of a team."

"Can do, Sir," I said. "You can count on me."

I then extended my hand to shake his. The minute I did it I realized I shouldn't have, that it wasn't exactly military protocol. But my hand was already out and I knew it would be worse to pull it back.

It took me more than a little by surprise, but he reached out and shook my hand firmly, nodding his head as he did so.

"Yup, I think we'll make a damn good team," he said.

Just then the ship rocked to the left. The waves had been growing larger for the past few hours, and the up-and-down movement of the ship as it made its way through them could really be felt now. Colonel Phillips leaned forward against the table and put his face in his hands. His words were muffled, but I could still hear him say, "If I don't get off this damn ship I'm going to die!"

"We haven't had a burial at sea yet," I said. "Might be good for the men to see."

He groaned again and said, "Shut up, Perkins. Remember we're a team now. If I go, I'm taking you with me."

The ship lurched to the right, and I guess that did it. Colonel Phillips, hand over his mouth, got up and ran across the floor and up the steps. I did my best not to laugh in case he looked back. The ice was being broken, and rather nicely I thought, but I didn't want to fall through completely before I found out if he'd reach down and pull me out. That was enough for now.

When Colonel Phillips had gone, I sat back down at the table. My thoughts were racing, and I wanted a few minutes to go over everything by myself. It felt good to know where we were going, but at the same time, the news was bittersweet. The battalion was going to be split up. This sort of thing happened all the time in war, but I never dreamed it might happen again to us so soon, especially after so many of the men in barracks N-1 had been shipped out and reassigned before we left Fort Bliss.

It also dawned on me that I was the one who knew the men best. I was the one who would have to split the battalion, would have to make the company assignments. This wasn't going to be like back at Fort

Bliss where I assigned the men to different baseball teams or back at Sumner where I put kids in different groups for science projects. This was no game.

This was war.

And now, at long last, we were a part of it. I prayed we were as ready as I thought we were—as ready as I bragged we were.

Time would tell.

That time started now.

21

RESPONSIBILITIES

Thick fog surrounded us and a steady, light rain fell as the SS *Livermore* brought us into the main harbor at Naples. I had given the men permission to stay out on deck so they could get a good view of the city as we came into port. However, the fog was so bad nothing could be seen but a few small warehouses in the dock area.

It didn't matter to them. They were so excited to finally see land they hugged each other, shook hands, and danced around the deck. Even in this excitement I could still see a cloud of sadness settling over them. The night before, Colonel Phillips had given me permission to tell them where we were going and a few details about what we'd be doing. They had been quiet and attentive—until I got to the part about the battalion being split up.

I called off the names on the battalion roster and announced to which company each of the men had been assigned. Many became emotional as the names were called. They immediately realized they would soon be saying good-bye to dear friends, friends who had become, in so many ways, their family. This was particularly hard on Brown and Davis, who had become like brothers. When they realized they were being separated, they hugged each other, patting each other on the back, tears filling their eyes. The men around them looked away as if they hadn't noticed.

As I looked out at the group, they reminded me of my Sumner students right before the end of the school year. The students were always excited about the prospect of being let go for the summer, but they were also sad to be saying good-bye to many friends they knew they wouldn't see again at least until the next term started—and some they'd possibly never see again.

The men now looked like they felt exactly the same way.

I had no idea if it was true or not, but near the end of the list I paused and told them these were "temporary" assignments until we could get the first part of our work done. I went so far as to hint that the battalion might be brought together again in a month or so.

Sergeant. Situational liar. Yes, I was getting better and better at combining the two.

I told them as much as I could about what their duties would be without going into too many specifics, but I could tell my words didn't do anything at all to make those who were sad feel better.

For the rest of the night, the ship was very quiet.

They didn't have long to think about this, however. The minute we got off the ship we were taken to the staging area at Bagnoli. There we were all given a quick going-over by doctors to make sure we were still OK after our sea voyage. Two of us weren't. Fletcher had contracted pneumonia and spent the last half of the voyage in sick bay. Simmons was absolutely miserable because of the little going-away present he had been given by one of the women at Hampton Roads. Both were taken immediately to the temporary hospital that had been set up in an old hotel nearby. We were told if they recovered well they'd be rejoining us. If not, they'd be shipped back home. They were taken away before I could say good-bye to them.

As soon as the examinations were finished—and of course after more shots—we were ushered out to two lines of trucks.

Two sergeants were assigned to help the men get aboard. The older of the two, a spooky looking man with a droopy left eye, immediately began shouting, "Form two lines in front of us! Able to the left! Baker to the right! We're going to call your names off and tell you which group you're in and which truck to get into. We don't want anybody to get lost. And if any of you can drive, let us know as your name is called. Now shut up and listen!"

As soon as he started calling off the names, I overheard Williams say, "Whose left? Theirs or ours?" The men around him who heard him pose that question immediately started moving back and forth from line to line, unsure of where they should be standing.

It was going to be a long day.

I turned to Colonel Phillips, who had just rejoined us after getting our updated orders at headquarters, and asked, "This is it? The men don't even get a chance to say good-bye to each other?"

"We don't have any choice. We have to move out right now. I was told German planes have been paying a visit most days about mid-morning, so they want us out of here before they show up. Truck convoys make mighty nice targets."

I thought about this for a second and a vision of a long string of trucks being shot at by German planes flashed in my mind. As soon as that registered, my sadness at not having time for a proper farewell melted into a desire to get everyone the hell out of there as quickly as possible. I jogged over and climbed onto the tailgate of the last truck on the left and shouted, "OK you lamebrains. You heard the man. Pay attention. Line up. Now! And I mean now! Move it! Move it! Move it!"

They all looked at me like I had lost my mind.

While the men were being checked in, Colonel Phillips motioned for Sergeant Ingram and me to come back over to him.

Shaking his head as he watched the men, confused now more than ever, moving back and forth from line to line, he said, "Come with me back to headquarters for a minute. We've got something we need to talk about. From the looks of things, it looks like we've got at least a few minutes."

When we got there he took us into a small room at the rear of the building and motioned us to a table where a map had been spread out.

"Look at this map and try to remember as much of it as you can," he ordered, sharply. "Let's get ourselves oriented."

The man who now stood in front of us wasn't the same man who had kept his head in a bucket practically the whole way across the ocean. His demeanor had changed dramatically once he got off the ship and had his feet firmly on land. He was all business.

"I need to fill you in on our new orders. Especially you, Ingram, since you're headed a different direction than we are. Come closer to the map so I can point a few things out to you."

He used the map to give us our bearings, then he motioned us to sit in the chairs in front of him.

"Listen up, and listen up good. We've got a big job ahead of us. First, let's talk about Baker Company. Ingram, you're going with them down to Salerno."

He pointed to the map to show us that Salerno was to the south and east of Naples but still on the Mediterranean.

He paused long enough to light a smoke and then continued, "The German raids have knocked the hell out of communications all down the coast. First you'll be resupplied in Salerno. Then your company will be in charge of repairing the lines used by the Tactical Bomber Command of the 12th Air Force. You'll start there in Salerno and work your way all the way back here. The Brits have been chipping in and lending a hand with this, but they'll be taking off as soon as you get there so they can rejoin their own units. Before they get out of there, if you get a chance, thank them for what they've been doing for us. I hear they've been doing a hell of a job."

He looked at Sergeant Ingram a minute and then reached out and put his hand on his shoulder, "And this is where it gets interesting."

"I thought it was already getting pretty interesting," I butted in.

"Well, hold onto your hats. Unless things change, Baker Company will then advance with our troops when they push ahead up the coast. You know what that means. It may take a while, but I think it's a safe bet to say you're going to Rome."

Sergeant Ingram smiled and said, "I always wanted to see Rome. Especially that big damn Colosseum. I've seen pictures of it in books. Maybe now I'll get my chance."

Colonel Phillips cleared his throat and said, dryly, "I think you'll see a lot more than that before you get there."

"That's what I'm afraid of," Sergeant Ingram replied, raising his eyes to the ceiling.

"One more thing. When you get to Salerno, a Colonel Hartley will be waiting for you. He'll take charge of everything. I was told only one thing about him, that this is his first duty, too. He's as green as I am, so go easy on him. OK?"

"Now you, Perc. Get closer to the map over here. You're taking Able Company up to Melito di Napoli. It's right here, just north of the main part of town. Technically, that'll be our home base, but it looks like we'll be on the move most of the time."

"You're not coming with us?" I asked.

"I've been ordered to stay here tonight for another briefing, so I'll join you at some point tomorrow morning. For the time being, you're going to be in charge. OK?"

I nodded. He then continued, "Able is going to be in charge of maintenance for all communications in the immediate area, and they really need us bad now. When we're not doing that, and when and if we can come up for air, we're also going to pitch in and help take care of some airstrips. There are two in particular that we'll have to have at least some of the men work on every day if these raids keep up."

He pointed to the map again and added, "The one here at Pompeii, and the main one here at Capodichino. Capodichino really got whacked yesterday. As soon as we get settled in we're supposed to head down there first and see what we can do to help out. Then, in our spare time we'll also be doing some line construction, too. The brass wants about ten miles of poles and line put up to Battipaglia, but we're supposed to wait and see if Baker can get back to do it first. If they get held up, then we'll take over and do it instead."

He put his hand back on Sergeant Ingram's shoulder again and said, sternly this time, "And I don't want to do that. You get Baker back up here as soon as you can so *you* can do it. Got that?"

"Yes, Sir," Sergeant Ingram replied. "We'll get it done."

"Any questions?" Colonel Phillips asked.

"Just one," I said. "Is there any chance the battalion will be put back together somewhere down the line?"

"Hard to tell," he replied. "Doubt it. It's rough for you guys who have been with the outfit a long time, but there's a lot to do and it'll be easier splitting up like this. OK, if you don't have any more questions, you need to get rolling. And please, make sure everybody gets into the right truck. Perc, I'll see you tomorrow. Ingram, see you when I see you—good luck."

He shook Sergeant Ingram's hand, then we both backed up and saluted him before turning and heading back outside. He called after us, "And keep your heads down!"

Only a few men were still in line when we got back. The others were already in their assigned trucks. At least I hoped they were in the right trucks. I turned and shook hands with Sergeant Ingram. Neither of us said a word to the other. We didn't need to.

I then walked down the middle of the two lines of trucks and said a quick "Good luck—see you soon" to the men as I passed. Saying good-bye to those who were going with Baker Company was hard. There was so much I wanted to say to them, but there was no time.

The truck engines started firing up, and I had just enough time to jump into Able Company's lead truck before it took off. The sergeant with the droopy eye who had been helping with the truck assignments, Sergeant Carlton, had jumped in right ahead of me. He was going to show us how to get to Melito di Napoli and where we were to be quartered once we got there. As I settled into my seat, I turned to introduce myself to him. It was then I noticed who was driving our truck.

Tyler.

"Here we go, Sarge!" he shouted in his high-pitched voice. The truck lunged forward, bucking like a wild stallion. I braced myself for what I knew would be one of the rides of my life.

* * *

As we pulled off the main road and into Melito di Napoli, those who still lived there, and there didn't seem to be many, ran for cover like frightened animals. That really surprised me, and I said something to Sergeant Carlton.

"I can't blame 'em," he said matter-of-factly. "First Mussolini's Brown Shirts came through and took just about everything they had. Then the Krauts came through and took what was left, including what they had left of their dignity. But at least they left the buildings standing. Then it was our turn. To take this area, we had to bomb the stuffing out of it. Now the Krauts are bombing it themselves to try to get it back. Ain't much left at all now. And you wonder why they hide when they see anybody coming? Can you blame them?"

I had to admit I couldn't.

Sergeant Carlton directed Tyler to pull down a narrow street on the left about halfway through the village, or rather what was left of it. Sergeant Carlton was right. We had bombed the stuffing out of it.

About half the buildings we passed were reduced to rubble, and the other half looked like a stiff breeze could have blown them down. A church in the middle of town was now nothing more than the frame for the front door and a huge cross that was somehow still miraculously perched above it. Piles of building stone were stacked at every intersection, grim reminders of deadly air attacks. Off in the distance, on a small hill overlooking the south edge of town, row upon row of homemade crosses marked the final resting places of those who had lost their lives as each wave of intruders made its way through their village.

Sergeant Carlton told Tyler to pull over near the end of the street in front of a building that looked remarkably unscathed. It had a bell tower above the entrance, and at first I thought it was another church.

"This was their school," Sergeant Carlton said. "Most of the children have been sent to live with relatives in other villages, so there's really no need for it now. Luckily for us, other than one big hole in the roof in the back, it hasn't been damaged at all to speak of. This is where you'll be staying while you're here."

He motioned me to get out of the truck and he followed. He moved out to the center of the road and directed the men driving the rest of the trucks to pull ahead and park along the other side of the street.

When they were parked, he came back over to me and said, "Have them unload everything they can find in the trucks and take it inside. You're going to live on that and what you brought with you until we can get more supplies up here. I don't know how it happened, but most of your supplies and tools accidentally got shipped to Bari yesterday. The first thing we've got to do is figure out how to get all that over here."

"Here's a map," he said, handing it to me. "If you can figure out how to get there, I suppose you can send some men to get everything yourself."

Here he paused, smiled weakly, and continued, "And you're going to have one other small problem. I'm supposed to take the trucks back with me to Bagnoli tonight. I can't say why, but we're going to need them again tomorrow."

"Then how are we supposed to get around?" I asked. "We're supposed to get to the base at Capodichino tomorrow morning. We're supposed to help repair the strip."

"Sorry, but not my problem," he replied. "It's only a couple of miles. A little walk will be good for you. It'll help you get your land-legs back. Now, let's get everybody to hurry the hell up. I'd like to get back as soon as I can. Oh, there's one other thing. I'll need to have some of your drivers help take the trucks back. They can then all pile in one truck and bring it back tomorrow. At least you'll have one you can use. Consider it a housewarming gift."

I bowed and said, "Anything else you want?"

"Probably. But I'll think of it later," he said, laughing.

I didn't find it funny.

The men quickly unloaded the trucks and brought our gear into the schoolhouse. It was small inside—and dark. There were a few desks still piled up in the back of the room, but other than that, it was empty.

"What are we going to use for beds?" Williams asked as he bumped into me on his way into the room.

"Look at that floor," I said. "Solid marble. Cool in winter and cool in summer. *That* will be our bed for the time being. Help me pass the word. Have the men spread their blankets in rows along the outer walls. Maybe this isn't the Chase Hotel in St. Louis, but it'll beat sleeping on the ground outside."

"Not by much it won't," he replied.

"Well, maybe you won't have to sleep here tonight," I said. I curled my finger and motioned him to come over near me again.

"I know that look, Perc. What do you want now?" he asked suspiciously.

"My friend, we need trucks, and we need them right now. I've got to talk over a few things with Sergeant Carlton before he takes off. It might not hurt if you took one of his trucks on a recon mission to see what else is around here and stay away until he leaves. You could even take a few guys with you."

"And while you're gone," I added, "maybe you could see if you could find another truck or two that isn't being used. I saw a couple on the way up here."

"Say no more," he said. "I'm already gone."

He almost crashed into Sergeant Carlton as he bolted from the room.

"Well, I think that's it," he said. "I better start back now."

"Please wait just a minute," I asked as politely as I could. "I'd really appreciate it if we could look over the map just one more time. I want to make sure I know which direction to go to get to Capodichino. I'm still kind of disoriented. OK?"

He looked at his watch and said, "OK, but just for a minute. Let's make it snappy."

"Thanks so much," I said, slapping him on the back. "You're a pal. Now just let me spread this map out on the floor…"

I heard a truck start up outside and roar away. Sergeant Carlton started to get up to take a look, but I grabbed him by the shoulder and held him down. "Is this Capodichino—or is it over there?"

When the truck could no longer be heard, he looked back down at the map and went over the directions again.

Sergeant. Situational liar. I was now fully in that club.

* * *

There were plenty of jobs to keep the men busy the rest of the afternoon. I assigned one group to clean the schoolhouse, especially the windows so some light could be let in. I sent another group outside to repair the hole in the roof. Clouds were moving in quickly and it looked like it was going to rain. The thought of sleeping on a wet marble floor wasn't appealing at all. I told the men to give the roof priority.

Back outside I saw Doc breaking up the school desks so we'd have wood for a fire later in the evening. I waved at the schoolhouse and said, "You know what this reminds me of? Davis-Monthan. Remember how the three of us were put in charge of getting the whole barracks ready back there? We thought that was pretty lousy duty, didn't we? Well, just maybe Uncle Sam knew what he was doing when he had us do that. Looks like we're doing the same thing here, only now we've got experience."

He wiped the sweat from his eyes and said, "Perc, how you can always find the good in everything I'll never know. You could find a gold nugget in a pile of shit. And speaking of that, you better take a look over there."

The outhouse had been flattened in one of the bombing raids, so another was going to have to be built. I rounded up a few more men and said to them, "I doubt you'll find much wood around here, so you're going to have to be creative. I'm sure you'll come up with something. Whatever you come up with, I want it done by tonight. Get busy."

Later in the afternoon Albertson came over and asked, "Sarge, what are we going to do for chow tonight?"

I raised my hand and pretended to shield my eyes as I looked around. "You know, I don't see a mess hall anywhere around here, do you? What do you think we ought to do?"

"I think we ought to go back to Naples. That's my opinion."

"You may have something there," I said. "But for the time being, we're stuck here. We've all got K rations. That'll be dinner tonight."

Albertson grimaced. "I'd rather eat dog."

"You won't find any of those around here, either. From the looks of things, I think the locals beat us to 'em."

Beaming as if an inspiration just struck him, he asked, "Sarge, how would you like some stew? We're going to have to boil the water before we drink it anyway, so why not get a big pot going and dump in the meat part of the K rations and whatever else we can scrounge up around here."

"Sounds good," I said. "You're now chief cook. Don't tell Williams when he gets back. He'll be plenty mad that you're cooking instead of him."

"I'll get on it right away," he said. "Leave everything to me."

I felt like I had just gotten the short end of the stick, but I wasn't exactly sure how so. But his stew idea did sound good compared to the alternative, so I took a chance. Actually, it didn't seem like much of a chance at all because the K rations usually tasted like cardboard. Anything would be an improvement.

* * *

Maybe it was because we were all hungry, but we all thought Albertson's stew turned out to be pretty darn good. He had scrounged up a few carrots somewhere along the line and added those to the K rations. He also added more than a little booze of some type, but I didn't want to know what it was or how he managed to have it with him. There are times when ignorance is bliss.

He called his creation "apple stew." I asked him how he came up with that name because it sure didn't taste like apples. He said, "Well, this is Melito di Apple, isn't it? So, this is "apple stew."

"That's Melito di Napoli," I corrected, drawing out the pronunciation. "But you know, I think I like the name "apple stew" better, so that it will be. Especially because I think I taste something a little like applejack in here, too, don't I?"

"Well, maybe just a touch of something like that, but just for flavor and to kill the germs. I don't want anybody to get sick."

The men laughed, and they needed it, especially after saying goodbye to so many friends earlier in the day. I laughed right along with them. I needed it, too.

Just as Doc got up for seconds, a plane roared overhead. A few men ran to the windows to look outside. "Here comes some more," Jamieson shouted. "Look at 'em go!"

"Sweet Jesus!" Doc shouted. "Get your heads down! Stay low! Those aren't ours!"

Less than a minute after they flew over, explosions could be heard to the east.

"Keep down!" I shouted. "They won't know we're here unless we do something stupid. Everybody crawl over by the wall and just stay there and cover your heads until I say otherwise. Now!"

It was nearing dusk, and flashes of light could be seen off in the distance along with the sound of more explosions.

"Someone's really gettin' an ass whippin'," Doc whispered.

"Yeah," I said. "And I think it's us. That's just about where Capodichino's supposed to be if I read the map right."

As quickly as the explosions had started, they stopped. The planes didn't come back our direction. We guessed they were making a big loop on their way back to where they came from to avoid antiaircraft fire. When the attack appeared to be over, I told the men they could get back to their stew. Slowly, they crawled back to the middle of the room, this time forming a tighter circle.

"That was close," Albertson said.

And it's going to get a lot closer," I added. "A lot closer."

Not too many of us got to sleep that night.

I sure didn't.

* * *

The next morning right at 0500 the sound of a truck skidding to a halt outside woke us all up. After the events of the previous night we were all jumpy, and several men, me included, ran to the windows to look outside.

It was still dark, but there was no mistaking the outline of the person who climbed from the truck. It was Williams. As soon as he stepped out, four more trucks came roaring down the street. Transportation would no longer be a problem.

I ran outside to greet him and asked, while hugging him, "I know I shouldn't ask, but where in the world did you find these?"

"Did you see the attack last night?" he asked. "Well, we were in that. I even got wounded."

He pulled open a hole in his uniform pants to reveal a spot of dried blood. He then pointed to the door of his truck and said, "Look at those machine gun holes."

"You got shot?" I asked.

"Well, not exactly."

Sanders interrupted him and said, "What he means is he ripped his ass when he jumped out of the truck and ran for the ditch. Funniest thing I ever saw."

"I'm still wounded," he protested. "How about putting me in for the Purple Heart?"

"It'd be more like the Pink Heart," Sanders teased. "You should have seen him run."

"Oh yeah," Williams shot back. "Who was it who nearly broke my neck when he dove in on top of me?"

"Never mind all that," I said. "You men OK?"

"I guess we're OK," Williams finally admitted.

"Then where in the hell did you get these trucks?"

"After the attack. We were right there next to the base when it happened. When it was over we drove over to see if we could help. These trucks were parked in a row of trees just off the base—probably being hid there. I just thought it would be better to get them out of there so they wouldn't get bombed."

"So, you were just *protecting* the trucks? That right?"

"Yeah, something like that," he said, a twinkle in his eye. "Anyway, here they are."

I just shook my head. "You little crook. Someday they're going to hang you, but in the meantime, I'm glad you're on our side."

Then I said to the others, "I'm proud of you. I'm also bettin' you've got to be whipped. Rescuing trucks will do that to a guy. Why don't you get inside and get some shut-eye. You've earned it."

As the others headed for the schoolhouse, I grabbed Williams by the arm. "One more thing. We're going to need one or two of those trucks to get some of us to Capodichino this morning—and maybe to Bari later on. Better find a way to cover up the ID numbers on them or they're going to know where we got 'em. Right?"

"What numbers?" he replied, shrugging his shoulders.

I looked closer at the trucks. The numbers were already gone.

22

HEROES

The weeks flew by as we settled in to what had become a regular routine. I could remember as a little boy knocking the dirt off ant mounds, only to discover them built up perfectly again the next morning. The work we were doing now reminded me exactly of that. One day we would reconnect downed communication lines or help repair one of the airstrips in the area. The next day the German Messerschmitts and light bombers would blast our repairs to smithereens. The day after that, we'd start all over again.

Ants rebuilding their mounds.

Repairing the strips and putting up line poles would not have been easy work under the best of circumstances. The ground in this part of Italy was so rocky the men joked that all one had to do was stub his toe on the earth and a rock came up. They may have been joking, but this seemed to be true more often than not. Strips became especially dangerous after a rain because rocks always came to the surface then. The morning following a heavy rain, a squad of men would stand across the head of the strip, each at arm's length apart, and walk the strip, looking for rocks and other debris. At the same time, they carried small yellow flags they would stick in the ground when they came across an uneven spot or a hole caused during the last attack, marking it for repair.

Keeping the strips level and smooth was the greatest challenge of all. The army engineers were bounced around from place to place as much as we were, so we were often asked to step in and take charge after raids, especially since Colonel Phillips's own background was in engineering. He was most often out front when we started the repairs, and the men were impressed by that.

During these repairs, after rocks were picked up and holes filled, steel rollers were attached to the backs of trucks and pulled down the strip to complete the smoothing of the surface. Steamrollers would have been much easier to use, but none had been brought up this direction yet. The flyboys we had were good, but there wasn't much even the most experienced pilot could do during a takeoff or landing if a tire blew from hitting a sharp rock or control of the plane was lost when a wheel dipped into a bomb crater. It was often our job to see that didn't happen, and we took great pride in keeping the strips manicured as best we could.

The field wasn't the only casualty of a German raid. We worked day and night to repair buildings that had been hit by bombs. During one attack, the flight observation tower at Pompeii had taken a direct hit, leveling it to a pile of ash. Four men who had been in the tower during the attack were killed instantly, their bodies consumed in fire. In the process of clearing away their remains, Albertson suddenly ran out to the field, fell to his knees, and vomited.

"What's got into him?" Jamieson asked.

"Over here. In the corner," Clark replied in a hushed tone.

There, resting on top of a charred shoe, was an eye.

Jamieson ran out and joined him on the field.

As soon as the area had been cleared, all of us who could drive a nail or carry tools pitched in that day, and by nightfall a new tower was operational, complete with new communication lines up and ringing. Times like this I felt we were the glue holding everything together in this part of Italy.

Vehicle repair was a constant problem at the airfields as trucks, jeeps, and planes were popular targets of the German pilots. There wasn't much we could do to help with rebuilding damaged planes, but truck repair was another story. The chief mechanic at the motor pool at Frattamaggiore was killed by machine gun fire while trying to get a jeep out of the way during a sudden attack. This left them with two men who could do light maintenance, but no one to do major repairs. They were in desperate need of help. When Colonel Phillips found out about this, he loaned Doc to them. For a week he worked in the motor pool there each day, returning to eat and sleep with us in the evenings.

I asked him one night how it was going, and he replied, "Perc, I hated it at first. The other mechanics wouldn't talk to me or even come near me. They acted like I was Typhoid Mary. Then the second day there I told those country boys to rub dirt on their faces so I'd feel at home. They laughed like hell and loosened up enough that we could finally work together."

"So it's OK now?" I asked.

"I don't know. I can't explain it. I feel good and bad at the same time when I'm over there. It's strange. Real strange. Do you know what I mean?"

I knew exactly what he meant.

Technically, we were assigned to the 12th Air Force. However, just as had been the case at Fort Bliss, we were left pretty much on our own. Everyone in our area wanted our services, but no one seemed to want us. I felt this more and more each day. I didn't say anything to the men. I didn't have to. We were starting to be known as the "Roving 449th," a nickname we could have done without. There were still fences, even here in Europe, even as bombs were exploding all around us.

Between communication maintenance and strip repair, the men worked most days from sunup to sundown. They badly needed a rest, but we had also discovered that war never took a day off. Even when there would be a short lull, our own equipment had to be maintained or replenished. This gave the men very little time to themselves to kick back and relax. We had brought our baseball gloves with us across the Atlantic, but there hadn't been time yet for one single game of catch.

Then suddenly, just when I thought the men were going to drop from sheer exhaustion, a break came, catching us all by surprise.

The air strikes stopped.

Word soon came that Allied troops were landing up the coast at Anzio. It was no secret that if we were able to take Anzio, the road to Rome would start to open. And if Rome fell, the rest of Italy would surely follow. We knew it. The Germans knew it.

It was going to be one hell of a fight.

The immediate result of the amphibious landing at Anzio was a decrease in the number of attacks in our own area. The Germans were no doubt throwing everything they had at our troops there to halt their progress. We were now small potatoes by comparison. As soon as that operation started, a new spirit gripped all of us in our immediate area as we switched from a defensive to an offensive mode of operation. Now, instead of spending most of our time helping with repairs of one type or another, we suddenly found ourselves among those helping set the stage for battle. We kept a crew standing by for strip repair, but the rest of the company geared up for stringing lines as our troops advanced up the coast to join those digging in at Anzio. This meant we'd be moving out of our schoolhouse—and sooner rather than later.

And now that we had our own fleet of trucks, thanks to Williams who kept "finding" and "rescuing" them, we were also one of the more mobile support units in this whole section of Italy, a fact that made us all the more popular. At times, I thought, a little too popular. Once word got around, we were bombarded with requests to help move everything from men to supplies. It got to the point where we were sending at least two trucks down to Naples each morning to pick up supplies that we would deliver to those waiting for them up and down the coast. Never in my wildest dreams did I think back at Fort Bliss that their driver's training would one day mean this much to so many.

Now it did.

Then, on top of everything else, the news came that we'd all just about given up hope we'd ever receive: Baker Company would be rejoining us. Colonel Phillips called us all together one evening just before lights-out to share the news. The men were overjoyed and cheered even louder than they had at their first sight of land after our sea voyage. That moment was pure bliss.

The colonel also went on to say that once the others got back, the battalion would be kept together, but squads would be formed and sent out daily to take care of each of the airfields and line routes in the area until we got our moving orders.

Very little of what he said that night registered with any of us. The important thing was the battalion would soon be whole again.

* * *

It was too good to last. The lull in the storm lasted exactly two days.

Reports filtered down that the Germans had been taken by surprise at Anzio. Once they figured out what was going on, however, they hit back with everything they had, including, some said, even the kitchen sink. They also figured out a good chunk of the air support for the Allied landing was coming from down our direction.

Then they doubled their strikes on the airfields.

Our communication poles and cables were being destroyed nearly as fast as we could repair them, so we started working in shifts around the clock. The men were nearly dead on their feet. We had been ordered to give this work first priority because, above all else, our forces had to maintain good communication. Without it, we'd be fighting blind.

Just after midnight on the second night of the renewed strikes, when we had finally completed repairs on nearly two miles of cable and were returning to Melito for a much needed rest, we saw a large crowd surrounding a building at the far edge of the village at Capodichino. It was a rare sight to see the locals in any of the villages, so we knew immediately something was up. As we approached the crowd, I told Tyler to pull over and stop. An older man wearing a long, black coat ran up to the truck and started screaming in Italian, obviously imploring us to help.

"Let's get out and take a look," I said to Tyler, who had now become my driver.

Doc, driving the truck right behind us, also pulled over and jumped out. "What gives?" he asked.

"Don't know yet. Whatever's going on, I'm guessing it's not good," I replied.

A young woman, wiping tears from her face, came over and put her arms around the man who had been screaming at us, trying to comfort him. Then, calmly and in broken English, she told us a family had been buried alive when their home had been hit by a bomb during the last German attack. They knew at least some were still alive because their cries could be heard through the rubble. The young woman explained they had started trying to dig them out but stopped when someone checking the second floor discovered an unexploded bomb lodged under a fallen wall. The front of the building had been blown off by the first bomb, and now the midnight blue tip of the unexploded one on the second floor could be seen from the street. It appeared the weight of the debris on top of it was all that was keeping it from falling to the ground below.

It had been a large two-story building, one of the few still standing in town, a fact that probably made it a logical target for the Germans. The woman explained that the family business, a bakery, was on the main floor, while the family lived in the rooms above. When the last attack started, the family had hurried down to the basement seeking shelter. However, a bomb hit the upper rear wall of the house, causing the side walls of the second floor to fall inward and the entire front wall of the building to blow out, leaving the house totally exposed from the front. The sudden weight of the collapsed walls had buckled the floors, and the bottom floor caved into the basement, trapping the family. The second bomb had landed almost immediately and almost in the same spot, but it hadn't exploded, lodging under the remains of what had once been the west wall. The badly buckled second floor looked like it was hanging by a thread. It was a miracle it hadn't fallen down when the front wall came off the building.

"Sarge, what are we going to do?" Albertson asked, suddenly appearing from behind Doc.

"I don't know," I replied. "But we can't just walk away from this."

I looked around at the crowd. Most eyes were now on us. We may not have been able to speak the same language, but the looks on their faces didn't need translation. These people needed help, and they needed it right now.

"OK, this is what we're going to do," I said, turning to Doc. "You get everybody back to Melito as quickly as you can. Load two trucks with lumber and tools and head right back here. Pick six men and bring them back with you. If Williams is back from his hunt for mattresses, roust him and bring him back with you, too. We may need his particular talents before this is all over. We'll get those people out of there."

Doc looked at me suspiciously. "You really think so? Look at that bomb again."

I grinned and said, "We're a construction battalion. Remember? If we can't shore up that second floor so we can dig those people out, then we've got no business being here at all."

An incredibly bright full moon filled the night sky, so visibility was quite good. I studied what was left of the building again and continued, "I've got this figured out. At least I think I do. We'll put cross supports down first over the front part of the foundation to make a level base. Then we'll wedge in the smaller line poles between the base and the second floor to keep pressure on it. That should keep it from collapsing while we dig out below. It should also keep that bomb up there. It better."

"And what if the bomb goes off while we're working?" Doc asked.

"You're a gambler," I said. "Let's roll the dice and see what happens."

"OK, if you say so. But I still say this is too chancy."

"Maybe," I said, "but we're the only chance they've got."

I then turned to Albertson and said, "Since Doc's going to be hotfootin' it to get back here, I'm putting you in charge of getting the other trucks supplied and ready when you get back. I know it's late, but we need them ready to roll if we get called to rush somewhere in the morning. When you're done, then have the men fall out and get some sleep. They need it. Do not come back here. You hear me? And if Colonel Phillips is still up, fill him in on what we're doing and tell him we'll get back as soon as we can. Then you get some sleep, too, OK?"

I then put my hand on his shoulder and said, gently this time, "If we don't get back before more orders come in, I want you to take over for me. I know you can do it."

"Thanks, Sarge. I'll do my best."

"I know you will. Now you and Doc get everybody the hell out of here. Tyler and I will stick around until Doc gets back."

Doc was already headed to his truck when I called out to him, "Make it snappy. I don't think we have much time."

As the trucks pulled out, Tyler came back over to me and asked, "What do we do now, Sarge?"

"We wait," I said. "And we pray."

I looked at Tyler, and he was already looking up at the sky. I joined him.

* * *

The minute Doc and the others returned, we rolled up our sleeves and got to it. The woman who spoke English came up to me and asked if there was anything the villagers could do to help. I shared our plan with her and asked her to help keep the others back while we worked. We'd be calling on them to help out once we had the supports in place. She nodded and headed back to the crowd to relay the information.

The immediate trick was to figure out how to build a section of floor without putting pressure on the rubble below. The entire front of the building was gone, but the rim of the foundation was exposed and still relatively intact. Doc, building upon my original idea, suggested we take our longest boards and cut them to fit lengthwise across the front of the foundation to make a smooth platform. That made good sense. Fortunately, the building was narrow, so the boards wouldn't give much even with weight on them, especially if we stacked them three deep.

After taking some measurements, the men quickly set up saw-horses and cut the boards to the right length. Moving carefully so we didn't disturb anything either below or above us, we placed the boards across the front of the foundation. When the last one was in place, I said, to no one in particular, "Well, I guess we better find out if it will hold some weight. Anyone want to volunteer to walk on it?"

"I will, Sarge," Tyler volunteered.

He weighed the least of anyone in the battalion, so he really was the logical choice.

"OK, but put that helmet back on first, " I scolded him.

"If that bomb hits me on the head, the helmet ain't going to make a bit of difference," he replied.

He had a point, but I made him put it on anyway.

The crowd moved back slowly as Tyler stepped up on the boards. I didn't understand the words, but it was obvious several of the villagers were praying. Others hugged each other. Still others silently wept.

The boards didn't give. Tyler bent his knees and bounced his weight gently up and down. The support was solid. Whether it was solid enough to support the poles was still anyone's guess. I was glad there was so much praying going on among the villagers. We needed all the help we could get.

A near disaster occurred when Jamieson slipped as he and Brown brought the first of the poles over to us. The pole slipped out of Jamieson's hands and Brown's forward motion caused it to fly forward, like a spear. It landed with a thud in the hard dirt just in front of the building. If it had landed a foot farther and hit the foundation or our new floor, the concussion might have been enough to cause the entire upper floor to come crashing down. The oddest part was that no one, not any of the villagers and not one of us, moved an inch while that took place. It was hard to tell if we were all just stunned or frozen by fear. Whatever it was, a collective sigh of relief could be heard when the pole was picked back up.

"Sorry, Sarge," they both said at the same time.

Jamieson added, "It was all my fault. I slipped. Won't happen again."

"It better not," I said. "I don't think we'll get a second chance, if you know what I mean."

He knew exactly what I meant, and as they lifted the pole into place they moved it slowly and cautiously, gently wedging it between our boards and the sagging second floor. As it was being put into place, the second floor was raised slightly, causing a small amount of plaster and dust to fall. But that was all that fell. The bomb hadn't moved.

It looked like prayers were being answered.

Four more poles were cut and put into place. That would provide enough support to keep the second floor from crashing down.

Once the second floor and the bomb seemed to be secure enough, we turned our attention to the basement. Only the front part of the main floor had given way in the explosion, crashing down toward the rear of the basement where the family had been hiding, trapping them against the back wall. In order to dig the family out, men would have to crawl across our boards and drop down into the front half of the basement, without bumping into the support poles, and start handing out what pieces of the caved-in floor could be moved. We hoped enough of the rubble could be set aside or lifted out so that we could find a way to get into the back part of the basement where they were trapped.

Every few minutes we could hear the muffled crying of one of the family members trapped below, but it was getting softer and softer in volume. We needed to hurry.

Doc and Brown, who were by far the strongest of all, suggested they be the ones to climb in and start handing out the debris. I thought about it a minute and realized it would be best to have the smaller men inside and the more powerful men outside. If the smaller men were able to lift up the pieces of the floor that had caved in, the larger men could then grab hold of them and use their strength to make sure the supports didn't get bumped into and knocked down. There was still the bomb to consider.

Tyler and Williams stepped forward and volunteered to crawl inside and start handing out the pieces of the crumbled floor.

"I know you've told us a million times not to volunteer for anything," Williams said. "I just think it has to be us."

I thought so, too. We wished them luck.

Breaths were held as they inched their way across the planks and dropped into the rubble below.

"Be careful where you step," I shouted as I dropped flashlights down to them. "You don't want to cause anything to shift."

Tyler called back out, "Don't worry—we're going slow and easy."

I could hear what sounded like boards and building stone being stacked toward the front of the foundation just below us. We couldn't see them, but the light from their flashlights moved regularly back and forth from rear to front, registering their movements.

After a few minutes I asked, "What's it look like down there?"

Williams stood on some of the rubble and popped his head up. "It looks good, looks like we're lucky. If we can move a few more boards and bricks we should be able to crawl into where they are. We can hear them, so we're digging toward their voices."

He wiped his forehead with his sleeve and added, "We better not stack anything else up down here or it's going to fall again. You ready for us to start handing stuff out?"

"We're ready. Just go slow and be careful. There's still that bomb up there."

"Don't you think I know it," he said, rolling his eyes upward.

From below him I could hear Tyler say, "OK, hold your breath. Here it comes."

For the next ten minutes they used every muscle on their skinny frames to raise boards and position them so Doc and Brown could grab them and ease them out without hitting the support poles. Next came large chunks of building stone, one after the other. The rest of the men and the villagers formed a line behind Doc and Brown and helped move everything away from the building.

Suddenly, all was quiet below. Too quiet.

I leaned in as far as I could and yelled, "What's going on down there? You OK?"

There was no response.

I called down again, "Are you OK?"

Tyler, covered in dust, scared me when his head appeared right in front of me.

"Hi, Sarge," he said. "Got something for you. You ready?"

Before I could respond, he lifted above his head a young child who looked about two years old. Doc reached over and gently took her into his arms. She looked like she was asleep.

"She's still breathing," Tyler said, his breath now coming in short bursts. "But she's got a pretty good knot on the side of her head. Doesn't look real good to me."

The child was unconscious and in need of medical attention, but at least she was alive. Doc handed her to a large woman standing off to the side.

"She's alive," Doc turned and said to the villagers. They may not have understood his words, but they understood his tone. They cheered and clapped.

"Got another," Tyler called out. "Here she comes."

This time all we could see was Tyler's hands as he lifted up another little girl, this one about nine or ten. She was sobbing softly as Doc and Brown each grabbed an arm and gently lifted her out. Brown held her close as he carried her out to the crowd. The villagers cheered again, many rushing over to pat Brown on the back.

A few minutes later Tyler yelled up to us, "I think this is the mom. Wow, is she heavy. I hope we can get her out of here."

Williams lifted her at her waist while Tyler pulled up on her arms. Doc leaned forward to grab her wrists and lost his balance, crashing down on the planks. Dust and plaster from the second floor rained down on top of him. At the same time, Williams and Tyler, startled, stumbled back, supporting the woman above them as they fell. Doc reached down to break most of his fall but hit his chin on the edge of a board, slicing it open. Blood streamed down his neck.

I ran over, reached down, and quickly pulled him away from the building. "You OK?" I asked.

"Yeah, just a scratch. Never mind me. How are they doing? Did I hurt anybody?"

"I think they're fine. Let me take a look at that. Some scratch," I said, wiping the blood away. "You're going to need a couple of stitches."

"Won't be the first time," he said. "Oh hell, I'm OK. Let's get back at it."

It was then we noticed the bomb had moved.

When Doc fell onto the plank, one of the support poles shifted, causing the second floor to sag slightly more toward the center. The bomb had moved with it and now didn't look nearly as secure as before.

"We've got to work fast now," I said. "I don't think that upper floor's going to stay put much longer, and we can't risk putting up more poles to hold it."

Williams and Tyler then raised the woman up again. This time Doc and Brown gently pulled her out. She, too, was alive but unconscious. There was a bad gash above her forehead, and the area around it had already started turning blue.

"Be easy with her," I said. "Take her over there by the truck and wrap her in blankets. Try to keep her warm so she doesn't go into shock."

Tyler appeared again, motioning me to lean down close to him. "We've got a problem," he said. "There's a man down here who's alive, but his legs are trapped under some boards. They're too heavy. We can't move them. What do you want us to do?"

"I'm going in," Doc said. "I'll get him out."

"You can't," Tyler said. "You're too big to fit through the hole down here."

I thought for a minute, then asked, "Is there room to pry up the boards and pull him free?"

"We better give it a try," he responded. "I don't think he's gong to last much longer if we don't."

"We'll get you a couple of long-handled shovels. Give them a try. Slip the blades under the boards as far as you can and then push down on the handles to make a lever. But be careful, OK? We don't want to loosen things up too much."

"You've got that right. Sarge, I can still hear wood cracking every time we take a step down here."

"I wish I could help them," Doc said to me as we handed them the shovels.

"Me, too," I said. "If anything happens to them."

Soon we could hear the faint sounds of boards creaking. The platform we had built also moved slightly. More plaster fell from the ceiling above. We held our breath as all eyes now focused on the bomb.

"We got him!" Tyler called out. "We got him!"

As Tyler and Williams raised him up, Doc and Brown reached in and grabbed him under his left shoulder, lifting him carefully across the planks before carrying him over next to the truck where the woman had been taken. As they lowered him slowly to the ground, the man raised an arm and pointed back toward the house. Then he closed his eyes and passed out.

Tyler motioned to me to lean in close to him. This time he whispered. "We've got two more down here. An old man and an old woman. They're both dead. What do you want us to do about them?"

"We're going to have to leave them. I want you two out of there, and I mean right now. We've got to get out of here before that bomb goes off or the building gives."

I motioned for Doc to lift Tyler out, then Williams. When they were clear, I shouted, "OK, everybody get back now. That's all we can do."

The woman who spoke English translated my words for the

others. I noticed a few asked her questions before she came back over to me. She asked about those who were still below.

"I'm terribly sorry," I said, lowering my voice. "They didn't make it."

She turned and said something to the villagers, who were just starting to back away from the building. They turned silent. The men who had hats removed them. Others crossed themselves and prayed. The large woman holding the youngest child sobbed as she rocked her back and forth.

"We'll get someone back here as soon as we can to take care of the bomb," I said to her. "In the meantime, I don't want anyone to go near the building. Please tell everyone to keep away. There's nothing more that can be done."

I then called Sanders and Clark over. "Get the family in your truck and take them over to the airfield. They've got a medic there. He'll take care of them."

Turning to the others, I said, "The rest of you—good job. Now let's get the hell out of here and go home."

What happened next was something none of us would ever forget. The villagers spread themselves out and formed a line in front of our trucks. They then walked toward us, each stopping to shake our hands and hug us. A few of the women kissed us on the cheek.

Williams and Tyler were standing next to the last truck. When the villagers got to them, they lifted them on their shoulders and cheered again as they carried them down the street, their outlines silhouetted in the soft glow of fading moonlight.

Doc put his arm around my shoulder and said, "Look at that. They're their new heroes."

"You know what?" I said. "They're mine, too,"

* * *

By the time we got back to the schoolhouse, the sun was just beginning to creep above the horizon. Those inside were still sleeping, so I told everyone, and especially our new heroes, to be quiet as they slipped inside for some much needed rest.

I was still so wound up I couldn't sleep. I sat down outside and leaned against the large apple tree next to the rock wall surrounding the schoolhouse. Doc had gone inside for a minute but soon returned, walking quickly toward me.

"Look at this!" he said, realizing he was talking too loud. "Letters from home!"

While we were away mail had been delivered to the battalion. Doc had received a letter from Judy. Mine was from Olivia. At the same time we tore open the envelopes.

It had been weeks since we'd received any mail, and I was craving news from home. Even so, I didn't read the letter right away. I held it in my hand and stared at it, thinking about how much I missed Olivia. How much I missed her touch. The smell of her hair. The softness of her lips.

Before unfolding the pages, I looked over at Doc, who was quickly scanning Judy's letter, a smile beaming across his face. He had it bad.

And so did I.

I smoothed out the pages of the letter and started to read, losing myself in the sound of Olivia's voice. She could have written about the weather back home and at that moment it wouldn't have made any difference to me. Just seeing her handwriting, the gentle loops of her "l's" and the high curve of her "s's" took me all the way back to St. Louis.

I closed my eyes and drifted back to the last time we had been alone together, the last time she had hugged me as tightly as she could, nestling her cheek against my neck. "I love you," she had said so gently, so warmly that afternoon. It wasn't just the words I remembered now. It was how she said them, putting emphasis on the "I"—drawing me closer to her as she said it, connecting the "I" and her touch. I didn't want to let go of her—ever. When she finally raised up to kiss me, she looked me deeply in the eyes but didn't say a word. When her lips touched mine I felt the love in ways words couldn't begin to describe.

Before I finished the first page, which was mostly gossip about friends back in the Ville, I noticed Doc refolding his letter and stuffing it back into the envelope.

"Perc," he said. "I'm an idiot. I should have married her when I had the chance. I've never felt this way about anybody in my whole life. You don't know what I'd give to be with her right now, right this very minute."

I smiled and said, "Oh, I think I know. I've got one of those over here, too." I pointed to my letter.

"All I can say is, if I get back, I'm going to get a license before I do anything else. Then we're going to get married and have six kids. Maybe seven. And every day when I come home from work we're going to do something different. I've been thinking about this a lot. We're going to go dancing, go on picnics, go to the movies."

Here he paused for emphasis and added, "And we're going to the zoo. We're not going to be like my folks, who never went anywhere or did anything. We're going to live—and we're going to love. We're going to do it all."

"That sounds really great," I said, "But I want to know something. How in the world are you going to feed all those mouths?"

"I've been thinking a lot about that, too. My uncle has already said he'd make me a partner in the garage if I stick with him. That's a start, but only a start. You're lucky in the Ville, and we're lucky in Kinloch. But there are so many places in St. Louis that don't even have a place to buy gasoline, let alone a place to get a car worked on—especially for us. If I can get a few dollars ahead, I think I'll try to add a few other places and hire people to run them for me."

"Like Monopoly?" I said, teasing him.

"OK, make fun of me if you want, but just you wait. We'll see who gets the last laugh. I'll feed all those mouths and *still* have money for dancing and movies. And maybe even a real vacation every year down to Mississippi to see the rest of my family. That would really be something."

More seriously now, I said, "Doc, I'll be damned if I don't believe you. One day you'll be the garage king of all St. Louis, and the rest of us will be coming to put the bite on you for money. I can see it happening. I can."

"And what about you? You made up your mind what you're going to do when you get back home?"

"I've been doing a lot of thinking, too," I said, leaning back against the rough bark of the tree again. "Colonel Ellis kept telling me to try for Officer Candidate School, and for a while I thought I might give that a shot."

Doc, making fun of me, groaned and rubbed his stomach like he was going to be sick.

"No, really," I continued. "This army isn't so bad, and if I was an officer the money would be pretty darn good. Shoot, eventually I'd probably even be able to get into some kind of training division like Ellis did. Like I said, that *sounded* good, and in some ways it still does. But it isn't where my heart is, so I've thrown all that out the window."

"Hallelujah!" Doc shouted, again realizing that he was making too much noise for this early in the morning. "So what are you going to do?" he asked again, almost whispering this time.

"I'm going back to Sumner. That is if they don't just up and fire Olivia for getting married and me for being so sneaky about it. That's where my heart is. That's where it'll always be. I may be wearing a uniform now, but inside this shirt is a teacher aching to get back to his old job. As strange as this is going to sound, I don't think I really appreciated what I had there until I started working with the men back in El Paso. After I got my stripes, I saw in some ways being a sergeant is like being a teacher, and in other ways it's just the opposite. And I learned the difference in a hurry. A sergeant is supposed to tell his men what to do and then expects them to do it—and without question. From the minute they made me a sergeant, I knew that wasn't me. I'm a teacher, plain and simple, and I hope I always will be. A teacher not only tells his students what to do, he helps them see *why* they're doing it. That's the part I like most. The minute my students understand the *why,* they've really learned something. They get more than just knowledge about *things.* They learn more about themselves. When that happens, the world will open up for them. That's what I want to do. I want to teach kids the *why* of the world. If I can help them with that, then the world will be a special place for me, too."

"I'm glad to hear you say that," he said, smiling again. "You're a great teacher, Perc. The best I've ever known. Go back to Sumner. They need you. Hell, we all need you. Just think about what you've done with these brickheads here. Where do you think they'd be if you hadn't shown up?"

Lowering his voice, he added, "To be honest, I didn't think any of us would end up doing anything other than 'watching the mail' like we did on the train that first night out of St. Louis. And now look at us. What we're doing is important. It's making a difference. Think about it. The 449th is keeping everybody and everything connected all the way up the line. No one would know what anybody else was doing around here if it weren't for us. *We're* doing that. We're keeping the airfields open. We're moving more men and supplies around than anyone else in the area. Hell, we're building everything in sight. And all of this is because of what you've done, Perc. It's true. I'm smart enough to know we'd all be digging latrines now if you hadn't been there to keep us together and teach us everything you've taught us. You are a natural-born teacher, and there aren't many of those around. Yeah, you've got to go back to Sumner when this war is over. And they'll be damn lucky to have you."

"Thanks," I said. "You're giving me way too much credit, but thanks for saying it anyway. That means a lot to me. It really does. And I'm smart enough to know whatever I've done, I couldn't have done it without you. And *that's* the truth. We make a damn good team, my friend. A damn good team."

I flicked a stick at him and said, "When we get home, I'm going to be teaching those Sumner kids to drive, and you'll probably end up working on their cars when they grow up. Won't that be something? We just might be teaming up for a long, long time."

"I like that thought," he said.

"So do I," I said. "So do I."

A light coming on in the schoolhouse caught my attention. A few of the men were beginning to stir. I looked again at Doc and pointed past him. "We can dream all we want about being back home, but in the meantime, we've still got to keep working on—what did you call them?—our brickheads? What a group!"

Doc laughed. "They're a collection, all right. They've still got a few rough edges on 'em, but look at how much they've changed already."

He was right. They really had changed. I thought back to the first night we were all together in El Paso, how frightened most of them were to be away from home for the first time. I also thought of all we'd been through together. Driver's training. Baseball games. Mexican adventures. Game nights in the barracks. Classes. Giant spiders.

Albertson's Last Stand. Ocean voyage. The war.

Yes, they had changed. They were now soldiers.

And they had become so much more than that.

They had become men.

No words could express how proud I was of them.

There was no telling what the future would bring, but whatever they did, these men would do it with pride and dignity.

They weren't men on a journey anymore.

They had arrived.

The sun was rising slowly over the mountain range to our east. A day of new beginnings and a day of new hope was being born.

The men of the 449th were ready for anything.

23

PASSAGES

JUNE 17, 1944

Master Sgt. Inman Perkins crawled slowly out of his tent, raising a hand to shield his eyes from the early morning sun. His back and legs were killing him. He moaned and cursed under his breath as he stood up, rubbing his stiff neck at the same time. He had barely slept a wink the night before, waking almost every hour to reposition himself, seeking a comfortable spot on the hard ground. The thin army-issue blankets offered little protection from the rocky terrain of Anzio. His own stove-up and bruised body was now proof enough of that.

He lit a Lucky, inhaled deeply, and looked down the long, irregular row of tents to his right. The men of the 449th had been ordered up from Melito two weeks before and were now bivouacked in a peach orchard just down the road from the main Allied headquarters at Anzio. Because most of the town had been leveled during the Allied landing and the German counterattacks that followed, no suitable structure could be found to quarter them. The few buildings still standing seemed for the most part on the verge of collapse, missing entire walls or sections of roof. Therefore, the 449th had been given tents and were told to search for a place to pitch them where they'd at least be difficult to spot by enemy planes. The peach orchard was one of the few places left in the immediate area that provided any semblance of cover, so they decided to hide the tents as much as possible under the trees there.

As Inman rubbed his back and tried to shake the kinks out

of his legs, he looked off in the distance. Half a dozen pillars of smoke still billowed skyward, reminders of a series of German air attacks the day before. There was no doubt in Inman's mind, as he heard the faint sound of a far-off explosion and watched a pillar of smoke catapult even higher into the air, that communication lines were down again and they'd soon be sent out to repair them. The Luftwaffe was doing one hell of a job during their strafing runs keeping the Allied troops occupied and, at the same time, knocking out communications so that the Allies' right hand had a tough time keeping up with what the left was doing. Inman quietly laughed as he spotted a downed pole just down the road from where they were camped.

"We're ants building our mounds again," he said aloud, shaking his head.

He looked up and down the row of tents and saw no movement. The men should be rousted so they could get on with the work of the day, but he just couldn't bring himself to do it yet. They had been working almost day and night since they arrived and badly needed the rest. He decided he was going to let them sleep as long as they could—and at least until someone at headquarters sent over the orders for the day.

He lit another cigarette and sat down on a pile of rocks next to his tent, removing a pencil and a carefully folded piece of paper from his shirt pocket. Unfolding the paper and smoothing it out on his leg, he quickly added a few lines to the letter he had started to Olivia the night before.

In that early morning hour, all around him was quiet.

It was then the first Messerschmitt came right out of the sun.

The lead plane swooped down directly over headquarters but didn't fire a shot. At almost the same instant, the air-raid siren pierced the heavy morning air, causing a sudden eruption of movement all around. The men of the 449th bolted from their tents. Inman screamed above the siren, "Wait! Don't move! Wait until I give the word—and then run like hell to the shelter!"

The men froze in their tracks, some only halfway out of their tents, and stared up at the sky. The second plane opened up, raking the main street with machine gun fire. Small puffs of dust rose from the ground in a steady stream as the bullets struck. Inman screamed again, "Hit the dirt! Cover up—and don't move!"

The instant the second plane roared by, Inman yelled, "Now! Let's go before the next one!"

He had noticed from raids on previous days that the planes seemed to come in intervals fairly uniform in length. He prayed that pattern would continue.

The men ran as quickly as they could across the street to a low, rectangular building still reasonably intact. Before the war, it had been used by one of the local grocers to store meats, cheeses, and vegetables. Its two-foot-thick rock walls had provided enough insulation to prevent quick spoilage of his goods. Now, the same building was providing protection—but of a vastly different kind.

Inman made sure the last of the men made it to the shelter and was just about to head across himself when the next plane dropped down. Just as he was backing up to hide behind a tree, he felt himself being grabbed by his belt. Startled, he turned to see Doc standing behind him.

"Hang on!" Doc shouted above the roar of the Messerschmitt's engine. "Here we go!"

With that, Doc half lifted and half jerked Inman with him as both tumbled over the remains of the front wall of the bombed-out building immediately behind them. Doc fell on top of Inman, knocking the breath out of him. He covered his friend's body with his own while scooting them both right up against the wall.

A steady stream of bullets clipped a large branch off the tree Inman had been crouching behind. It fell to the ground with a thud just a few feet away from them.

When Inman finally caught his breath he gasped, "Holy shit! I could have been killed! I should have been killed. And you—you dumb idiot—what do you think you're doing? Why aren't you in that shelter with the others?"

"So that's the thanks I get," Doc responded, smirking. "And don't you think I'm completely out to save your ass. If you get drilled, they just might make me a sergeant, and I sure as hell don't want that. Saving you is saving me. Get it?"

Inman smiled and reached out to shake his friend's hand. "By the way, did I say thanks?"

Doc took his hand and squeezed it so hard Inman let out a yelp. At the same time, both ducked again and hugged the wall as the last plane peppered the air with its machine guns. This time the peach orchard was blasted. One after the other, the tents collapsed slowly, like balloons with small leaks, finally resting flat on the ground. Fortunately, none of the men had remained in them. If they had, they wouldn't have stood a chance.

At the tail end of the last burst of fire, a bullet ricocheted off the back wall of the building and lodged in the wall a foot above Doc's head.

"Damn, that was close!" Doc cried, feeling up and down his legs and chest to make sure he was still all there. "You OK?" he then asked.

As the air-raid siren continued to blare, Inman replied, "Close? I felt the wind from the propeller! If he'd come in any lower we'd have gotten the 'big haircut.'"

Doc knew exactly what he meant and nodded. "We've got to get out of here," he said. "We might not be so lucky when the next one comes."

"I think that's it," Inman said. "Listen. I think they're going away."

As quickly as they had struck, they vanished back into the sun. An eerie calm followed, punctuated only by the crying of a small child coming from a building at the far end of the street.

As soon as the all-clear sounded, the men slowly and cautiously climbed from the shelter. Inman walked over to meet them, to make sure they were all OK. No one had been hit, but Tyler had thrown up, and the smell, in the close quarters of the building, had also set off a few of the others. The first men out of the building had their hands over their noses and mouths.

"Geez, Sarge. Can't you do something about Tyler?" Brown complained, gagging. He then continued, "For such a small guy, he can sure put up one hell of a big smell. He darn near killed us all in there. I think next time I'd rather take my chances out here with the Germans."

Tyler was the last one out of the shelter. The others immediately surrounded him, as if waiting for an explanation of some type. He didn't disappoint them.

"Hey, guys. I really wasn't scared. I got some bad K rations last night, and they made me sick. That's all. Really."

A collective groan passed across the men as they rolled their eyes and headed back toward their tents.

"Honest," Tyler continued his protest. "I wasn't scared."

Inman walked over to Tyler and put his arm around his shoulders. "Maybe you weren't scared," he said, "but I was. Scared all the way down to my GI socks. I want everybody to be at least a little afraid. Maybe it will keep us all alive."

Then he patted Tyler lightly on the back and said, "You better go eat something if you think you can keep it down. I think we're going to be at it a long time today, and you look like you're running on empty."

Inman turned and was going to tell the men the same thing, but Tyler's stomach was already ancient history. They were standing as a group, either arms folded or hands on hips, staring at their tents—at least what was left of them.

"Holy Moses!" Jamieson shouted. "We've been creamed!"

Albertson was the first to reach his tent and screamed to no one in particular, "Those sons of bitches! They shot my girlfriend!"

He held up a large picture of his girlfriend that now had a bullet hole the size of a half dollar right where her breasts had been. Jamieson yanked it from his hands, held it up to the sky, and said, "Well, you wouldn't be seeing them anytime soon anyway."

Albertson didn't find it funny. He kicked at the ground, sending rocks flying into the men gathered around him. They knew the look on his face and knew they were best off not saying anything. They moved down the row to their own tents to see what destruction awaited them.

Inman crossed the road and walked slowly down into the peach orchard, pausing at each tent to offer words of encouragement to the man whose belongings had been shredded.

"Listen up," he finally said, drawing the attention of the group. "I'll give you each five minutes to crab about this, but then I don't want to hear any more about it. It could have been your ugly behinds that got shot up instead. Think about that a minute. We were all lucky. Damn lucky."

He paused long enough to reach down to pick up one of Jenkins's socks that had been blown out of his tent. He smelled it and in mock disgust said, "Whew! Maybe they did us a favor after all."

That seemed to break the tension. Sensing that, he continued, "Let's pick up the pieces. Albertson, I'm putting you and Jamieson in charge of trash detail. Get something to gather up all the stuff that got shot up. Sanders, you and Clark supervise the work on the tents. Get 'em back up as quickly as you can. Let's get this place in order again before we head out this morning. I don't know about the rest of you, but I don't want to come back to this tonight. And besides, it's going to rain. Look at those thunderheads to the west. I don't want anybody sleeping in water tonight. If any of you get pneumonia, you're going to have to answer to me. Now get going—all of you."

Turning to Doc, Inman said, "Let's get to Headquarters. We better find out where they think we can do the most good today."

"I have the feeling we'll be busy," Doc said, pointing to the

new pillars of smoke off in the distance.

"So do I," Inman replied. "So do I."

* * *

The orders of the day for the 449th were plain enough. The German raids the past two days had destroyed nearly five miles of forward lines. Repairs had to be made immediately to keep the ground troops in contact with the Allied air forces, and a scouting party had to be sent out to assess the damage and make preparations for repairs. Without that communication, those on the ground would be forging ahead at great risk of attack not only from the Germans but from their own planes as well. The 449th shared the responsibility of making sure the lines of communication were kept open all the way from Anzio to Rome. It was no easy job, but it was a job they relished and in which they took great pride. From the time they had arrived in Italy, they had performed many functions, from construction to flight support, but communications work turned out to be their niche.

The men of the 449th Signal Construction Battalion were seasoned veterans, having contributed significantly to the battle for Anzio. They distinguished themselves during this battle by providing support for the 12th Air Force while stationed near Melito, helping form the protective shield over Anzio during the landing there, a landing that produced huge surprises on both sides of the battle line. The Allies, expecting heavy fighting during the landing, were surprised to find themselves ashore with much less resistance than intelligence had suggested they would face. The Germans, on the other side, were caught off guard because they hadn't anticipated the location of the landing and hadn't moved troops up to defend the area.

The plan for the landing at Anzio, code-named "Shingle," had been put together by Winston Churchill. It called for the Allies to first dig in upon taking the beach and then fight their way steadily through the German defenses, with the ultimate goal of taking Rome. The initial resistance had been so light in comparison to what they expected, the digging-in stage really hadn't been needed. Troops could have been moved forward almost immediately, and strategic positions, especially those on higher ground, could have been taken while resistance was almost nonexistent. The Allied troops, instead of advancing while the opportunity presented itself, had dug in and waited, and the waiting was costly. This gave the German commander, Field Marshal Albert Kesselring, time to draw reinforcements to the area, and the fighting that ensued was bloody beyond even the most pessimistic of expectations. Nearly eight thousand American soldiers lost their lives during the "foot at a time" battle that ensued after the initial surprise on both sides had worn off.

The battle for Anzio was now, after nearly four months, for all intents and purposes, over. By the end of May, the Allies had finally broken out of the beachhead, pushed back the German defenses, and struck forward mightily, the first tanks rolling into Rome the morning of June 4. German planes still harried the Allied forces all the way down to Anzio on a fairly regular basis to slow their forward progress, but even the German high command knew the attacks were futile. It was just a matter of time before Italy was lost.

And the 449th, through its work in keeping communications open, was a vital cog in the advancing Allied forces.

Sgt. Inman Perkins was well aware of this when he returned from Headquarters and gathered the men to explain the orders of the day.

He looked around the anxious faces before him and said, "Everybody listen up. Plans have changed. I've got good news—and some bad news. The good news is most of you are getting the day off."

He paused and changed his tone, sounding like someone shilling for a summer resort. "You can lounge around, pitch horseshoes, play ball, take a nice, long, relaxing nap. I've even arranged it so you can go in the shelter if it starts raining so you won't have to stay in those damp tents. What more could you want than that?"

A few of the men hooted and cheered. Others knew better and stood there with blank expressions on their faces, waiting to hear the rest of it.

Inman then added, deadly serious this time, "We really got hammered up the way this morning. Lines are down everywhere. We're not going to be sent out today because HQ thinks we're in for a few more visits from the Luftwaffe, and after last week you know what kind of target a line of trucks can make. I still can't believe none of us were killed. I don't know about you, but I'm still shaking from that little trip. And if that wasn't reason enough to hang around here today, storms are also rolling in. Rain and planes. I know, I know. What a great combination."

He paused, then continued, "Well, that's the good news—for most of you anyway. Now the bad news. I'm going to take a couple of you 'volunteers' with me this afternoon to check out the damage and make plans for repairs. Then tomorrow, if the weather blows through, we'll all head up that way. I'm sorry, but it looks like we'll be working around the clock again to get everything up and running from here to about half-way to Rome. Tomorrow we'll take supplies with us and camp along the way. So, get some rest today. Trust me, you're going to need it."

He turned and started to leave, but stopped short. "Oh, and one more thing. I almost forgot. I need a couple of volunteers. Oh, let's say, how about Doc, Albertson, and Tyler. The rest of you can start your goldbricking now."

Before the men started leaving, Albertson raised his hand and shouted, "Hey Sarge. Since I'm going to be in those storms today, you think I need to take my raingear?"

"You'll drown if you don't."

The men howled.

Looking at his watch, Inman continued, "OK, enough jerking around. The rest of you get out of here. A few of us have got *work to do."*

Doc, Albertson, and Tyler hung back as the others crossed the road and headed down toward their tents. They gathered around Inman, waiting for his instructions.

"Tyler, I want you to drive. I'll be up front with you. Doc, you and Albertson are going to be our lookouts and protection today. I want you armed to the teeth. Doc, I want you to grab that BAR Williams found last week. Hell, I'd take a cannon with us if we could get it. There are reports of German patrols crossing our lines all over the place, and I don't want us to be caught with our pants down."

"Got it," Doc responded, running off toward his tent.

Albertson looked around to make sure no one was listening and said, almost in a whisper, "I don't know where he got 'em, but Williams also got some grenades the other day. You want me to get them?"

"As many as you can carry," Inman replied. "With the way Doc can throw, those might just come in handy if we run into trouble."

He then turned to Tyler and asked, "What about you? Got anything up your sleeve?"

Tyler smiled and said, "No. But if we come across any Germans, they better get out of my way. I can do a lot of damage with a truck, you know."

"You're telling me," Inman chuckled. "I've already seen that."

Tyler mimicked steering a wheel hard to the left while making skidding noises.

Inman just shook his head and rolled his eyes.

* * *

It was mid-afternoon when they drove out of camp, weaving slowly around fallen trees and craters in the road as they went. Less than a mile out, the sky opened up. The rain came down so hard and so fast the first drops hitting the road caused puffs of dirt to rise up in the same way the machine gun bullets had earlier that morning. The clouds to the west suddenly turned dark green and seemed almost to be touching the ground behind them. The wind picked up and whistled past the truck. Doc and Albertson were riding in the back, and Inman and Tyler both laughed out loud as they heard them cussing and moaning as the rain swept in on them.

"They'll be like drowned rats," Inman said, reaching over and slapping Tyler playfully on the arm.

"I hope so," Tyler replied, slowing down to navigate around a pothole on the left and a fallen tree on the right. As he steered the truck back and forth to dodge more limbs that had blown into the road, he added, "Albertson's getting what he deserves. He still owes me ten bucks he borrowed back in Virginia."

He laughed again and jerked the wheel sharply left, which caused his passengers in back to lose their balance, fall off their seats, and roll to the other side of the truck.

"Hey—what the hell is going on up there?" Doc shouted.

"You trying to kill us?" Albertson added.

Inman tried not to laugh. As sternly as he could manage, he said to Tyler, "OK, that's enough of that. Keep your eyes on the road."

"Sorry. Couldn't resist, Sarge. Now if I never get my money back I've had ten bucks' worth of fun."

"And then some," Inman added, shaking his head again.

They drove in silence for a few miles. Tyler was doing a good job of dodging debris in the road, and Inman complimented him. Finally, through sheets of heavy rain that were coming now almost parallel with the ground, Inman could see up ahead the faint outline of a fuel depot. The depot had been the first one set up outside the Anzio beachhead during the advance toward Rome. Now that Rome had been taken, it was the farthest back down the line and of little use, except as a place to keep fuel in reserve. Plans were to move the fuel up to Rome, but the trucks needed to transport it were being kept busy enough supplying the front lines. A single squad of men had been left in charge of guarding the fuel. Sergeant Jackson, a man in his mid-thirties with a week's growth of stubble on his chin, got up from a bench near the entrance to the depot and walked over to meet Inman's truck as it pulled up.

"You here to move us out?" Jackson asked excitedly, wiping the rain from his eyes.

"Sorry," Inman replied. "We're not transport." He pointed to a pole snapped almost exactly in half but still supporting its wires near the entrance to the compound and added, "We're checking out damage today. We're the new repair group."

"Damn!" the sergeant groused. "All we do is sit here on our duffs and watch everybody going back and forth in front of us. I'm telling you, it's like watching horses going around a track. If we don't get out of here, we're going to go nuts. Look at my men. You ever seen a group that looked more bored than that?"

His squad hadn't even gotten up when the truck arrived. All were in full rain gear and were huddling under a long stand of trees just east of the depot. Inman saw a row of sagging tents behind them and at once understood why they were under the trees.

Inman shook his head and said sympathetically, "You'll be out of here soon. Scuttlebutt has it we're all moving up to Rome in a week or so. I wish I could help, but for the time being, we're stuck here, too."

"Thanks anyway," Sergeant Jackson said. "We'll just have to rough it out I guess. More like swim it out if this rain doesn't quit soon. Anyway, you take care. Be seeing you, Mac."

Just as Inman was ready to order Tyler to drive on, Sergeant Jackson shouted, "Hey, wait a minute. As long as you're here, can you take a look at something for me?"

"What is it?" Inman asked, pulling his collar up close to his neck to keep the rain from splashing down his back.

"Over there. Behind that big tree on the other side of the compound. The pole is leaning right on the fence. Looks to me like if it fell the rest of the way the whole damn fence would come crashing down. And what if the wires then hit the fuel cans? I haven't slept for three days thinking about that. What do you think? Got anything to prop it up?"

Inman shielded his face from the raindrops as he got out of the truck and walked over to study the pole. Sergeant Jackson was right. If it fell, not only would it cause another line break, it also looked like it would collapse the rest of the fence on that side.

"What the hell," Inman said, shrugging his shoulders. "We're all going to be soaked to the skin soon anyway. We'll get this before we leave."

"Thanks. You don't know how much I've been worried about this."

"We'll have it fixed before you can say Louis Armstrong."

Inman called over for Doc and Albertson to bring some tools and a ladder. Inman remained there, trying to decide the best way to reset the pole.

With a booming crack of thunder following almost simultaneously, a lightning bolt pierced the sky.

In a flash instant, flames arced skyward as row after row of fuel cans ignited.

The sky turned white. Then red. Then black.

The concussion had been so violent, Doc had been blown across the road, landing back first into a drainage ditch overflowing with the warm rain. He never lost consciousness, but the force of the blast made him dizzy to the point of being nauseous. A steady ringing filled his right ear and a stream of blood oozed from his left. He started to sink in the water, and when it reached his face, he threw out his hands to steady himself against the edge of the ditch.

Off to the right he saw Tyler on his hands and knees next to the truck on the side opposite the flames. The canvas on the truck was on fire. Tyler was looking up at it, but he didn't move. Turning his head from the truck, he opened his mouth as if trying to speak. He pointed toward Doc—and collapsed.

Albertson had been lucky. He had dropped a shovel at the

back of the truck and had bent down to grab it at the exact moment of the blast. The tailgate of the truck had shielded him from most of the concussion that followed. On pure instinct, he had raised up to see what was going on and cut his forehead on the edge of the tailgate. Blood pooled in his right eye as he wiped it away, blinking rapidly. A lump was already rising there, but he was still too stunned to feel the pain.

Sergeant Jackson's neck was snapped in the blast. He was lying, facedown, a section of fence on top of him. His men had been resting under the row of trees on the other side of the compound and had jumped behind them right after the blast. None were seriously hurt.

The haze slowly lifted in Doc's brain. As he became more aware of his surroundings, he realized something was missing.

His best friend.

It was when Doc tried to stand up, putting weight on his left arm, he realized it was broken just below the elbow. Grimacing, he rolled to his right and crawled to his knees before standing up, fighting the dizziness as he rose.

Another bolt of lightning lit the sky. As the flash faded, Doc saw him.

Inman was on his side, curled in a ball, his back resting against the chain-link fence of the compound. He wasn't moving. To Doc, he looked so peaceful he appeared to be sleeping.

"Perc!" Doc shouted, his voice sounding like a plea. "It's me. It's me."

Doc ran over to his friend, picked him up quickly but gently, and carried him away from the smoke now billowing around them. He carried him over to where Tyler had collapsed and placed Inman next to him. Unbuttoning Inman's shirt as quickly as he could, he leaned down and put his ear to his chest.

He was still alive.

"Get up," Doc said matter-of-factly to Tyler. "I need you to drive. Where's Albertson?"

Tyler sat up awkwardly and, after looking around, pointed to the rear of the truck. "He's there. Hey, Jim. You OK?"

Albertson, still stunned, waved back, weakly.

"He's OK," Tyler said. "How about Sarge?"

"He's bad. Real bad. We've got to get him out of here right now. Get the truck started."

Doc, his arm throbbing, picked Inman up and carried him to the back of the truck.

"Help me put him in," he said to Albertson, who was dazed but now standing.

When all were in the truck, Doc kicked on the floor with his feet and yelled, "Get us out of here!"

He cradled Inman in his lap, holding him tightly, all the way back to Anzio.

* * *

The men milled around silently outside the field hospital, anxiously waiting news from the doctors. Word had already come that Tyler and Albertson would be fine. However, there had been no news of either Doc or Inman.

Williams had tried to sneak into the hospital to check on his friends, but two MPs quickly caught him and ushered him back out. He tried to bribe the MPs with packages of cigarettes, but they would have none of it. Williams persisted until, finally, one grabbed two packs from him and said, "You stay here. I'll see what I can find out."

He returned a few minutes later and said, "One's OK. They're still working on the other."

"Which one's OK?" Williams asked.

"That's all I know," the MP replied. "Sorry. I'll check again later."

Williams relayed the news to the others. They clustered into small groups, finally talking but in hushed tones.

"They'll be OK, won't they?" Jamieson asked loudly enough that all turned and looked at him.

No one said a word. At this point, there was no need to. All *they could do was pray.*

A short while later, Doc, his arm in a sling, appeared in the doorway, steadying himself against the taller of the MPs. Tears streamed down his cheeks. He started to speak, but looked down instead, covering his face with his hand.

"Oh my God!" Williams cried, rushing forward to hold up his friend, who was now on the verge of collapse. "Please, God, no!"

Williams put his arm around Doc and held him close as both sobbed against each other's shoulder.

Inman Perkins was gone.

* * *

At 2300 hours, the storms settled into a soft rain almost as fine as a mist. Jim Albertson had been released from the hospital earlier in the evening after receiving twelve stitches to close the gash on his forehead. He wasn't sure why, but he couldn't leave the area around the hospital. He smoked cigarette after cigarette as he paced slowly back and forth in front of the main entrance.

The MPs, feeling sorry for him and the loss of his friend, called him over and told him he could go back inside for a short visit with Doc and Tyler if he promised not to tell anyone. He was just on his way up the steps as the orderlies appeared carrying a stretcher. Albertson looked up to see they were carrying Inman out to the hospital jeep that would take him to the temporary morgue across town.

"Please, don't leave yet," he begged the orderlies. "Give it five minutes. Please, you've got to do this."

He then ran down the road and dropped from sight as he entered the peach orchard.

The orderlies looked at the MPs as if asking what they should do. The MP who had taken Williams' cigarettes shrugged and said, "You can give him five minutes. It's OK. Here, have a smoke while you wait."

It didn't take five minutes before Albertson returned. The orderlies hadn't had time to finish their cigarettes.

When they looked up, they saw Albertson standing, in full uniform, at attention, across the road from the hospital.

"What now?" one of the orderlies called across to him.

Just then, the rest of the men, each also dressed in full uniform, marched quickly up the road from the peach orchard, forming a line next to Albertson.

Doc and Tyler suddenly appeared in the doorway of the hospital, edging past the stretcher holding their friend. The MPs tried to block them, but Doc, using his broken arm, pushed them aside as he said, coldly, "Not this time."

They looked into his eyes—and backed off.

Tyler went ahead of him and climbed into the driver's seat of the jeep.

Doc walked slowly across the street and stood between Albertson and Williams.

"OK," was all Albertson then shouted across to the orderlies.

The orderlies carried the stretcher to the jeep and buckled it securely to the platform on the back. When they finished, they climbed in behind Tyler, each reaching an arm back to hold the stretcher more firmly in place.

Tyler started the engine, gently let out the clutch, and the jeep eased forward smoothly.

Starting with Albertson, one by one the men snapped to attention and saluted as the jeep passed them.

Williams, choking back tears, turned toward Doc and said, "He always said we don't salute sergeants."

"This one we do," Doc answered softly. "This one we do."

As the light rain continued to fall, the men tightened their salutes one last time and watched the jeep fade into the night.

Epilogue

Word of Inman's passing reached Olivia one month later to the day. She was watering her dianthus when the minister of her church, whom she had taken into her confidence and told of her marriage, walked up, holding a Western Union telegram. After seeing only the envelope, she collapsed.

She kept to her bed for two weeks. Because their marriage had been kept a secret, it took almost that long before others understood fully what Inman's death meant to her. When word finally spread, her friends and neighbors in the Ville attended her constantly until she felt well enough to reenter the world.

Four weeks after the telegram arrived, Olivia walked into Sumner High School and said she was ready to return to teaching in the fall— if they would still have her. They would, and they did. That fall she returned not as Olivia Merriwether, but as Mrs. Inman Perkins. She remained at Sumner for a teaching career that spanned forty years. She vowed that summer of 1944 to keep Inman's spirit alive by putting a little of him into every student who would cross the threshold of her classroom.

She kept that vow. Her students became her life. Through the years, Olivia touched the lives of thousands of students. Among the more distinguished students who thrived at Sumner during her career there were Arthur Ashe, Tina Turner, and Chuck Berry. Olivia cared deeply for all of her students, but her favorite student of all was a young man by the name of Richard "Dick" Gregory, who went on to become one of America's treasures through his work in everything from the civil rights movement to the world of literature. Mr. Gregory kept in touch with Mrs. Perkins through the years, often staying at her home while traveling across the country.

In recognition of her work at Sumner, in 1975, Olivia Merriwether Perkins was included in Sumner's centennial list of "The 100 Most Outstanding Teachers" in the school's history.

Olivia never remarried. She kept her love for Inman fully in her heart until the day she died, July 6, 1995. She was buried in Oak Grove Cemetery in St. Louis, Missouri, not far from her beloved Sumner High School.

* * *

Today, Sumner MEGA Magnet High School continues to build upon its rich tradition of excellence. Still today, as Inman Perkins once described it, it is a school where students are taught "to be proud of themselves, their families, and their heritage." For Sumner, that description will always hold true.

* * *

The area of St. Louis called the Ville, where Sumner is located, exists to this day. Though not hard and fast by any means, most consider its boundaries to be Taylor Avenue on the west, Sarah Street on the east, St. Louis Avenue on the north, and Dr. Martin Luther King Drive (formerly Easton Avenue) on the south. Beginning with the 1960s, the Ville became a microcosm of the cycle of urban change, in terms of both decay and renewal, found in most major cities across the land. Today, buildings which have not fared well over time are slowly being replaced. The apartment where Inman lived on Easton Avenue is now gone. Olivia's home at 4341 West Belle Place, technically a few blocks south of the Ville proper, is also gone, a vacant lot now at its former location.

But even as the winds of change swirl, the soul of the Ville continues to grow stronger with each passing year. Today, the future of the Ville looks as bright as ever.

* * *

The 449th Signal Construction Battalion, which had initially been called the "449th Colored Signal Construction Battalion," provided invaluable support during the Italian campaign. After breaking out from Anzio, the Allied forces struck for Rome. This was significant because the battles for Anzio and Rome kept German forces in Italy and their attention away from a little place in France called Normandy. Two days after Rome fell, and while German forces were being rushed to halt the forward advance of the Allies in Italy, the D-Day invasion began in earnest on June 6, 1944. In many ways, the Anzio beachhead had been a trial run for the main invasion of Europe—a costly and bloody one, but a necessary one. As the Italian campaign drew to a close, the 449th was sent to France the next spring. From there, they also served in Belgium and Germany, mostly in the area of communication support, before war's end.

Not quite a year after the end of the war, the 449th was at the center of one of the ugliest and most controversial incidents involving Allied occupational forces in Europe. Accounts of the incident differ greatly and are sketchy at best, but a common thread in the reports indicates that men of the 449th were taunted by some French soldiers in the French Occupational Zone in Germany. Words were exchanged and fighting broke out. A French officer was hit by a rock or knocked unconscious by a punch, depending on which version is to be believed. Whatever actually happened, the French officer reported the incident to his commanding officer, who then demanded the men of the 449th be disciplined for their actions. Several members of the 449th were court-martialed, and the battalion was removed from the French Zone. Did the men of the 449th deserve to be court-martialed and the rest removed from the Zone—while none of the French were disciplined? The true story of that incident will perhaps never be known.

The battalion eventually returned to the States. They were transferred in late 1948 to Lockbourne Air Force Base in Columbus, Ohio. Finally, on July 5, 1949, the 449th was deactivated, ending a proud and stormy history.

* * *

After the war, Doc and Judy married and moved to Jackson, Mississippi. There they eventually owned a chain of six service stations, one for each child they brought into the world. Doc and Judy's lives, as he had dreamed, were full of love and laughter.

* * *

For their actions in helping rescue the civilians from the collapsed building near Capodichino, Williams and Tyler were recommended for the Soldier's Medal. The recommendation was never acted upon.

Williams returned to the diner in Kinloch after leaving the army, but he didn't stay there long. He made use of the GI Bill to take cooking classes at night. After working his way up through several smaller restaurants around the Midwest, he eventually became a chef at a large hotel/casino in Las Vegas, Nevada. He finally got his restaurant where gravy wasn't served on everything.

* * *

Through the years, Olivia made several attempts to have Inman returned to St. Louis, but all of her efforts ended in failure. He was never brought home. He was buried about forty miles south of Rome in the Sicily-Rome American Cemetery in Nettuno, Italy. He is resting today in Plot D, Row 3, Grave 18.

* * *

Long after the last train pulled out of St. Louis's Union Station, the Whispering Arches, where Olivia and Inman professed their love for each other, still stand, just inside the north entrance to the station. It is said when couples whisper "I love you" to each other inside those arches, an echo can be heard. Maybe it's not an echo at all. Maybe, just maybe, it is the voices of Olivia and Inman calling to each other still today. An endless echo—a timeless love. Intertwined forever.

* * *

And finally, just as Inman lived in Olivia's heart the rest of her days, their legacy will live on in ours whose lives they touched so deeply—now, and for all time.

ACKNOWLEDGMENTS

As this manuscript was prepared, I was given help by many wonderful folks, and I would like to thank them now. For assistance in locating educational records, I'd like to thank Sharon A. Dolan, Records Center Supervisor/Archivist for the St. Louis Public Schools; Myrtle Love, former Principal of Sumner MEGA Magnet High School; Ernest Hill, former Assistant Principal, Sumner MEGA Magnet High School; Tinnie Collins, former Registrar, Lincoln University; Constance Williams, Vice President for Student Affairs, Lincoln University; Philip Patton, Registrar, University of Northern Iowa; Melanie Allsup, Library Assistant, Chemistry Library, University of Iowa. For help in sourcing historical information, I'd like to thank Jason Stratman, Research Librarian, Missouri History Museum Library and Research Center; Marc Griffin, General Manager, Borders Books, St. Louis, Missouri. For help with military history and assistance in deciphering military records, I'd like to thank former sergeant major John Griffin, 1315th Engineering Construction Battalion (WWII), U.S. Army; Patricia Higdon (President) and Sonny Higdon of the Dyersburg Army Air Base Memorial Association, Inc., Halls, Tennessee; Lt. Col. Chris Lukasiewicz and Lt. Col. Robert Stavnes, University of Northern Iowa Army Reserve Officer Training Corps; Judy G. Endicott, Organizational Histories Branch, Air Force Historical Research Agency; Rebecca Raines, Chief of the Force Structure and Unit History Branch, U.S. Army Center of Military History (Washington, D.C.); Alan Knight, Curator, Old Fort Bliss Museum, El Paso, Texas. For background related to Inman and Olivia's family history, I'd like to thank Chloe Williams and Sarah Leigh. For assistance with manuscript preparation, I'd like to thank Gail Moehlis and Kris Knebel. I'd also like to thank Linda Van Vickle for believing in me and for her constant enthusiasm and support.

A special thank you to my parents and my aunt, Judy Hartley, for sneaking back to the table at the Belleville flea market to purchase the rest of the letters for me—and for their encouragement during all phases of this project. I'd also like to thank Mrs. Verda Crump for providing valuable family history related to many of the characters in this story. I would also like to thank Mr. Dick Gregory, an inspiration to us all.

Finally, I wish to thank Rosemary Yokoi of Paragon House for believing in this project.

My thanks to you all.

Sources of Background Material

The journey to write this book, an enjoyable experience in and of itself, was also not without its share of twists and turns and potholes along the road, detours which often made the experience ever that much more challenging and rewarding. The nearly 150 letters, the letters upon which the story is based, written by Sgt. Inman Perkins between the fall of 1942 and late spring of 1944, were incredibly detailed. They provided a wealth of information in such areas as what travel was like for the common soldier, the hectic nature of life in an army barracks, the daily routine and training of enlisted men in a racially segregated battalion, an individual, personal chronicle of what was going on in all aspects of American society at the time, and the hopes, fears, and dreams of men in service, many of whom were away from home for the very first time. The letters, perhaps above all, through Sergeant Perkins' eyes and voice, conveyed the pulse of a nation in the throes of a great conflict. Sergeant Perkins was a gifted and talented letter writer whose prose contained a natural beauty and rhythm. His eye for the small details produced vivid images that conveyed the swirling emotions of a complex man during an explosive time in American history.

However, as detailed and descriptive as the letters were, they alone were not enough to tell Inman's story. Military censorship guidelines regarding personal letters, established to prevent sensitive information from falling into the hands of the enemy, set specific boundaries upon what could, and could not, be shared with those back home through written correspondence. In addition, individual, personal accounts, by their very nature, seldom provide comprehensive context and background to events described within them. Soldiers did not wish to share information about the dangers they faced in the war, so as not to pile worry upon worry.

In order to fill in these essential pieces of the story, background details were still needed to supplement the letters and shed light on the many events described within them. This proved especially difficult, at first, because uncovering information about what many during the World War II era called the "colored battalions" was like chasing shadows. These battalions played important, often vital, roles in the war effort, but their contributions more often than not went unreported. Whether this was a direct result of the segregation still such a part of the fabric of American life of the time—and strict segregation in the military in particular—or whether it was because the "colored battalions" were simply overshadowed by the larger military units they were attached to and supported during the war is debatable. Whatever the reasons, the records of these battalions are sketchy at best, and in some cases, they have not survived at all. Sadly, if their deeds weren't recorded at the time of the war, they have now become more than ever the invisible men of that great conflict. A part of this is also no doubt due to the fact that even though the Army Air Corps was a part of the Army during World War II, the records of many of the groups that served within the Army Air Corps were later transferred to the U.S. Air Force in 1947 when that group was finally given independent status within the structure of the United States Armed Forces. In other words, some of the records that did exist and did survive were kept by the army, and others were moved to a new branch of the military where they were recataloged, reindexed, and refiled, making the records that much more difficult to access. It took digging and perseverance, but the records finally came to light.

In order to gather the additional background information and supporting details necessary to complete the story, a number of sources, many of which overlapped in terms of the type of information they held, were consulted.

In terms of both overview and specific background related to the duties and responsibilities of the Army Air Corps during World War II, the resources of the Force Structure and Unit History Branch, U.S. Army Center of Military History in Washington, D.C., proved to be invaluable. Through this clearinghouse, details were gathered related to such areas as military terminology, army rules and regulations, aircraft used by the army, and descriptions of and uses of everything from weapons to military transport vehicles to military gear and supplies. They also helped provide information about military rank structure.

The Department of the Air Force's Air Force Historical Research Agency: Organizational Histories Branch, Maxwell Air Force Base, Alabama, was also consulted for specific information related to the 449th Signal Construction Battalion, Army Air Corps, the battalion in which Sergeant Perkins served. Through this organization, I was able to acquire the short, but detailed, official military history (mostly in narrative form) of the 449th Signal Construction Battalion. This included such information as when and where the 449th was stationed, the specific training the men in the battalion received, the duties they carried out during the war, and the specific units they were attached to during the war and throughout the remainder of the battalion's history. This information wasn't declassified until 1993, and as far as could be determined, I was the first one to read the account since the end of World War II.

For much needed geographical context to help illuminate many of the activities described in the letters, two specific sources were also consulted. The Old Fort Bliss Museum, El Paso, Texas, houses a comprehensive history of the base and its role during World War II; Fort Bliss was where Inman and the 449th were stationed while receiving much of their training. Many of the activities on the base described in Inman's letters became much more clear after this context was added. In addition, the officers of the Dyersburg Army Air Base Memorial Association, Inc., provided further geographical reference and background information related to both the "air support" training and travel experiences of the 449th. The Dyersburg Army Air Base, in Halls, Tennessee, where several men of the 449th received special training on their way to joining the battle in Europe, now consists of a wonderful museum—and thousands and thousands of feet of silent airstrip, now dotted with weeds growing up through its rich history.

In addition, to gather supplemental information about the everyday lives of those who served in the army during World War II, interviews were conducted with current military personnel (military historians) and those who saw active service during the war. One gentleman in particular, Sgt. Maj. John Griffin, 1315th Engineering Construction Battalion, U.S. Army, Ret., had served in a segregated battalion, and the stories of his time in the army were breathtaking, his insights detailed, precise, and often poignant.

In contrast to the challenge of gathering information related to the military side of the story, information about the private lives of the main characters was readily accessible. The Missouri History Museum and the Missouri History Museum Archives, both in St. Louis, Missouri, were storehouses of information about the section of St. Louis called the Ville, the focal point and heart and soul of the African-American community; it was also the community where Sergeant Perkins and Olivia Merriwether lived while teaching at Sumner High School. In addition, two newspapers published specifically for the African-American community residing in and around St. Louis, the *St. Louis Argus* (published continuously 1912 to present) and the *St. Louis American* (published continuously 1922 to present), were consulted to check names, dates, and geographic locations associated with events described and referred to in the letters. Both newspapers were invaluable in providing background information related to everything from the work done by those on the home front in St. Louis to support those in military service to the thoughts about racial segregation, in mainstream American society and in the military, felt by those of the African-American community. In addition, details of the teacher training received by Sergeant Perkins and Olivia Merriwether were confirmed by offices at the University of Iowa (Sergeant Perkins) and Lincoln University (Ms. Merriwether). The teaching records of both were found through the exceptional help provided by officials at Sumner High School and the St. Louis Public Schools Record Center Archives. The St. Louis Public Schools Record Center Archives also provided lists of classes taught by each and pictures of both while at Sumner High School, as well as an overview of the curriculum presented at Sumner High School during the war years. Detailed information about the personal lives of both at the time period of this story were gathered from interviews with relatives, ranging from a niece to a grandniece to family members of a grandnephew. Finally, former students and colleagues from Sumner High School were interviewed to complete research into that area of their lives.

No matter how deeply I dug into the other sources of information, the letters kept calling me back, back to the voice of Sgt. Inman Perkins—back to a time in our history when the clouds of war darkened every aspect of American society—and always back to his story, a timeless story to be told at last. This was *his* story, based upon events described in the letters combined with the background details provided through the groups and individuals noted above. At the same time, it is also now *our* story, a slice of our history and heritage that should never be forgotten.

JSC

The 449th Signal Construction Battalion, Army Air Corps

A Brief Chronological History

November 1, 1942	Battalion activated, Davis-Monthan Field, Tucson, Arizona.
June 6, 1943	449th transferred to and reformed at Fort Bliss, El Paso, Texas. (Additional troops added, training and preparation for overseas duties)
December 9, 1943	Battalion transported by troop train to Dyersburg Army Air Base, Halls, Tennessee. ("Ground support" training and acquisition of supplies)
January 4, 1944	449th arrived at Camp Patrick Henry, Hampton Roads, Virginia. (Prepared and outfitted for overseas crossing. Boarded and shipped out on SS *Livermore* on January 13)
February 20, 1944	Arrived Naples, Italy. (Assigned to support 12th Air Force Service Command, 12th Air Force)
March 1944— February 1945	Battalion served in Italian campaign March 1944 through March 1945. (Air-ground support, construction, communications, transport)
March 1945— May 1947	Continued support duties postwar in France, Belgium, and Germany. (Construction, communications, transport)
May 25, 1947	449th returns to United States. Stationed at Langely Air Force Base, Langely Field, Virginia.
November 16, 1948	Battalion transferred to Lockbourne Air Force Base, Columbus, Ohio.
July 5, 1949	Battalion deactivated.

PICTURES

Olivia and Inman in front of Charles Sumner High School in St. Louis, Missouri. The picture was taken while he was home on leave.
Photo Courtesy of Jeffrey S. Copeland

Charles Sumner High School, St. Louis, Missouri.
Photo Courtesy of St. Louis Public Schools Archives

Sumner High School faculty, 1941.
Inman Perkins (2nd from right, 3rd row up from bottom)
Olivia Merriwether (2nd from left, 4th row up from bottom)
Photo Courtesy of St. Louis Public Schools Archives

Inman's and Olivia's students standing on the steps of Sumner High School, 1941.
Photo Courtesy of St. Louis Public Schools Archives

Inman Perkins before promotion (right) and friend, saluting. Taken at Davis-
Monthan Field in Tucson, Arizona, 1942—just after they reported for duty.
Photo Courtesy of Jeffrey S. Copeland

Inman Perkins in his sergeant uniform after his promotion. Picture taken at Fort Bliss in El Paso, Texas.
Photo Courtesy of Jeffrey S. Copeland

Inman Perkins (far right) seated with two of his friends in Melito di Napoli, Italy, spring 1944.
Photo Courtesy of Jeffrey S. Copeland